Renaissance Florence

RENAISSANCE FLORENCE

GENE A. BRUCKER

University of California Press
Berkeley, Los Angeles, London

University of California Press
Berkeley and Los Angeles
University of California Press Ltd.
London, England

Copyright © 1969, by John Wiley & Sons, Inc.
Supplements copyright © 1983, by the Regents of the University of California

ISBN 0–520–04695–1 paper
       0–520–04919–5 cloth
Library of Congress Catalog Card Number 82–40097
Printed in the United States of America

6 7 8 9

The paper used in this publication meets the minimum requirements of American
National Standard for Information Sciences—Permanence of Paper for Printed
Library Materials, ANSI Z39.48–1984. ∞

For MARK, WENDY and FRANCESCA
and for HARRIET

PREFACE

A book on Renaissance Florence does not require an elaborate justification. But the particular form of this study reflects certain interests and prejudices of the author, for which the reader deserves an explanation. This book is not a survey of Florentine Renaissance history, although I have attempted to describe the main outlines of that story from the time of Dante (1265-1321) to the age of Machiavelli, Leonardo da Vinci, and Michelangelo in the early sixteenth century. I have concentrated upon one segment of that two-century span, the years between 1380 and 1450, often described by historians as the "early Renaissance." These years witnessed significant changes in the patterns and configurations of Florentine experience, most distinctly in the cultural sphere, but also in social and political institutions, in attitudes and values.

Save for the final section, the epilogue, the chapters treat substantive topics which have been carved, somewhat arbitrarily, out of the total context of Florentine history. The beginning chapter on the physical city—which examines Florence as a complex of buildings, streets, and monuments— is followed by chapters which analyze the city's economic life, social and political structures, and, finally, religious and cultural phenomena. Inevitably, this format does violence to the reality of human experience, which is never organized so neatly. I have sought to minimize the effects of these artificial divisions by tracing connections between the various dimensions and by suggesting causal relationships.

In writing this book, I have been selective and specific rather than comprehensive and general. Each chapter contains an introductory section, which summarizes the background; I have then selected particular themes to define and illustrate the subject, analyzing, for example, the problems of the woolen cloth industry and the international merchant in the chapter on the Florentine economy. While this selectivity does permit a relatively thorough and detailed examination of particular issues, it has forced me to ignore, or to treat very sketchily, other significant facets of the city's history. Two particularly important subjects which have been slighted are the rural hinterland surrounding the city, and the urban poor. It is natural for the historian to focus his attention upon the rich and the powerful, upon that patrician class which dominated Florence's economy and government, her religious and cultural life. The evidence concerning this urban aristocracy is more extensive than the surviving fragments of information about the lower strata of Florentine society: the artisans and shopkeepers, the wage laborers in the textile factories, the denizens of the underworld. The historical role of these urban "underprivileged" and their rustic cousins in the outlying areas deserves more careful study than it has hitherto received.

Much of the book's illustrative material I found in the Florentine *Archivio di Stato*, that vast and wondrously rich depository of historical debris, which is housed in the lower floors of the Uffizi Palace. For the early chapters (those dedicated to economic, social, and political developments), I have relied heavily upon archival documents. While I have consulted, and profited from, the writings of scholars who have worked in these areas, both my evidence and my conclusions derive largely from the sources. These chapters represent a summary of a more detailed and comprehensive analysis of Florentine politics and their social context between 1380 and 1434, for which I have been gathering material during the past decade. In those areas of Florentine history where my knowledge is meager, I have been more dependent upon secondary studies (where they exist) and upon the fragmentary gleanings of my research, in those fields which have not been thoroughly explored.

GENE BRUCKER

Princeton, New Jersey, March 1969

Appended to this edition are *Notes on Florentine Scholarship* and a Bibliographic Supplement.
1983

CONTENTS

LIST OF ILLUSTRATIONS

LIST OF MAPS

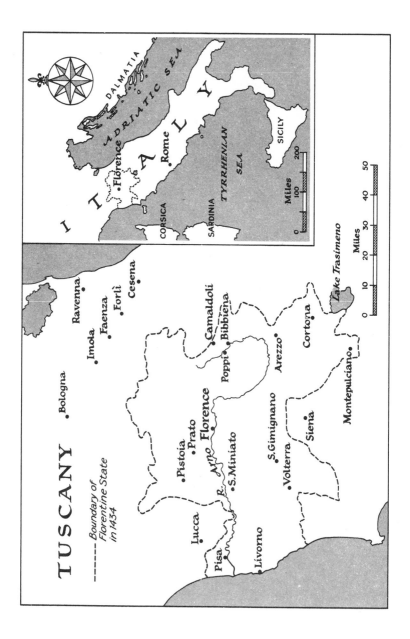

ONE

The Renaissance City

THE SETTING

In 1400, a traveler approaching Florence along the main roads did not encounter that striking view of the city and its environs which is so admired today. Winding through the steep hills north of the Arno river, the road from Bologna offers some impressive glimpses, but the view is truncated by the ridges which protrude like fingers into the plain. The ideal vantage point was Fiesole, the hill town overlooking Florence from the north. From that elevation, one could enjoy an unobstructed view of the entire city, and also of the Arno valley stretching westward to the sea. Visible too were the particular features of this urban complex: the walls and towers, the river and its bridges, the network of roads which had given birth and nourishment to Florence, the countryside which was linked to the city by a thousand bonds.

Florence's river location, some fifty miles from the Mediterranean Sea, was her most distinctive physical feature. Most Tuscan towns of any size—Siena, Volterra, Cortona, S. Gimignano—are located on hilltops, from which they dominate the surrounding plain. Centuries of political disorder following the barbarian invasions had dictated the site of these hill towns, which were more easily defended than settlements in the lowlands. With the sole exception of Pisa, a port city, the lower Arno valley did not attract large urban concentrations in the Middle Ages. The plain was swampy, poorly drained, and vulnerable to floods, and not until the late thirteenth century was it reduced to the condi-

View of Florence from Fiesole. (Alinari-Art Reference Bureau)

tion of fertility and easy communication it possesses today. And, then as now, Florence was not immune from the danger of flood waters; medieval chronicles describe the periodic devastations of the Arno, swollen by the heavy autumn rains. Once or twice in every century, the river would take a heavy toll of human life and property.

Even though the Arno occasionally brought death and destruction to the city, it also conferred substantial benefits upon her inhabitants. Florence was never troubled by the water shortages that limited the size and growth of Siena, Perugia, Cortona, and other hill towns. If the Florentines enjoyed some measure of sanitary and hygienic superiority over the Sienese and the Aretini, this was due to the proximity and availability of river water. The city's elevation and distance from the swamps of the lower Arno valley protected the inhabitants from malaria and the other marsh diseases which decimated Pisa's population in the fourteenth and fifteenth centuries. Fish from the Arno was a staple product in the Florentine diet; the flour mills located along the river and its tributaries ground the meal for the city's bread. That Florence —and not Siena or Perugia—became the largest center of cloth manufacturing in central Italy was due in part to her river location. Washing, fulling, and dyeing cloth all required a plentiful water supply, which taxed the river's capacity only during the annual summer drought.

The river was an important route of trade and travel, linking Florence with Pisa and the sea, and also with the Apennine hinterland. The Arno, however, was not an ideal artery of communication. Its volume and rate of flow fluctuated sharply from season to season; it was shallow and sluggish in summer, swift and often unnavigable during the autumn and spring floods. Silt forming at the Arno's mouth also impeded river traffic and increased the cost of transporting merchandise by water. Upstream, the only important urban center near its course was Arezzo, fifty miles to the southeast, but the river was—and is—too shallow for large boats in the summer months. Travelers preferred the land route paralleling the river. Downstream toward Pisa and the sea, river travel was heavier, but the summer drought also hampered this traffic, as did the artificial barriers and sand deposits along the Arno's course. Early in the fourteenth century, a road suitable for year-round travel was built between Pisa and Florence, and travel on this highway was as heavy as barge traffic on the river.

Matching the difficulties and hazards of river communication were those encountered by merchants who utilized the land routes radiating from Florence in every direction. Tuscan terrain is hilly, an interminable succession of ridges and valleys, not rhythmic and regular like the Appalachians but uneven, contorted, chaotic. The major roads which linked the city to other Italian regions were not noted for their ease of transit, but they were better than most alternate paths. Florence was the southern terminus of a major route across the Apennines. Traffic from the Lombard plain, from Milan and Venice, converged at Bologna and then followed the roads over the mountains to Florence, sixty miles away. From there, travelers proceeded to Rome and the southern provinces along two main arteries, one by way of Siena, the other following the course of the Arno along the old Roman road, the Via Cassia, through Arezzo, Perugia, and Assisi to Rome. The route across the peninsula followed the Arno valley to Florence, then over the Apennines via Bologna or Forlì, to the ports on the Adriatic Sea, the gateway to the Levant.

From the city's center, these roads ran through districts (now disfigured by urban sprawl) that were still rural: a complex of hamlet, farm, villa, and monastery. The villages surrounding the city—Sesto, Peretola, Rifredi, Settignano, Fiesole—were all small, their inhabitants and vitality drained by the powerful magnet of Florence. Only Prato, ten miles to the northwest, was able to withstand this pressure, to grow and to maintain an independent economic existence. These villages did not alter the essentially rural character of the landscape, nor did the ecclesiastical foundations, which were numerous but small. The largest of these monasteries—Settimo and Ripoli, the Certosa at Galluzzo, Vallombrosa and Camaldoli in the Apennines—were all several miles from Florence. The one large monastic complex in the immediate vicinity was S. Salvi, the ancient Vallombrosan convent near the Arno east of the city walls.

The beauty of this rural landscape has been extolled by generations of writers, by men as diverse in their tastes as the fourteenth-century humanist Coluccio Salutati and the nineteenth-century esthete John Ruskin. Over the centuries, the ingredients of this *bellezza* have changed little: the variety of terrain, from flat plain to rolling hill to rough Apennine slope; the combination of brilliant blue sky, dark green cypress, and silvery olive; the sensitive arrangement of land contours, buildings, fields and trees. The Tuscan countryside is displayed in the backgrounds of many Florentine paintings, for example, in works by Gozzoli, Fra Angelico, and Leonardo da Vinci. Leonardo was particularly successful in depicting the misty, ethereal atmosphere, still one of the most distinctive features of the Tuscan landscape.

The relationship between town and country is one of the most significant themes in Italian urban history; it influenced social structures and values, economic activities, political institutions and developments. For many Italian cities, the predominant theme in this relationship was the strong influence exercised upon urban life by powerful feudal families with estates outside the walls. Genoa's political and social history bore the sharp imprint of the great feudal dynasties which dominated her rugged Apennine hinterland, and both Rome and Milan felt the strong pressure of their potent noble clans: Colonna and Orsini, Visconti and Della Torre. Venice was a unique case; she possessed no close ties with the mainland before the fifteenth century, a fact which contributed to the social homogeneity of her ruling class. The Venetian patriciate was preoccupied with mercantile affairs, and the city's politics were not disturbed by eruptions of feudal disorder or by quarrels between town and country interests.

The pattern of urban-rural relationships which evolved during Florence's medieval period corresponded quite closely to that of other inland cities. Florence expanded by tapping the resources of her hinterland. Emigration enlarged her population; surplus grain, oil, and wine from Tuscan farms fed the growing urban populace. The aristocracy which governed the commune in the twelfth and thirteenth centuries was an amalgam of social groups, each of which had close ties with the rural areas surrounding the city. One part of this ruling class had descended from the feudal nobility which still possessed large estates in the *contado**; another segment was formed by descendants of an affluent rural bourgeoisie who had migrated into the city, invested capital in commerce and industry, while retaining land and social contacts in the district from which their ancestors had emigrated. By the end of the fifteenth century, the typical agricultural unit in the rural areas around Florence was the *podere,* a compact bloc of land assembled and fructified by a heavy injection of urban capital, sufficiently productive to sustain the family of peasant cultivators as well as the landlord's family living in the city. The development of this *mezzadria* or sharecropper system provided a secure food supply for the propertied classes in the city, and it created exceptionally stable conditions in the Tuscan country-side. The system also contributed to the formation of intimate and remarkably permanent ties between the urban and the rural populace, based upon a community of economic interest and a tradition of cooperative effort.

The city's formal boundary was defined by its walls. This for-

---

*The *contado* was the rural area surrounding the city, which formerly had been under the jurisdiction of the feudal power and later came under the commune's control. Florence's *contado* extended from Empoli and Prato in the west to beyond the Arno and Sieve rivers on the east. The district (*distretto*) comprised those parts of the Florentine dominion which lay beyond the *contado,* and which had come under the commune's control more recently.

tification, some five miles in circumference, was erected during a fifty-year period from 1285 to 1340. On the Arno's north side, the bastions formed a rough parabola. Joining the river at its western boundary beyond the Porta al Prato, the walls curved inland to the Porta S. Gallo, over a mile north of the Arno, and then cut sharply back toward the river. These walls were torn down in the 1860s, but their location is clearly marked by the girdle of wide boulevards which circles the inner city, dividing the old town from the modern suburbs. On the river's south side, the walls enclosed a more restricted area, for the hills were a formidable barrier to urban development. From the Porta S. Niccolò, where river and wall met at the city's southeastern corner, the line of fortifications moved abruptly inland to the Porta S. Piero Gattolino (now Porta Romana), and then rejoined the river farther west at the Porta S. Frediano. Traversing rough terrain unsuited for building or communication, these walls have survived into the twentieth century. Nostalgic spirits seeking to relive the past will find sustenance for their reveries in that section of wall which runs from Porta S. Niccolò to the Belvedere fortress. The path alongside this barrier is narrow, rough, little traveled. It does not follow the contours of hill and valley but, like a Roman road, moves sharply up the ridges in a straight line. The wall itself, some twenty feet high, is interspersed at regular intervals with towers, originally more than 100 feet high, which were truncated in the sixteenth century.

These imposing fortifications were clearly visible to an observer stationed on Fiesole's hill, but the other urban landmarks would not be so easily distinguished in the dense clot of masonry within the walls. Close to the river were the bell towers of the palace of the Signoria (Palazzo Vecchio), which housed the legislative and executive organs of the commune, (p. 15) and the palace of the podestà, the most important magistrate and police official. These massive edifices were constructed in the late thirteenth and early fourteenth centuries, and their austere, fortress-like appearance reflects something of the temperament—hard, assertive, suspicious—of the Florentines of Dante's generation, who had built them. They were conceived as bastions of defense; their purpose was to protect the communal government against attack from any quarter: whether from the feudal nobility, subdued but not destroyed, or from a proletarian mob, or from a Sienese or Pisan army.

Today, the most distinctive feature of the city's skyline is the cathedral or Duomo (p. 14), located some 400 yards north of the Piazza della Signoria. This giant structure, begun in 1296, was still not finished a century later. The architectural and engineering problems of building the cupola baffled the officials in charge of construction. Not until the 1420s were these problems finally solved by Brunelleschi, who developed the plans for this architectural breakthrough (the first large dome to be constructed in Latin Europe since Roman times) and supervised the early stages of construction. In the absence of the dome, the Fiesole observer who (in 1400) viewed this scene could locate the city's ecclesiastical center by identifying the cathedral campanile, begun by Giotto in 1334. To the west of the cathedral were two other important elements in this ecclesiastical complex: the Baptistery and the episcopal palace. Florence abounded in sacred foundations large and small, from great monasteries to tiny hospitals and parish churches, like the minuscule S. Maria in Campo a few yards from the cathedral. To the left of the Duomo was the tower of the Badia of S. Stefano, the ancient Benedictine monastery near the palace of the podestà. More imposing, visually and architecturally, were the great basilicas built by the Dominicans (S. Maria Novella) and the Franciscans (S. Croce). As if by tacit agreement, these rival orders established themselves on opposite sides of the city: the Dominicans in the northwestern quarter, and the Minorites along the eastern wall, near the Arno.

We have a more precise impression of what the viewer from Fiesole saw, thanks to the survival of the Bigallo fresco painted in 1342 (p. 16). This work is not distinguished for its realism, but the artist did convey two striking features of the urban landscape: its "spiny" character derived from the proliferation of towers, and a sense of compression and density—the lack of free, open space. These impressions were valid. Medieval Florence was a city of towers, both ecclesiastical and secular, and her central zone was a solid, dense block of masonry, broken only by thin lines of alleys and narrow streets, and by occasional courtyards and squares. But neither of these features survived into the sixteenth century as permanent characteristics of the urban milieu. The towers gradually declined in number, their tops lopped off by communal ordinance in 1250, or demolished to make room for other buildings. The transformation of the urban center into a more spacious area, with larger squares and wider streets, was a gradual process, not finally completed until the nineteenth century. This transformation gathered momentum in the fifteenth century and was a result not only of economic pressures but also of changing values, both public and private, which are associated with the emergence of the Renaissance.

BUILDINGS, STREETS, NEIGHBORHOODS

Florence has many old buildings, a few ancient streets, but no medieval quarter. There is no district of the city which communicates that sense of the medieval past which one experiences in S. Gimignano or Gubbio or the S. Pellegrino quarter of Viterbo. In these smaller, less "progressive" towns, old buildings and monuments have not been sacrificed, on a massive scale, to the requirements of the modern world. As late as the mid-nineteenth century, Florence still retained its traditional character, its harmonious blend of medieval and Renaissance architecture, with scarcely a trace of later building styles. The first major step toward modernization was taken in the 1840s, when the Calzaiuolo—the street connecting the cathedral square with the Piazza della Signoria—was widened and straightened. Twenty years later, the city walls were torn down, and wide boulevards (*lungarni*) were constructed along the banks of the Arno. These streets facilitated communication, but they also destroyed the pleasantly rustic character of the river banks, a favorite subject of artists in the early nineteenth century. The most flagrant desecration occurred in the 1880s when, in the name of progress, the authorities ordered the destruction of the district surrounding the Mercato Vecchio, the Old Market. In 1944, the German army added the finishing touches to this century of vandalism, when it blew up all of the Arno bridges except the Ponte Vecchio (p. 17). The Wehrmacht blocked both ends of that venerable monument by dynamiting the adjacent areas, and thus pulverized some of the remaining fragments of "old Florence."

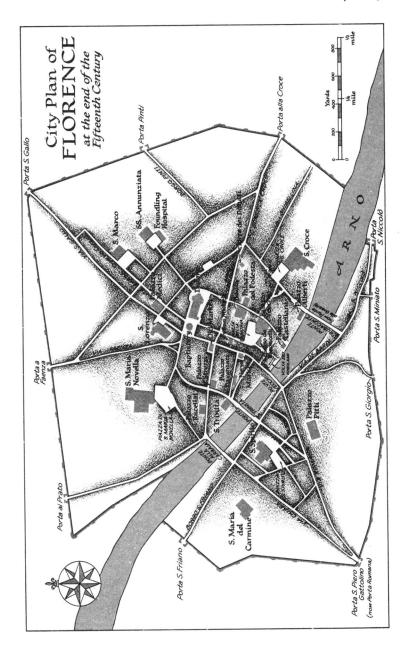

City Plan of
FLORENCE
at the end of the
Fifteenth Century

The scars of war had not been entirely obliterated when, on November 4, 1966, the city experienced the most destructive flood in its history. The Arno inundated the historic center of Florence, the waters reaching heights of fifteen to twenty feet in some buildings, and extending more than a mile inland on the north, beyond the lines of the old city walls. None of the bridges collapsed, although the shops on the Ponte Vecchio were gutted by the rampaging waters. The city's major architectural monuments survived, but they all suffered some damage. Flood waters weakened building foundations, and crude oil from furnace reservoirs discolored stones and frescoes. The flood's toll in human suffering and property damage was enormous, but the loss to Florence's cultural patrimony is particularly grave. Even though only a small part of the art treasures, manuscripts, and books have been irretrievably lost, the city's museums, archives, and libraries must devote years of effort to the task of recovery and restoration.

One method of describing medieval Florence is to focus upon the great monuments which have survived: the Duomo, the churches and monasteries, the public palaces, the major streets and squares. Here we adopt a different approach, searching for fragments of the old city in various locales and utilizing evidence from literary and artistic sources as well as physical artifacts. These glimpses and impressions may lack coherence from being jumbled and blurred, but they often convey a more vivid sense of the past, of a world that is lost, than do the views of grandiose palaces and basilicas.

The Old Market and its environs, razed some eighty years ago, was a characteristically medieval quarter; photographs taken of the district prior to its destruction reveal its distinctive features (p. 17). The Market was a rectangular square, in the center of which was a pavilion (erected in the fourteenth century) where butchers sold their viands. In this pavilion and around the periphery, vendors of other commodities set up their stalls. Surrounding the square was a network of streets and alleys which reflected the chaotic and disorderly character of medieval Florence. Here were the stumps of the towers of the nobility, their upper stories dismantled in the thirteenth century by a hostile populace which feared the power of these feudal clans and the immunity from control which these fortresses signified. Here too was urban construction at its most congested. Houses were packed together, built in those decades before the construction of the last circle of walls provided the inhabitants with adequate living space and protection. Streets twisted and meandered through the district, following no rational pattern. Building heights fluctuated crazily. Wedged between two massive towers eighty feet high might be a minuscule one-story cottage, uneconomic from the viewpoint of land utilization, but allowing a small amount of light and air into a district habitually dark, damp, and fetid. The area was festooned by a network of arches, which bolstered the less substantial buildings, and also served as the foundation for another room or two, to provide the residents of this district with additional living space.

A stone's throw from the Piazza della Signoria there survives a tiny enclave of the old city, or rather fragments of an enclave. Since medieval times, this zone has frequently been the scene of urban renewal projects. Buildings were systematically razed in the fourteenth century to make room for the Loggia dei Lanzi and for the enlargement of the Piazza della Signoria. Another wave of urban demolition occurred in the sixteenth century to provide space for the Uffizi palace. But surviving this destruction is the Chiasso dei Baroncelli, a medieval street which connects the Piazza della Signoria with the Via Lambertesca. It is a narrow lane, only eight feet wide at its southern exit, lined on both sides by tall buildings which effectively block out the light. Two arches curve above this alley at its southern end, emphasizing the antiquity and fragility of the walls they support. A few yards to the south of the Chiasso dei Baroncelli, paralleling the river, is the Volta dei Girolami (p. 18), likewise spanned by two arches, which serve as tunnels under buildings to permit passage through this very congested area.

The district around the Piazza S. Spirito (p. 19), on the Arno's southern bank, has undergone relatively little change over the centuries. This quarter has some remnants of Quattrocento architecture and some traces, too, of a past way of life. The tree-lined piazza, facing the old Augustinian church, is one of the most attractive in Florence. It has also maintained its traditional social function as the physical core of a neighborhood, with its outdoor market, its small shops and cafes catering to residents rather than tourists, its benches for the elderly, its playing space for children. The streets adjacent to the piazza —the Via Toscanella and the Borgo Tegolaio, for example—are lined with buildings constructed 500 years ago. On the ground floors of these ancient structures are shops (*botteghe*), many of which retain their original arched doorways. Here Florentine artisans ply their trades: the ancient crafts of carpenter, silversmith, and cabinetmaker as well as the modern skills of mechanic and electrician. In these shops, and in the work of these talented artisans, there survive some of the few links between contemporary Florence and its past.

Time and progress have wrought less havoc in the Oltr'arno quarter than in the regions north of the river. Many of the houses on the Via S. Niccolò, which connects the Porta S. Giorgio (p. 19) with the Porta S. Niccolò, were built during Brunelleschi's lifetime (1377-1446). These structures form a solid façade of brick and stucco, without a breach, along a street 100 yards in length. Each dwelling, however, has its distinctive physiognomy, its peculiar dimensions and character. The façades are high and narrow, some no wider than twelve or fifteen feet, but rising three or four stories to fifty feet and more above street level. From the vantage point of the Porta S. Giorgio, one can see the rumps of these structures, which are adjacent to the city wall. They present a striking view of broken lines and irregular forms; of decrepit attic rooms, chimney pots, and tile roofs; of ancient, weathered brick surfaces from which the stucco has peeled.

The anatomy of the "typical" Florentine house of the Renaissance can best be seen from the north side of the Arno, near the Ponte alle Grazie, looking south across the river. Here the terrain, rising abruptly from the Arno bank, provides three-dimensional views of these dwellings. Florentine houses retained the form and some of the character of their architectural ancestor, the medieval tower. Very tall and narrow, often rising to five stories, they extended well back from the street, their depth often three times greater than the width of the street façade. Windows were few in number and small in size; they provided the barest minimum of light and air for the lower stories. A distinctive feature of these houses was the covered balcony or terrace on the top floor, which opened out onto the street and permitted inhabitants to escape from the gloomy interiors. These terraces and the *sporti*, the projecting upper stories, are Florence's particular contribution to Italian domestic architecture.

If such houses, or smaller and humbler cottages, provided the living space for most Florentines, aristocratic families could afford more elegant and more spacious quarters. Many descendants of ancient families continued to live in the primitive towers inherited from their ancestors, the stumps of which still survive, particularly in the zone north of the Piazza della Signoria. The most notable of these venerable relics, the Torre Donati (p. 20), still stands in the Piazza di S. Piero Maggiore in the eastern quarter of the old city. This tower marks the urban habitat of that turbulent noble family, so intimately involved in the factional struggles of Dante's time. But in the second half of the fourteenth century, new styles of domestic architecture evolved, heralding the changing patterns of aristocratic living in the Quattrocento. The Davanzati palace (p. 21), built by the Davizzi family in the fourteenth century and now converted into a museum, illustrates the architectural tastes of the Florentine aristocracy in the late fourteenth century. Its external appearance is traditional: a high, narrow façade crowned with an open balcony, severely simple lines which recall the primitive austerity of the towers. It is the interior that reveals the progress made toward a new style of living. A small, open courtyard introduced limited quantities of light and air, those two rare commodities of medieval urban housing. The ground floor was reserved for shops, and for storing the produce of the family's country estates. Living quarters were located on the two stories above ground level. Each floor contained the full complement of rooms required for a household, for among the Florentine upper classes, it was common practice for fathers and married sons to live under the same roof. The main rooms of these apartments faced the street. These spacious, elegant halls spanned the length of the palace, and they were used for formal occasions: the banquets, receptions, and family gatherings that played an important part in Florentine social life. Adjacent to the main salon was a smaller dining room, and then leading toward the rear of the house,

Aerial view of the Cathedral (Alinari-Art Reference Bureau)

Palazzo Vecchio and the Piazza della Signoria. (Alinari-Art Reference Bureau)

Detail of fresco of the Madonna della Misericordia in the Loggia del Bigallo showing view of Florence in 1342. (Alinari-Art Reference Bureau)

Ponte Vecchio

Old Market prior to demolition. (Alinari-Art Reference Bureau)

Volta dei Girolami. (Alinari-Art Reference Bureau)

Piazza of S. Spirito. (Alinari-Art Reference Bureau)

Porta S. Giorgio showing old city wall. (Alinari-Art Reference Bureau)

Donati Tower. (Alinari-Art Reference Bureau)

Davanzati Palace. (Alinari-Art Reference Bureau)

a series of bedrooms for members of the household. Toilets were located in antechambers adjoining the bedrooms, and although these were not provided with running water, they were a sign of refinement in aristocratic circles, and the abandonment of more primitive hygienic customs which still prevailed among the lower classes. Interior decoration in this palace was lavish, opulent, and colorful. Frescoes and tapestries adorned the walls, and the furniture would not have been out of place in royal palaces in northern Europe.

Adequate evidence from documents and buildings survive to describe the aristocratic mode of living in Renaissance Florence, but information on lower-class housing is scantier and more fragmentary. The dwellings inhabited by the urban poor were primitive and unsubstantial; they have not survived the ravages of time. Tax records, however, do provide some data on housing and living conditions among the lower strata of Florentine society. Most artisans and laborers lived in small houses of two or three stories (one room per story) or single-room cottages. A typical worker's lodging was the cottage in the parish of S. Piero Maggiore on the eastern periphery of the city owned by a schoolmaster, Girolamo di Bartolo, who in 1427 received an annual rent of 3 florins* from his tenant Neri, a laborer in a soap factory. Tax records contain a few references to buildings in which rooms or stories were rented out to several individuals or families, but the apartment house was a rare phenomenon in fifteenth-century Florence. However, the tax declaration of

---

*Florence had two systems of coinage, one gold (the florin) and the other silver. Silver money was based upon the medieval system of coinage of *lire* (pounds), *soldi* (shillings), and *denari* (pence): 12 *denari* to the *soldo*, 20 *soldi* to the *lire*. Gold coins tended to appreciate in terms of silver; in 1400 a florin was worth approximately 75 *soldi*, or 3¾ *lire*. The florin contained 3.536 grams of gold, worth approximately $4 at the current price of $35 per ounce, but worth much more in terms of purchasing power. Daily wages for laborers and artisans ranged between 7 *s.* for unskilled workers to 20 *s.* (1 *lire*) for masters. The average monthly wage of a minor official in the communal bureaucracy was approximately 6 fl. Senior officials in the government and distinguished university professors might receive annual salaries as high as 300 fl. or more. The price of a bushel (*staio*) of grain fluctuated between 15 *s.* (in times of plenty) to 60 *s.* and more in times of famine.

Alessandro Borromei in 1427 does contain a portent for the future. A wealthy Pisan émigré with large real estate holdings, Borromei had purchased a palace which once belonged to the noble Amieri family. He converted this structure into a multiple-unit tenement, renting shops on the ground floor to merchants and artisans, and single rooms in the upper stories as living quarters. From his real estate investments, this prototype of the modern urban landlord earned annual revenues of nearly 1000 florins.

A remarkable feature of Renaissance Florence was the social and economic heterogeneity of each district and neighborhood. No sections of the city were reserved exclusively for the rich, no ghettoes inhabited solely by the poor. Each district was a mélange of palace and cottage, of cloth factory and retail shop, of parish church and monastic foundation. Then as now, the ground floors of elegant palaces were rented out to shopkeepers and artisans; rich bankers and industrialists lived on streets inhabited by shoemakers, stonemasons, indigent cloth workers, and prostitutes. This pattern was a result of the disorderly character of Florence's expansion, and also of social tradition. Each prominent family was closely identified with a particular neighborhood, where the first urban generation had settled—its members banding together for protection—in the twelfth and thirteenth centuries. By 1400, the danger of physical attack from a rival house or faction was less real, but the pressures to remain in the ancestral neighborhood were very strong. For in its own district, a family could muster the support among relatives, dependents, and friends which enhanced its political role in the commune.

In one sense, therefore, this urban community was a complex of hundreds of family nuclei, each representing a focus of power and influence within its own neighborhood. Along the Borgo degli Albizzi southeast of the cathedral were several palaces belonging to the Albizzi; the Piazza dei Peruzzi near the Franciscan church of S. Croce was the public courtyard of that prominent mercantile house, whose palaces fronted upon the square. The banking family of the Bardi had its power base on the south bank of the Arno along the Via de' Bardi. The Medici were the leading family in the parish of S. Tommaso adjacent to the Old Market, although some members owned property in the vicinity of the church of S. Lorenzo. One of Florence's largest families, the Strozzi (comprising some thirty-five urban households in 1378) was established in a zone near the Arno, surrounding the monastery of S. Trinita. A prominent banking house in late fourteenth-century Florence was that of the Alberti, who inhabited a dirty, noisome quarter of cloth-dyeing and wool-cleansing shops near the Franciscan church of S. Croce. The Alberti might have preferred a more attractive setting for their elegant palaces, away from the sounds and smells of cloth production. But they could not abandon their ancestral hearths, the neighborhood which was a bulwark of their political power.

Some degree of specialization, by occupation and economic function, did exist in certain urban districts. Shops engaged in some phase of cloth manufacturing were located in every part of the city, but they were concentrated in two zones: the Via Maggio in the S. Spirito quarter, and the S. Martino district near the cathedral. Subsidiary industries of dyeing, wool-washing and soap-making flourished along the Arno near S. Croce. Most of the shops and forges belonging to artisans who manufactured military equipment—swords, shields, and armor—were located in the quarter of S. Giovanni north and east of the cathedral. Communal legislation stipulated that slaughterhouses and tanning factories be located in the city's outskirts, where brick kilns and fulling mills were usually established as well.

Rents for both houses and shops were naturally higher in the center, and they tended to diminish as one moved toward the periphery. Commanding very high prices were shops located near the Piazza della Signoria and the Piazza del Duomo, or along the streets connecting these squares. A retail cloth shop near Orsanmichele rented for 118 florins in 1427; a barber shop located on the Piazza della Signoria brought the landlord a handsome return of 27 florins annually. Rents of 25 florins were common for houses in central Florence, while in the outskirts, tenants rarely paid more than 10 florins, and usually less. Although every district had its quota of urban poor, the peripheral areas contained the heaviest concentrations of cloth workers, servants, and casual laborers. Tax records indicate that the parish of S. Frediano in the Oltr'arno quarter south of the river was heavily populated by wool carders, beaters, and combers. In this slum area, rents were minimal (1 or 2 florins per year), and the quality of the accommodations was certainly as low as the rent. After five centuries S. Frediano is still predominantly a working-class neighborhood.

THE CHANGING FACE OF FLORENCE, 1350–1450

Our knowledge of Florentine building patterns in the late thirteenth and early fourteenth centuries is derived from evidence in chronicles, notarial and ecclesiastical records, laws and statutes, and from the surviving architectural remains. Although data are sparse and fragmentary, they suffice to prove that these were years of intense building activity, both public and private. The guild regime established in 1282 initiated one major project after another: the reconstruction of the old Badia and the third circle of walls in 1294, the cathedral in 1296, the palace of the Signoria in 1299. Work on the cathedral and the walls progressed very slowly in the early fourteenth century, but the tempo of construction quickened in the 1330s when the walls were finally completed. The foundations of the cathedral campanile and the loggia of Orsanmichele were laid down in 1334 and 1337; the reconstruction of the Ponte Vecchio began immediately after its collapse during the 1333 flood and was finished twelve years later. Meanwhile, the great basilicas of the mendicant orders, S. Maria Novella and S. Croce, were being completed, subsidized by the contributions of pious Florentines and also by occasional grants from the communal treasury.

The scale of private building in these decades was even greater than in the public and corporate sphere. Providing shelter, however poor and inadequate, for 100,000 inhabitants (Giovanni Villani's estimate for 1338) represented a massive investment of money, labor, and raw materials. Competing for these resources utilized in housing were the industrialists who needed capital to construct their factories and warehouses. Even in this age of primitive technology and low wages, it required a substantial investment to build the cloth shops, fulling mills, stretching sheds, and dye plants for an industry which employed some 30,000 workers in the 1330s. Also contributing to the building boom were the fires that periodically ravaged sections of the city.

According to the chronicler Giovanni Villani, a fire in 1303 destroyed 1700 buildings in the city center. Political conflict also played a role in urban renewal. Guelfs who had been driven into exile in 1260 returned six years later to find that some 600 of their houses had been damaged or destroyed by their Ghibelline enemies. The Guelf commune then demolished the palaces and towers of Ghibelline families, and either sold the confiscated property, or gave it to the Parte Guelfa, the political society of the triumphant faction.

By the middle of the fourteenth century, however, urban construction had slackened considerably. The plagues of 1340 and 1348 had reduced Florence's population by one-half, and only part of this loss, perhaps one-third, was recovered in the second half of the century. This demographic contraction sharply reduced the demand for new housing. While describing the prosperous state of the city in the 1330s, Villani wrote that the citizens "were continually renovating [their buildings] for greater comfort and luxury, importing designs from abroad for every type of improvement." But in the 1340s, large numbers of construction workers were unable to find employment. Two carpenters wrote to an acquaintance in Avignon in 1344 to inquire whether they could find work there, explaining that "the condition of the artisans and lower classes in Florence today is miserable, for they can earn nothing." For the first time in many decades, the city enjoyed a housing surplus. Urban rents plummeted in the 1340s, and did not rise again until after 1360.

Private building did not cease entirely in the decades following the Black Death, but its scope and character changed significantly. Before the plague, urban construction was heavily concentrated in the peripheral areas adjacent to the walls, where immigrants found shelter within the city's fortifications. After 1348, these outlying zones were no longer required to house the shrunken population. Orchards, gardens, vineyards, and even wheat fields covered much of this area; the 1433 tax return of a blacksmith, Antonio di Giovanni, described his property within the walls, from which he received ten bushels of grain annually. The population decline also transformed building patterns in the central zones. Many of the cheaper and flimsier cottages and shacks were torn down; by 1400, so many wooden

structures had been replaced by stone buildings that fires were
no longer a serious hazard. Other changes resulted from the
declining fortunes of many noble families, debilitated by economic crises and political persecutions. The massive blocs of
towers and palaces once inhabited by the Amieri, Donati, and
Pulci families disintegrated into fragments as a result of con-
fiscations and inheritance divisions. Some of this property fell
into the hands of mercantile families whose fortunes were not
damaged by depression and bankruptcy, or it was acquired by
the newly rich who invested some of their money in urban real
estate.

After the Black Death, the commune focused its attention and
its resources upon three aspects of Florence's topography. First,
it continued and expanded previous efforts to develop a coherent
plan for urban development. Second, it launched a program to
expand and embellish the Piazza della Signoria. Finally, it invested a large sum of money in the languishing cathedral project,
which, like the palace of the Signoria and its square, had become
a symbol of Florentine grandeur.

The documented origins of urban planning in Florence date
from Dante's time, at the end of the thirteenth century. In 1299,
the poet was a member of a communal commission which received authority to widen and straighten the city streets. A
decade earlier, in 1288, the commune authorized the acquisition
of property to permit the enlarging of the square in front of
the Dominican church of S. Maria Novella. The impulse to
regulate and control the physical character of the city was thus
manifest at an early date, as were the articulated goals of urban
planning: to facilitate communication, and to provide a more
attractive environment for the inhabitants. This latter ideal was
expressed with particular clarity in a Sienese proclamation of
1309: "Those who are charged with the government of the city
should pay particular attention to its beautification. An important
and essential ingredient of a civilized community is a park or
meadow for the pleasure of both citizens and foreigners. . . .
The cities of Tuscany . . . are well endowed with these ameni-
ties. . . ."

During the years of Florence's greatest growth, the commune
was endeavoring to impose some degree of order and coherence

upon the urban chaos. A primary goal was the establishment of public jurisdiction over the network of secondary streets and alleys in private possession. But the task was enormous and the resources limited; in times of crisis, the revenues authorized for civic improvement were often diverted to subsidize the construction of walls and fortifications. Although Dante's commission of 1299 had received broad authority to improve the city's thoroughfares, the money then available to purchase condemned property and rebuild streets was sufficient for only a few yards of roadway. But this initial phase of urban reconstruction did gain momentum, particularly in the early decades of the fourteenth century. Communal records for these years are replete with descriptions of street improvements and other public works projects. In the 1320s, for example, the commune provided funds for the rebuilding of the Via S. Gallo north of the Baptistery, "to increase the beauty and utility of the city of Florence, and in particular [to make] the streets rectilinear and attractive, and so that merchants transporting grain from the Mugello and Romagna [regions north of Florence] can reach the market in the loggia of Orsanmichele more readily. . . ." A petition presented to the Signoria in September 1317 described the area adjacent to the Carmine church as "a filthy place, a dumping ground for trash," which contaminated the entire neighborhood. The petitioners appealed to the commune to acquire this property and transform it into a public square, "so that what is now unsightly and vile will be made attractive for the passersby."

One cannot assume that these projects of urban renewal were always completed, or that the goals of the city planners were fully realized. The language of the regulatory legislation suggests an official resolution and fixity of purpose which did not always accord with reality. A law of 1324 described the Via de Panzano as "sordid, filthy and noisome," even though 7500 *lire* had already been spent on its improvement, and another 150 florins were required to finish the project. In 1351, the commune authorized the construction of a loggia in the Piazza della Signoria and appointed four officials to supervise the work; twenty-five years passed before this project was actually begun. The large corpus of legislation dedicated to city planning has contributed to the myth of a spectacular metamorphosis from disorder, chaos, and filth to order, symmetry, and beauty. This legislation was highly restrictive; it would excite the admiration and envy of any modern zoning commission. Many provisions, however, required such intensive scrutiny and control that they were probably unenforceable. An example is the law stipulating that a minimum of 100 florins be spent in the construction of a new house, and another stating that all buildings on public streets must be faced with stone to a height of seven feet. The commune waged a lengthy campaign against the *sporti*, those ubiquitous upper stories which projected over Florentine streets. They were first banned from the main thoroughfares—for example, the Via Maggio—on the legitimate grounds that they hampered communication and blocked light and air from the lower floors. But many property owners preferred to pay fines rather than dismantle their *sporti*; Giovanni Villani reported that in 1338, these penalties amounted to 7000 florins.

In its efforts to create an orderly and attractive urban environment, the commune had made substantial and visible progress by the end of the fourteenth century. But the magnitude of that achievement has been exaggerated by the rhetoric of some contemporary authors, and by our projection of modern images into the past. Salutati's description, in his *Invective against Antonio Loschi* (1403), is typical of humanist eulogies: "What city, not merely in Italy, but in all the world, is more securely placed within its circle of walls, more proud in its palazzi, more bedecked with churches, more beautiful in its architecture, more imposing in its gates, richer in piazzas, happier in its wide streets, greater in its people, more glorious in its citizenry, more inexhaustible in wealth, more fertile in its fields?"

Florence in 1400 was a more cluttered and disorderly city— in an architectural sense—than we imagine. Unfortunately, the records of the "officials of the towers," the public works commission, have not survived in quantity, for these would have provided us with more specific information about concrete achievements in the realm of city planning. From the extant fragments of evidence, we do receive a rough impression of the commission's activities, but little sense of its broader goals and accomplishments. In June 1397, the tower officials imposed fines

of 10 *lire* each upon three men who failed to obey their instruc-
tions to dig a cesspool to prevent water and sewage from running
into the street. Four years later, the officials ordered their chief
engineer to straighten and pave the Via Benedicta in the parish
of S. Paolo, and also fined three inhabitants of the street who
had impeded this work. In August 1415, the commission granted
Recco Capponi a thirty-day period of grace either to repair or
dismantle the dilapidated roof of his house or to pay a fine. In
that same year, the butchers in the Old Market were fined 100
lire unless they repaired the roof of their pavilion within a
month. In 1421, the commission supervised a more ambitious
project of urban renewal: the construction of a square between
the church of S. Simone and the city prison. The commune had
initiated this enterprise "for the beauty and utility of the city
and the church of S. Simone, and for the preservation of the
communal prison. . . ." A house in the Via dell' Anguillaia was
so decrepit that it constituted a menace to passersby, according
to a commission edict of May 1432, and its owners were told to
demolish or rebuild it. Occasionally, the tower officials had to
be prodded by their superiors. In July 1436, the Signoria reprimanded the commissioners for not repairing two streets near
the Old Market, Via Vecchietti and Via del Cocomero, and imposed fines upon them unless they finished this task during their
tenure of office.

With such sparse documentation, it is difficult to trace the
evolution of an urban ideal in the fourteenth century, to describe the Florentine vision of what the city should become.
Since Dante's time, the beautification of Florence was mentioned as a primary objective of every communal building project.
Furthermore, the ingredients of civic beauty—order, symmetry,
spaciousness, cleanliness—remained constant from the late thirteenth century to the fifteenth century. The commune's pursuit
of these goals may have intensified after 1350, but this cannot
be proved from the documents. Yet the completion of particular
projects did stimulate public efforts to create a more esthetic
environment by providing the citizenry with specific examples
of civic beauty. Although the construction of the cathedral proceeded at a snail's pace throughout the fourteenth century, this
enterprise did encourage the authorities to provide a more at-

tractive setting for this symbol of Florentine grandeur. Buildings were demolished to provide an unimpeded view of the church, and the adjacent thoroughfares were widened to 70 feet, "so that this cathedral will be encircled by beautiful and spacious streets . . . redounding to the honor and the utility of the Florentine citizenry." Inspired by the project to remodel the interior of S. Lorenzo, a group of citizens petitioned the Signoria in 1436 to embellish the church's exterior by tearing down some unsightly dwellings and enlarging the square in front of the basilica. From this larger piazza, so the petitioners had argued, the beauty and grandeur of the church would be more appreciated. They also claimed that the moral character of the neighborhood would improve, since the houses scheduled for destruction had been inhabited by prostitutes and other inhabitants of the Florentine underworld.

The transformation of the Piazza della Signoria, the city's political nucleus, was a slow process which required more than a century to complete. The two oldest elements in this complex were the Signoria's palace—completed in 1314—and the square, the site of the razed buildings of an exiled Ghibelline family, the Uberti. The square had been paved in 1330 and the palace enlarged in 1342-1343, but not until the last quarter of the century did there emerge a coherent plan for this area. The construction of the Loggia dei Lanzi (1376-1382) adjacent to the palace provided a dignified setting for official ceremonies such as the swearing-in of a new Signoria and the reception of foreign ambassadors. But the construction of the loggia also emphasized the cramped and irregular form of the piazza, and in the 1380s and 1390s the commune enlarged it by leveling buildings on its southern perimeter. An earlier law of December 1372 had authorized the tower officials to renovate the north side of the piazza, to reduce the height of some buildings and raise that of others, and to rebuild a wall so that this perimeter would be "beautiful and decorous, with a minimum height of 30 feet." In 1377, the commune enacted a provision "concerning the perfection of the loggia . . . and the cleaning of the Piazza della Signoria . . . and also the other streets of the city . . . which have been seriously neglected." Romolo Bianchi was appointed to a one-year term as "supervisor" of the loggia, responsible for maintaining the square and the city streets in a clean and sanitary condition. Apparently, this office did not become permanent, and its impact upon urban sanitation was probably quite limited and temporary. But subsequent legislation revealed the commune's persistent interest in the embellishment of the piazza and its environs. For example, a provision of December 1385 forbade the passage of carts through the square and also prohibited the dumping of detritus by furriers and tanners.

The construction of the Duomo, the cathedral, was the city's most ambitious building project; this enterprise engaged the hearts and minds, as well as the resources, of eight generations of Florentines. Its vast size and marble exterior, and above all its spectacular dome, were manifestations of the community's determination, first articulated in a statute of 1299, to build "the most beautiful and honorable church in Tuscany." Construction was frequently delayed during the fourteenth century by the diversion of resources to other projects, by disagreement over building plans, and by public indifference and inertia. The cathedral was primarily a civic, not an ecclesiastical enterprise; the commune provided most of the money for the project, and delegated the responsibility for the building to the Lana guild, the corporation of cloth manufacturers. The guild appointed four of its members as *operai*, with six-month terms of office, to supervise the work. These *operai* frequently requested advice from citizens with specialized knowledge—builders, sculptors, painters, goldsmiths—and on a few occasions organized a referendum on building plans in which "every person in the city of whatever status or condition" was invited to participate. Construction began on the façade opposite the Baptistery in the early years of the fourteenth century, and proceeded slowly eastward. Most of the façade and the walls of the nave had been completed by 1355, interior pillars and the vaulting over the nave a decade later. In 1366 and 1367, the *operai* approved plans for a fourth bay and an octagonally shaped choir. The implementation of these plans, however, required another fifty years, before the last and most difficult problem was solved: the construction of a dome to cover the huge aperture—140 feet in diameter—over the choir.

The decision to build a cupola of such proportions had been

made by 1367, and an artist's vision of the completed church crowned by its dome (painted about 1365) was visible for all to see in the Spanish Chapel of S. Maria Novella. Yet, none of the architects and builders before Brunelleschi could solve the technical problems of constructing a cupola of such dimensions, and instead concentrated their efforts upon other parts of the basilica. When the base of the cupola, the drum, was finally completed in 1413, the prospect of vaulting the huge octagon had to be faced. The opening was so wide that it could not be spanned by a wooden framework, the device used by medieval architects to build smaller cupolas. Furthermore, the weight of the projected dome was too great to be supported by the existing drum. Brunelleschi's model provided for the construction of two interior shells, which lessened the weight upon the foundation. He also devised a plan to construct the cupola in consecutive layers, tying each one to its predecessor, and thereby strengthening it so that it could serve as a base for a succeeding tier. Work on the dome proceeded throughout the 1420s and, except for the lantern, was essentially complete when Pope Eugenius IV dedicated the cathedral in 1436.

Not all public expenditure for ecclesiastical buildings was absorbed by the cathedral. From the late thirteenth century, the commune subsidized the construction of the churches being built by the mendicants and other religious orders: S. Maria Novella, S. Croce, S. Spirito (Augustinian Hermits), S. Maria del Carmine (Carmelites), and S. Maria de' Servi (Servites). These grants were usually made directly to the chapters of friars or monks, but in the second half of the century, a different pattern of communal subsidy developed. In June 1361, the commune intervened directly in the construction of the Franciscan basilica of S. Croce, which had progressed very slowly. This church, so the provision stated, "had been founded by the commune of Florence, and if it is not completed, will seriously mar the city's image." By implication, the friars were blamed for their failure to complete the basilica, and henceforth responsibility for the building was vested in the Calimala guild. Soon other religious foundations recognized the fiscal advantages of associating the laity with their building projects. In June 1383, the Vallombrosan monks of S. Trinita petitioned the commune to authorize the appointment of six men, residents of their neighborhood, to collect money and supervise construction within their monastic complex. Fifty years later (February 1422), the Dominican friars of S. Maria Novella appointed their first lay building committee, "in order to imitate the other churches and to work for the embellishment of the convent."

His reputation enhanced by his work on the cathedral dome,

The Foundling Hospital. (Alinari-Art Reference Bureau)

Brunelleschi participated in much of this ecclesiastical renovation. During the crucial stages of the cupola's construction between 1419 and 1423, he directed two other important projects: the Foundling Hospital for his own guild of silk manufacturers and goldsmiths, and the rebuilding of the collegiate church of S. Lorenzo. In the loggia of the Foundling Hospital, Brunelleschi introduced those principles derived from classical antiquity which revolutionized Florentine—and Italian—architecture in the fifteenth century. Brunelleschi's patron in S. Lorenzo was the wealthy banker Giovanni di Bicci de' Medici, who paid for the construction of the Old Sacristy, which then served as his family's burial vault. Although this structure was completed in 1428, the building of the main body of the church was interrupted for several years until 1441, when Cosimo de' Medici

S. Lorenzo, interior. (Alinari-Art Reference Bureau)

decided to subsidize the work. Brunelleschi did not live to see
the completion of S. Lorenzo or his last major project, the Augustinian church of S. Spirito. The *operai* chosen to supervise
its construction proceeded at that deliberate and fitful pace which
seemed to characterize all of Brunelleschi's architectural enterprises, and indeed much of Florentine building in these years.
The work on S. Spirito proceeded so slowly that only one column
had been erected when the architect died in 1446, and the church
was not finished until 1482. Of Brunelleschi's projects, only two
—the cathedral dome and the Foundling Hospital—produced
significant changes in the urban landscape, the latter serving as
the inspiration and the nucleus for the superb square of SS. Annunziata. The bulk of the great architect's work was hidden
behind church or convent walls, or has survived only in the
sketches of those projects which, like the church of S. Maria degli
Angeli, were never completed.

The fifteenth century marks the beginning of Florentine palace construction on a large scale. Perhaps a score of Quattrocento palaces have survived, without being so radically transformed by the taste or neglect of later generations that they are unrecognizable as Renaissance creations. Of these, a handful—the Medici, the Pitti, the Rucellai—have achieved renown either because of the reputation of their owners or their architects. But palace construction is poorly documented; private family papers have not been as well preserved as the communal records, which have described, however incompletely, the construction of the great public monuments. Some of these early Quattrocento palaces were created by combining and remodeling existing structures; the Lapi and Spinelli palaces are examples. But more commonly, the building of a new palace was a lengthy and complex process which involved first the patient acquisition of real estate, then the razing of existing buildings, and finally the actual construction. Agnolo and Carlo di Messer Palla Strozzi spent more than twenty years (1435-1457) purchasing the land for their palace, the Strozzino, before they dug the foundations. The scene of a major building project of the late fifteenth century has been graphically described by the druggist Luca Landucci, whose shop was located across the street from the site of the Strozzi palace:

[20 August 1489]. They finished filling in the foundations on this side, in the Piazza de Tornaquinci. And all this time they were demolishing the houses, a great number of overseers and workmen being employed, so that all the streets round were filled with heaps of stone and rubbish and bringing gravel, making it difficult for anyone to pass along. We shopkeepers were continually annoyed by the dust and the crowds of people who collected to look on, and those who could not pass by with their beasts of burden.

The construction of these palaces transformed the city in two important ways. Demolition of old towers and houses eliminated pockets of medieval jumble and clutter; it contributed to the development of a neater and more orderly—if less picturesque —urban scene. These Quattrocento palaces also inaugurated a new style of domestic architecture, characterized by the introduction of the classical principles of order, symmetry, and proportion—and such classical devices as the column, arch, and capital—which Brunelleschi first developed in the loggia of the Foundling Hospital and the Old Sacristy of S. Lorenzo. Brunelleschi's name has been connected with several palaces—the Busini, the Medici, the Pitti—but no solid evidence of his work for private patrons has survived. According to a story reported

Medici Palace on the Via Cavour. (Alinari-Art Reference Bureau)

by Vasari, he constructed a palace model for Cosimo de' Medici, who rejected it on the grounds that it was too sumptuous and grandiose. But Michelozzo, whom Cosimo hired to build his house on the Via Larga (now Via Cavour), incorporated many of Brunelleschi's ideas in his plan. Like all Florentine Renaissance palaces, this building was based upon the traditional form exemplified by the Davanzati palace of the late fourteenth century. Structurally, the differences between the Davanzati and the Medici palaces are minor, but architecturally, they are highly significant. Order, harmony, and spaciousness had been the articulated goals of Florentine planners for more than a century; in the Medici palace and in the interior of S. Lorenzo, these objectives were realized.

PEOPLE

Surviving buildings and monuments help us to visualize the physical character of Renaissance Florence, but they contribute little to our knowledge of the city as a stage for human activity. From contemporary works of art and literature, one receives glimpses, vignettes, fleeting impressions of the human scene, but the images are usually blurred, not sharp and clear. In the fresco cycle devoted to the life of St. Peter in S. Maria del Carmine, Masolino painted a Florentine street scene with a square and its adjacent houses. The architectural details are reproduced with great accuracy and fidelity, but the scene is stylized and artificial: it lacks the human dimension. The square is nearly deserted; except for the Biblical characters, one sees only two elegantly dressed aristocrats and a few isolated figures in the distant background. During the hours of daylight, the streets of Renaissance Florence were crowded, pulsating with activity and movement. Today, the characteristic qualities of public life in that past age are most visible not in Florence with its tourist crowds and its normally sedate atmosphere but in the popular quarters of southern Italian cities, in Rome's Trastevere or the Spacca of Naples.

Life in the Renaissance city was regulated by the sun. After the gates were closed and the curfew imposed at sunset, no unauthorized persons were allowed in the streets. Officials possessed special licenses which allowed them to circulate at night, but except for these privileged citizens, and the members of the police watch, the streets were empty from dusk to dawn. Nocturnal crime was quite rare. For offenses committed during curfew hours, the statutes prescribed double penalties. But this was probably a lesser deterrent than the walls and fettered gates, which prevented escape from the city, and the locked doors of shops and houses, which limited the opportunity for thievery and assault.

Dawn was heralded by the peal of church bells and the opening of the gates, which restored the city's communication with the outside world. Passing through the gates first were peasants from local farms driving their donkey carts laden with produce for the markets. Mingling in the streets with the carts and pack animals were devout souls hurrying to early mass, and the stragglers who had chosen to drink and gamble all night rather than risk a fine for violating the curfew. Morning mass was a major social event as well as a religious ceremony in the Florentine day. In those relaxed moments after the consecration of the Host and before the day's routine began, men could discuss political events informally, exchange fragments of news which had arrived from abroad, and even settle business transactions. For respectable Florentine ladies, the mass was a precious interlude of freedom in a cloistered day, which allowed few opportunities to escape from the confines of home and domestic burdens.

As the sun moved higher above the hills on the eastern horizon, the tempo of activity and the volume of sound in the streets increased. From the working class districts of S. Frediano and Camaldoli came the laborers who toiled from sunup to sundown in the cloth factories. Others hurried along the streets to begin their day's work in the retail clothing shops along the Calimala, or in the goldsmiths' *botteghe* in the Via delle Oche. From the dark interiors of the armorers' and blacksmiths' shops came the smoke of fires lit in the forges, and the first clangs of hammer against anvil, which resounded throughout the day. By mid-morning, the narrow streets were clogged with men and animals. Peasants with empty carts were returning to their farms; merchants from Pisa and Bologna were bringing cargoes of cloth and spices into the city; employees in the cloth factories were delivering consignments of wool, yarn, dyestuffs, and cloth from one shop to another.

Detail of Masolino's fresco in Brancacci Chapel, S. Maria del Carmine. In the background is a row of Florentine houses. The subject of the fresco is

The scene in the Old Market, one of the busiest and most congested districts in Florence, was graphically portrayed by the fourteenth-century poet Antonio Pucci. Pucci's eye was attracted by the great variety of products sold in the market, and also by the motley throng which filled the square. Every comestible of the Tuscan countryside found its way to the market: vegetables and fruits in season; meat, fish, and game of every variety; delicacies imported from abroad. Market women with their baskets of chestnuts and pears competed with the shopkeepers who rented permanent stalls: butchers, fishmongers, poultry vendors, sellers of china and glassware, cloth and kitchen utensils.

the resurrection of S. Tabatha. (Alinari-Art Reference Bureau)

> Every morning the street is jammed
> With packhorses and carts in the Market,
> There is a great press and many stand looking on,
> Gentlemen accompanying their wives,
> Who come to bargain with the market women.
> There are gamblers who have been playing,
> Prostitutes and idlers,
> Highwaymen are there too, porters and dolts,
> Misers, ruffians and beggars.

By their speech and dress, the individuals in this crowd revealed their provenance, social rank, and occupation. Mingling with the peasants from the *contado* and the artisans and laborers were the inhabitants of the Florentine underworld: prostitutes and their pimps, beggars and thieves, pickpockets and sorcerers. More sober and respectable were the members of Florence's business community—bankers, merchants, and industrialists—whose simple dress and unpretentious demeanor disguised the fact that they constituted the dominant element in this society.

Contributing to the variety and heterogeneity of the street crowds were the clergy in their distinctive garb and the communal officials, whose costumes identified their functions. A visiting feudal baron, the lord of Poppi or the count of Dovadola, would ride through the streets accompanied by a large band of retainers, which indicated his social importance. The soldiers recruited for the city's defense came from every part of the Italian peninsula and also from Germany and Hungary. They were particularly ubiquitous in times of crises, standing guard in the city squares, and bargaining with shopkeepers for the purchase of weapons and supplies. For an inland city fifty miles from the sea, Florence was very cosmopolitan. Merchants from Catalonia, southern France, and the Adriatic port cities, as well as a handful from more distant places, formed part of the transient population. The cloth industry attracted hundreds of workers from Germany and the Low Countries, many of whom settled permanently in the city. The most unusual element in this society were the slaves from the Black Sea region. Their visages and complexions betrayed their Tartar and Mongol origins, just as their bizarre and violent behavior and peculiar religious customs marked them as mysterious and dangerous outsiders. Slaves who had been emancipated or had run away from their masters blended easily into the Florentine underworld.

The Old Market was a mercantile forum; its activity embraced a broad range of commercial activities, from the purchase of a cabbage from a peasant girl to the negotiations for a cargo of English wool worth thousands of florins. Here men discussed other matters, some private and intimate, others public and general; but the main subject was business. The topics of conversation which could be overheard in the city's political forum, the Piazza della Signoria, reflected more accurately the wide spectrum of Florentine interests and concerns. That square was the natural arena for political discussions by officials and councilors on their way to meetings in the palace and by others who were curious and concerned. The Merchants' Court (*Mercanzia*) and the headquarters of two magistrates, the captain and the executor, were all located in this square, which thus served as a meeting place for lawyers, police officials and persons involved in civil litigation. If only a minority of the population was regularly involved in political affairs or court proceedings, a larger number paid taxes and thus made frequent visits to the headquarters of the gabelle collectors, the officials who levied forced loans, and those in charge of the commune's funded debt, the *Monte*. Citizens assembled in the Piazza della Signoria to discuss political issues, but also to conclude business transactions, to negotiate marriage alliances, and to obtain help and sympathy for personal problems. Gambling was prohibited in the square, and prostitutes were not allowed within 100 yards of the Signoria's palace. But some diversions were tolerated, as Leon Battista Alberti noted in his comments on the loggia's social utility: "One of the greatest ornaments . . . is a handsome portico, under which old men may spend the heat of the day, or be mutually serviceable to each other; besides that, the presence of the fathers may deter and restrain the youth, who are sporting and diverting themselves in the other part of the square, from the mischievousness and folly natural to their age."

The character and tempo of activity in Florentine streets and squares, in loggias and public buildings, changed with the seasons. Winters in Florence are cold, damp, and bleak; natives accustomed to the climate curtailed their activities and, whenever possible, remained indoors. The coming of the celebrated Tuscan spring brought a revival of energy and spirits, and also an influx of foreign visitors: pilgrims on their way to Rome, merchants eager to buy and sell, vagabonds and pickpockets attracted by the larger crowds and bulging purses. This pattern is quite similar to that established by tourist migrations today, which reach a peak at Easter and another in midsummer, when the exodus of natives during the August holidays temporarily reduces human congestion. Since the fourteenth century, Florentine patricians have spent their summers in country villas, away from the stifling heat and nauseous smells of the city. In late September and October, they returned to their urban palaces to enjoy the mild and pleasant autumn weather before the onset of the chill winter rains.

The cycle of religious festivals also left its mark upon Florentine life. In Protestant countries today, the impact of the religious calendar upon life and work is limited to the casual and irregular observance of Sunday as a day of rest and of Christmas as a public holiday. Americans and Britons who live in Italy soon become aware of the greater frequency of religious holidays: the feast days of St. Joseph, Sts. Peter and Paul, the Immaculate Conception, Ascension, All Saints Day. But the dozen holy days which are still observed in Florence represent only a small portion of the forty holidays (not including Sundays) enjoyed by the Renaissance city. These numerous holidays, with their enforced cessation of labor and their requirement of public participation in cult ceremonies, contributed to the formation of an irregular living routine, quite different from the standardized patterns of industrial societies. Religious fervor was particularly intense during the Lenten season, and between Christmas and Epiphany (January 6). Thousands flocked into the cathedral every evening during Lent to hear the sermons of famous preachers, who were hired by the commune for the season. Each religious holiday featured a public ceremony in which both clergy and laity participated. One high point in the city's festival cycle was the feast day of Florence's patron saint, John the Baptist (June 24). The celebrations began on the eve of the feast day with a massive procession through the streets. Leading this cortege were the members of the Signoria and other public officials, the clergy, who displayed the relics from their churches, and representatives of the religious confraternities. Later, a second procession of dignitaries—communal and guild officials, delegates from rural parishes, feudal lords who owed allegiance to the commune—brought their gifts of wax candles to the Baptistery.

Besides these cyclical variations in the urban routine, there were numerous special events and incidents which gave color and drama to Florentine life. Chronicles and diaries are valuable sources for these happenings. In the year 1386, for example, an anonymous chronicler noted the public occurrences which attracted his attention. When the new bishop, Bartolomeo Uliari of Padua, approached the city on January 28, he was escorted with traditional pomp and ceremony to his palace near the Baptistery by a group of communal officials and distinguished citizens. In his account of the reception of an ambassador from Hungary, on February 8, the chronicler described the public and ceremonial aspects of this occasion:

> The knights of the Parte Guelfa rode out to meet the envoy, on horses caparisoned with beautiful cloths. They accompanied the ambassador to the Piazza della Signoria. There they jousted and broke lances and unfurled their banners in the square. . . . Afterwards, they went to the Palace of the Parte Guelfa with much feasting and revelry. That night, the Signoria, the Parte Guelfa and the entire citizenry lit bonfires in honor of King Charles.

Similar processions and ceremonies were organized to honor a papal envoy who visited the city on December 15, and to celebrate the triumphal entry (July 12) of a Florentine mercenary captain, Giovanni degli Obizzi, who had waged a brief but successful campaign against the lord of Urbino, Antonio da Montefeltro.

These ceremonies were structured events, organized by the commune to satisfy the populace's craving for bread and circuses, and also to stimulate the community's pride in itself and its achievements. Unexpected and bizarre occurrences also interrupted the normal routines of life and were reported in the chronicles. The birth of two lion cubs on December 15, 1386 was an occasion for general rejoicing, for these symbols of Florence's Guelf allegiance were regarded as omens whose fortunes were linked to the city's. On August 20, the anonymous chronicler described the arrival from Hungary of the severed heads of three men who had been implicated in the assassination (in February) of King Charles of Hungary. These grisly specimens were in the house of a shopkeeper in the Via degli Spadai, "who showed them to whoever wished to see them." Although so common and frequent that they were rarely noticed by the diarists, public executions invariably stimulated popular interest and excitement. Persuaded that the witnessing of such horrors served as a detterent to crime, the authorities gave maximum publicity to these executions. In August 1379, the chronicler described the last hour of a slave girl named Lucia, who had poisoned her master. She was not taken directly to the execution site, but was placed in a cart and driven through the main streets of the city, her flesh torn by hot pincers, before she was burned at the stake.

From the accounts of chroniclers and diarists, as well as from official records, we are well informed about the Florentine response to the major crises of these years. They were of two general types: those arising from internal disorders or from external military threats; and the occurrence of natural disasters—floods, famines and visitations of the plague.

Protected by her walls, Florence was relatively secure from attack by enemy troops. Occasionally, a marauding band of soldiers would ravage the unfortified villages and farms on the city's outskirts, but rarely did an organized military force penetrate the outer ring of defense fortifications on the hills surrounding Florence. However, every invasion threat sent crowds of refugees laden with goods into the city. The danger usually passed within a few days, so that urban life was not seriously disrupted by abnormal congestion or price inflation. More dangerous were the internal disorders—the political conspiracies and the riots of hungry workers—which threatened public order and security and sometimes led to the downfall of the government. Between June 1342 and August 1343, the communal regime was thrice overthrown by force, while another outbreak of revolutionary violence occurred in the summer of 1378, during the uprising of the cloth workers, the Ciompi.

This proletarian revolution is the best known internal crisis in Florentine history.* It will serve to illustrate the general phenomenon of urban disorder and mass violence, even though it was more traumatic, and its consequences of greater significance, than the other revolutionary spasms which the city experienced. At the first signs of trouble, in June 1378, the shops and factories closed, and business activities all but ceased. Many

*The economic aspects of the Ciompi revolution are discussed in Chapter Two.

prominent citizens fled to their country estates, and the natural reaction of those who stayed in Florence was to remain indoors and out of sight. But artisans and workers gathered in the streets to discuss the latest events, and to voice their fears, apprehensions, and hopes for the future. With the shops and factories barred and shuttered, the number of idle workers multiplied, as did the threat to public order. Unemployment was a serious problem throughout the summer, and so too was the threat of famine. For despite the strenuous efforts of communal officials, the normal flow of victuals into the city was seriously disrupted. The revolutionary atmosphere was a deterrent to everyone involved in food distribution: from the wholesale grain and meat dealers, to the peasant women who brought a dozen eggs or a basket of salad greens to the market.

The specter of anarchy haunted many Florentines, and particularly men of property, in these tense weeks. The ingredients were ominously present and visible: the crowds of unemployed and hungry poor, many of whom possessed arms; the atmosphere of fear and tension; a weak and insecure regime which maintained a very tenuous control over the city and its restive inhabitants. On three specific occasions—in mid-June, mid-July, and the end of August—a complete breakdown of public order seemed likely. On June 22, a throng of artisans and cloth workers set fire to the palaces of a dozen aristocratic families. But other outbreaks of rioting and looting were repressed by the authorities, who summarily executed two Flemish looters in the streets, as an object lesson to potential troublemakers. A month later (July 21 and 22), there occurred a second explosion of violence; palaces were gutted by fire, communal and guild records were destroyed, a police official was lynched by a mob. But violence did not spread further, and a new regime led by the wool carder, Michele di Lando, desperately sought to reduce tension and placate the discontented. Six weeks later, however, crowds of unemployed cloth workers again assembled in the streets to protest the government's failure to provide them with work and food. Wild rumors circulated that the workers were planning to sack the city. Lending credence to these stories were the confused and aimless movements of laborers through the streets, the fiery speeches of proletarian orators, and the organization of a committee of "eight saints," which had some vague plan to make the regime responsive to their needs. But these undisciplined workers were easily routed in street battles with guildsmen (August 31), who were determined to resist these pressures for a more egalitarian political order.

The only natural disaster which, in its impact upon the city, rivaled these disturbances was the plague. Although famines occurred quite frequently in the fourteenth century, they were usually of short duration, and their effects were mitigated by the commune's policy of importing grain. But pestilence struck the city regularly, on the average of once per decade, beginning in 1340. Not every plague was as deadly as the Black Death of 1348, but each epidemic killed several thousand inhabitants and seriously disrupted the social and economic order and, to a lesser degree, the political structure.

Florence's ordeal during the Black Death has been graphically described by three authors: the chroniclers Matteo Villani and Marchionne Stefani, and Giovanni Boccaccio in the preface to his *Decameron*. The most immediate and direct consequence of the plague was the closing of shops and factories, as the city's economy stagnated. Even taverns shut down, and only a few doctors' offices and druggists' shops remained open in the stricken city. The breakdown of the food supply undoubtedly increased the death rate among the poor, who were deprived of sustenance and medical care, and who had no choice but to await death in their fetid, crowded slums. Wealthier citizens had a greater range of choices, one of which was to flee to their country villas, or to other, healthier regions. Among the few signs of life in the silent, deserted streets were the carts and horses of the rich in flight. The city resembled a vast hospital and charnel house; as the plague toll mounted, the care and concern for both the living and the dead declined sharply. Doctors, druggists, and the surviving purveyors of food charged exorbitant prices for provisions and services to the sick. "Blessed was he," commented Stefani, "who could find three eggs in one day's search through the entire city." Boccaccio wrote a grimly realistic account of the treatment which the plague victims received:

It was the common practice of most of the neighbors, moved no less by fear of contamination by the putrefying bodies than by charity towards the deceased, to drag the corpses out of the houses with their own hands . . . and to lay them in front of the doors, where anyone who made the rounds might have seen, especially in the morning, more of them than he could count; afterwards they would have biers brought up. . . . Nor was it once or twice only that one and the same bier carried two or three corpses at once; but quite a considerable number of such cases occurred, one bier sufficing for husband and wife, two or three brothers, father and son, and so forth. And times without number it happened that, as two priests bearing the cross were on their way to perform the last office for someone, three or four biers were brought up by the porters in rear of them so that, whereas the priests supposed that they had but one corpse to bury, they discovered that there were six to eight, or sometimes more. Nor, for all their number, were their obsequies honored by either tears or lights or crowds of mourners; rather, it was come to this, that a dead man was then of no more account than a dead goat would be today.

Those who survived the plague commented on its deleterious effects upon human behavior. Both Stefani and Boccaccio remarked that some men spent their days and nights drinking and carousing with friends. More disturbing was the spectacle of parents abandoning their children and husbands their wives; entire families would flee in the night, leaving a stricken relative to die alone and unattended. But fear and panic did not demoralize all members of this community; some heroic men and women sacrificed their lives in the service of others. There were certainly many parents like the Sienese chronicler, Agnolo di Tura, who wrote that he had buried five of his children with his own hands. The tribulations of the survivors did not cease with the passing of an epidemic. In addition to rebuilding their private worlds shattered by the loss of parents, children, relatives, and friends, they also had to restore those collective institutions —commune, guild, church, confraternity—which were threatened with disintegration. Perhaps the most demoralizing aspect of this reconstruction was the realization that pestilence would recur, that the struggles to rebuild might be futile. What were the thoughts of men who had survived the plague in their youth, to be menaced by another epidemic in their prime, or worse, to see their children succumb to a malady which a decade before had claimed their parents? In that age, which was accustomed to misery, pain, and death, the plague—by its mystery and its virulence—brought its special brand of fear and anxiety to five Florentine generations.

TWO

The Economy

THE FOUNDATIONS

The most important source for Florentine history before the Black Death is the chronicle of Giovanni Villani (d. 1348), which describes the city's growth from rural village to a metropolis of 100,000 souls. Villani's narrative is structured chronologically; it moves systematically from year to year and from month to month. But in the midst of describing the wars, factional disputes, and urban building enterprises of the 1330s, Villani paused in his story to provide his readers with a statistical survey of his native city. Only a merchant possessing a wide experience with numbers, and a sense of their importance, would have attempted this analysis. Thus we owe this valuable and informative survey to the chronicler's business background, as well as to his patriotism. For he justified this statistical excursus on practical grounds, "so that our descendants in days to come may be aware of any rise, stability and decline in her condition and wealth which our city may experience, and also so that . . . [our descendants] may strive to increase her power, seeing our record and example in this chronicle."

These statistics which Villani records are truly impressive. In 1338 Florence ranked among the five most populous cities in Europe; only Paris, Venice, Milan, and Naples were larger in size. Each day the residents consumed over 2300 bushels of grain and drank in excess of 70,000 quarts of wine. Some 4000 cattle and 100,000 sheep, goats, and swine were slaughtered each year to provide the city with meat. A large segment of the population was directly sustained by the woolen cloth industry, which employed some 30,000 workers, and which produced cloth valued at 1,200,000 florins annually (nearly $5,000,000 at the current gold price). Exported cloth worth 350,000 florins was processed and refined in the workshops of the Calimala guild. Although Villani did not estimate the number of merchants who lived and traded within the city walls, he did calculate that over 300 Florentines engaged in commercial activity abroad. Ministering to the financial and legal needs of this large business community were some 80 banking and money-changing firms and 600 notaries.

One dimension of the Florentine story which does not emerge clearly from Villani's chronicle is the rapid rate of growth. Florence developed much later than the maritime ports of Pisa, Genoa, and Venice; it was also more backward than the great Lombard center of Milan. When, in the twelfth century, merchants from neighboring Pisa were establishing their maritime hegemony over the western Mediterranean, participating in the profitable Crusade traffic, and establishing colonies in the Levant, Florence was still a small, provincial town. She was strongly influenced by the rural, feudal world of Tuscany; her economy was essentially local. Until the end of the twelfth century, Pisa surpassed her inland neighbor in size, population, and wealth. When Florence began construction of a new girdle of walls in 1172, the circumscribed area measured only 200 acres, just two-thirds of the space encompassed by Pisa's fortifications. By the middle of the thirteenth century, however, Florence had overtaken her rival. In 1284 she began construction of a third wall, a massive project which was not completed for a half-century, and which enclosed over 1500 acres, nearly 2½ square miles.

The beginnings of the city's economic expansion are not well documented. We may assume that Florentines constituted some small part of that diaspora which sent waves of Italian merchants and seamen along the Mediterranean trade routes to the Levant, the Black Sea, and the north African coast in the eleventh and twelfth centuries. But they were not reckoned among the pioneers who established Italy's commercial and maritime empire, and until the thirteenth century, their achievements and wealth were overshadowed by the mercantile communities established in Pisa, Genoa, Venice, and Milan. Florence's inland position was a serious handicap in this early phase of Italy's commercial revolution. Indeed, the city was not particularly favored either by location or by natural resources. The main traffic artery from northern Europe to Rome, the *via francigena*, ran west of the city, between Lucca and Siena, and Florence gained small profit from the throngs of pilgrims traveling to the shrines of the Eternal City. While the land around Florence did provide sustenance for a growing urban population, the soil was not particularly fertile, and the hilly terrain was more suited to vine and olive than to grain, the indispensable staple of urban masses.

Two significant developments for the city's growth in the thirteenth century were the establishment of close ties with the papacy and the Angevin kingdom of Naples, and the rise of her woolen cloth industry to a position of preeminence in Europe and Asiatic markets. These were the crucial factors which enabled her citizens to amass large fortunes. Wealth from these sources was utilized to build housing for the flood of immigrants, and to fight the wars which established Florence's hegemony in Tuscany. The architectural monuments of her medieval past —the Palazzo Vecchio, the cathedral, S. Croce, S. Maria Novella —were built by the profits accumulated from the sale of Florentine cloth, and from the transactions of Florentine merchants and bankers in Rome and Naples, in Venice and Palermo.

Florence's economic connection with the papacy and the kingdom of Naples was formed in the last decades of the thirteenth century. It was forged only after years of bitter strife between Guelf (papal) and Ghibelline (imperial) factions within the city, and after the Guelf powers had finally triumphed over their Ghibelline rivals in the peninsula. The conclusion of this lengthy and complex struggle represented a victory for a group of aggressive merchant families in Florence which used their Guelf ties to crush their local enemies, and also to obtain valuable economic concessions from their allies throughout and beyond the peninsula. They took over the papal banking monopoly from their Sienese rivals and established themselves as tax collectors for the Holy See throughout Latin Christendom.

The Florentine share of the proceeds from this lucrative enterprise was substantial, but these merchants also used their protected position to monopolize international banking and trade in ultramontane areas. The late thirteenth and early fourteenth centuries witnessed the rise of the great Florentine mercantile companies—Scali, Amieri, Bardi, Peruzzi, Acciaiuoli—each with capital resources far greater than any earlier business firm, and with networks of subsidiary branches which blanketed Latin Christendom. In Bruges, London, and Paris, in the Mediterranean ports of Barcelona, Marseille, and Tunis, in the Levantine marts, Florentine merchants bought and sold, invested, exchanged coins, and sent home the profits from their varied activities. The kingdom of Naples was most intensively exploited by these entrepreneurs. Florentine companies possessed a monopoly of the region's grain trade; their personnel collected taxes and rose high in the bureaucracy. The Angevin kingdom was to Florence by the early fourteenth century what India was to be for England 500 years later.

International merchants and bankers contributed significantly to Florentine prosperity, but their activity was not the main factor in the city's economic growth and the quadrupling of her population during the thirteenth century. This miracle was wrought by the woolen cloth industry, which provided employment for thousands of workers, producing cloth of such quality that it commanded the highest prices in the fairs, markets, and bazaars of three continents. To this enterprise, as to commerce, the Florentines came late, long after other regions—for example, Flanders and Lombardy—were firmly established as cloth-producing centers. Florentines first developed their skills by refinishing cloth imported from abroad. Their techniques and greed sharpened by this experience, they quickly developed their own system for producing cloth from imported wool. In their struggle for supremacy, Florentine manufacturers were aided by good fortune. The Flemish cloth industry was declining in the late thirteenth century, just as Florence's own production was expanding. Moreover, the city's mercantile network contributed to the growth of the cloth industry by supplying capital, by arranging for the purchase of high-quality wool in England and Spain, and by efficient and aggressive marketing of finished cloth.

But these favorable circumstances do not detract from this remarkable achievement, which was based ultimately upon the entrepreneurial talents of the manufacturers, and the technological skills of their workers.

The props which supported the Florentine economy—her mercantile empire and her cloth industry—were frequently shaken in the early decades of the fourteenth century, but they did not collapse. But a series of disasters in the 1340s did reverse the trend of economic expansion which had continued for nearly three centuries. The bankruptcies of the Bardi and Peruzzi companies, the two largest mercantile organizations, were serious blows to the city's economy and shook the confidence of the entrepreneurial class. Yet the effects of these business crises were minuscule by comparison with the impact of the Black Death in 1348. This pestilence still reigns unchallenged as the single greatest catastrophe in European history, more deadly than any war or natural disaster. According to the most recent estimate, some 40,000 Florentines died in this plague year. As an isolated phenomenon, the pestilence was a major catastrophe. But it was also a portent for a host of other scourges: recurring epidemics and famines, wars, political disorders, and social unrest.

The economic scene confronting these Florentines who survived the plague did not change significantly during the next century. The city had lost one-half of its population, and perhaps one-third of its market. Thereafter, whenever the population curve began to inch upward, the increment would be snuffed out by another epidemic. Seven times between 1350 and 1430, the city was struck by plague. Fed sporadically by immigration after each visitation of the scourge, the urban population fluctuated between 50,000 and 70,000. But not until the eighteenth century did the city again reach the size it had attained during Giovanni Villani's lifetime. Florence's plight was also Europe's: a population reduced by one-third, a shrunken market, a sluggish and stagnating economy. To these adverse economic conditions was added another negative factor, the intensification of political disorders. Throughout Europe, the merchant seeking to ply his trade was harassed by armed bands of soldiers and adventurers, spawned by the wars which broke out with increasing frequency and ferocity. If that perennial nuisance, feudal lawlessness, had largely disappeared from the European scene by the thirteenth century, its successor, the depredations of the armed companies, was an equally serious menace to the merchant and to his customers.

Florence lived through the disasters which threatened to overwhelm her in the 1340s, and, indeed, the city maintained her position as a leading mercantile and industrial center. Surviving the pestilence and the bankruptcies was a hardy group of entrepreneurs, some enriched by legacies from plague victims, who worked hard and effectively to repair the damage. Important segments of Florence's economic structure remained intact: most of the capital investment, the entrepreneurial and technical knowledge of merchants and artisans, and the competitive spirit and desire for profit, which had not been quenched by adversity. Fortified with these assets, the cloth manufacturers reopened their shops, enticed immigrant workers into their *botteghe,* and produced cloth for a market that was sluggish and unpredictable but did not disappear. Although business prospects and opportunities were never bright, neither were they universally bleak. Some areas were more prosperous than others; some markets were expanding while others declined. In this uncertain economic climate, intelligence, astuteness, and enterprise were at a premium, and Florentine businessmen were well fortified with these qualities. By employing their talents to the utmost, they were able to maintain a relatively high level of productivity and prosperity throughout these years. Their efforts secured the city's independence and provided the resources for the brilliant cultural achievement of the fifteenth century.

VARIETIES OF BUSINESS ENTERPRISE: THE CLOTH INDUSTRY

In textbook descriptions of urban economic life in medieval and Renaissance Europe, much stress is placed upon the rigid supervision and control of economic activity by secular and ecclesiastical authorities. These accounts point out that the affairs of each merchant and artisan were closely scrutinized and regulated by the guilds, which controlled production, fixed wages and prices, and sought to guarantee to each guildsman a fair share of a limited market. In this hierarchical scheme of business enterprise, each individual pursued a single trade or profession —lawyer, physician, merchant, druggist, baker, innkeeper— throughout his life. He gradually worked his way up in his métier, from apprentice to journeyman and ultimately to master. His shop was normally located in that section of the city reserved for his trade, so that medieval towns were divided geographically into distinct compartments of economic activity. Guild officials were not the only regulatory agents in the towns, for communal magistracies also supervised trade, exchange, and industry. Allied with these secular authorities were the officials of the bishop's court, intent upon detecting and penalizing usurious loans and other illegal business transactions.

The realities of Florentine economic life were quite different from this neat, stereotyped picture. Regulation, whether secular or ecclesiastical, was neither as close nor as rigid as the guild statutes or the canon law codes might suggest. The surviving records of business companies indicate that the operations of these firms were not seriously hampered by the imposing body of regulatory legislation in the statute books.

In yet another respect, Florentine business practice varied from the norm. The occupations and activities of the mercantile class were not narrowly defined or irrevocably fixed by guild membership. Most Florentine entrepreneurs engaged in a wide variety of economic pursuits, often enrolling in two, three or more guilds concurrently. Their business interests frequently included both mercantile and banking operations, the ownership of a cloth factory as well as shares in the commune's funded debt (*Monte*). A merchant's investment in real estate might include a palace and several shops in the city, a villa and vineyard in nearby Settignano, a cluster of houses in Prato, farmland in the Arno valley near Empoli, and perhaps some parcels of forest and grazing land in the hills above Pistoia.

An eminent lawyer of the late Trecento, Messer Alessandro dell' Antella, did not limit his activities to politics and legal practice, but was also a partner in an Avignon trading and banking firm. When the outbreak of war terminated that enterprise in 1375, he formed another partnership to buy Greek wine in bulk and sell it at retail in Florence. It is true that artisans and shopkeepers tended to pursue a single trade, and to pass their métier on to their sons. But tax records reveal some mobility even among these conservative groups; for example, Luca di Niccolò, a graindealer, became a *lanaiuolo,* and Piero di Nardo pursued two occupations, stockingmaker and cloth manufacturer.

The tempo and direction of the business activity of the Florentine mercantile community was constantly changing, according to inclination, opportunity, and circumstance. A merchant might temporarily abandon his moneychanging table in the Mercato Vecchio to invest his capital in foreign trade. Or he might decide to withdraw from the manufacture of woolen cloth, to concentrate upon the more profitable production of silk. Changing market conditions or ill health might induce him to divest himself of all entrepreneurial interests and live off the revenues of real estate and investments in communal bonds. Rarely were the economic interests of Florentine merchants, particularly on the higher levels, fixed irrevocably. The business world was in constant flux.

In no medieval city did the guilds incorporate within their membership all forms of economic activity. And in large urban centers like Florence, substantial segments of the economy escaped guild control. For example, stonemasons and carpenters possessed their own guilds, but laborers in brick factories and street pavers were not enrolled in any corporation. Grain dealers and bankers were organized, but not the operators of flour mills along the Arno and its tributaries. Moneychangers who maintained their tables in the Mercato Vecchio were under the jurisdiction of the Cambio guild, but their fellows who lived and traded outside the city were exempt from the guild's control. A remarkable catalogue of specialized trades and occupations, not described in any guild statute, can be compiled from the commune's fiscal records. Among the unusual occupations described in the tax declarations of 1427, the *catasto,** are a fencing

---

*Introduced in 1427, the *catasto* was a system of tax assessment based upon a detailed record of the property owned by Florentine citizens. The head of each household was required to compile a complete list of his assets (real estate, business investments, communal bonds, cash, and loans) and his

master, the director of an actors' school, an artisan who made
glass windows, and one Domenico di Lorenzo, who manufactured
gunpowder for cannon. Neither these tax documents nor any
guild matriculation list identify the members of yet another important profession, prostitution. But the *catasto* volumes do reveal the names of bordello proprietors, like Rosso di Giovanni
de' Medici, who rented six rooms to *femine mondane* for 3 or 4
florins per month, a price equal to the rent of a small house
for an entire year.

If the guild system did not impose serious limits upon the
direction and variety of economic pursuits, neither did it de-
marcate clearly the economic "classes" in Florence. There were,
to be sure, wealthy merchants and industrialists in the seven
greater guilds, and below them in the economic hierarchy, artisans and petty shopkeepers, enrolled in the fourteen lower
guilds. At the bottom of the scale were the cloth workers, ped-
dlers, servants, and beggars, who were not organized into any
corporation. But these categories were roughly drawn, and each
contained a broad spectrum of wealth and status. Some of the
richest Florentines belonged to no guild, and did not engage in
any trade, but lived off the income of their investments. Matriculated in the guilds of cloth manufacturers (*Lana*) and bankers (*Cambio*) were men who had made large fortunes, and
others who were destitute. And within the ranks of the artisans
and petty shopkeepers in the lower guilds could be found affluent
winesellers and ironmongers whose fortunes might have come
from an inheritance windfall or a lucky investment, or through
the slow and patient accumulation of capital. The *catasto* records of 1427 identify these wealthy representatives of the petty
bourgeoisie; men like the tanner Antonio di Antonio, and the
wine dealers Salvestro and Piero di Leonardo, whose gross assets
exceeded 6000 florins.

Binding together the units of this economic system was a vast
and complex network of relationships, which encompassed a
large geographical area, and which linked together men of every

---

debts and obligations. His assessment was calculated at 0.5% of the value
of his assets, minus his obligations and deductions for dependents and
living quarters. The tax was based upon property value, not income.

class and social stratum. The operations of Florence's great mercantile companies extended over the whole of Latin Europe, as well as the African and Asiatic coasts of the Mediterranean. The records of the Prato merchant Francesco Datini contain notices of transactions with 200 cities, from Edinburgh and Stockholm in the north, to Beirut, Alexandria, and the Caspian port of Tana to the south and east. But the economic orbit of small businessmen was also much larger than is often assumed. An old-clothes dealer matriculated in the lower guilds, Giovanni di Goggio, was also active in the grain trade with Naples. The profession of ironmongering would seem to be essentially local and domestic in character. But in the 1370s, Lorenzo di Giovanni and Francesco Pasquini formed a partnership in this métier, in which Lorenzo remained in Florence to operate the shop, while Francesco went abroad "to buy merchandise pertaining to this trade, and to sell the goods which came into their hands." Francesco's peregrinations in pursuit of business opportunities took him to Genoa, over 200 miles from Florence.

The most complex set of relationships in the Florentine economy existed within the woolen cloth industry. Linked together in this industry were capitalists, managers, factors, dyers, fullers, weavers, and spinners, men (and women) belonging to the highest and lowest strata of Florentine society. The key figure in the production process was the *lanaiuolo*, whose role corresponded to that of the president of a modern manufacturing company. Most of the 200 cloth-producing firms in Florence were associations of two or more *lanaiuoli*, who provided the capital for the plant's operation. Rarely did these manufacturers personally direct the daily operations of the shop; this position was normally filled by a salaried factor. It was his responsibility to organize and supervise the transformation of the raw material, the fleeces imported from England or Spain, into the finely woven and brilliantly dyed cloth that commanded premium prices in the European and Levantine markets.

The complexity of this industrial enterprise, and the large network of economic relationships it created and nourished, can be seen by tracing the stages of the production process. Upon arrival in the *lanaiuolo*'s shop, the wool was first prepared for spinning. Most of this work was performed in the shop itself, by workers whose activities were supervised by foremen. Spinning was done by women in the *contado*. Thus the rural areas surrounding Florence were drawn into the industry's vortex. Serving as intermediaries between the *lanaiuoli* and the spinners were brokers who delivered the wool, collected the yarn, and paid the women on a piece-rate basis. The yarn was given to weavers, who operated looms in their shops or private dwellings. The finished cloth was then sent to another category of subcontractors, the fullers, who operated their mills along streams in outlying areas. Most of the final stages of the production process —dyeing, shearing, mending—were also carried out in small shops by independent masters. Each of these petty entrepreneurs constituted a nucleus of economic activity, for they frequently hired apprentices or laborers to work in their shops. Each, too, nourished subsidiary industries, crafts, and markets. The wool washers were serviced by soapmakers, who in turn obtained their supplies from oil vendors. Dyers either purchased woad and other dyestuffs directly from the Lana guild, or from merchants who traded in these commodities. Blacksmiths and ironmongers provided some of the tools utilized in the production process, while other Florentines earned their bread by constructing the stretching sheds, the looms, spinning wheels, combs, and other instruments of this primitive industrial plant.

From extant business records, it is possible to analyze the internal operations of these cloth manufacturing firms. An account book survives, a record of income and expenditure, belonging to Niccolò di Nofri Strozzi and Giovanni di Credi, who operated a cloth *bottega* from October 1386 until January 1390. Although the ledger does not furnish production figures, this partnership must have operated one of the largest cloth factories in Florence, producing at least 200 bolts annually. The company's average yearly expenditure for labor, wool, and other production costs exceeded 9000 florins. The most interesting transactions in this account book pertain to labor expenses; they describe payments to a veritable army of employees and subcontractors who were involved in the various stages of the production process.

Many disbursements were made to subcontractors who operated their own *botteghe,* and who were paid on a piece-rate basis. Regular payments, for example, were made to a wool carder identified only as Fruosino, who received 10 *soldi* for each load (*salma*) of wool carded in his shop. His annual gross income from the Strozzi firm exceeded 100 florins annually, a very respectable sum for a small businessman. Other payments were made to operators of dye vats, stretching sheds, washing plants, and looms. The firm engaged a large number of weavers, including several women and three Germans, Anichino and Gherardo of Cologne and Ermanno [Herman] Dati. The lowliest category of laborers hired by the Strozzi firm were the female spinners. In a single day, over twenty women received their pittances for the wool which they had spun. Thus monna Nicolosa earned 2 *lire*, 13 *soldi*, for 43 pounds of spun wool, while monna Margherita, a widow, earned the cost of 3 bushels of grain (2 *lire*) for her consignment of 10 pounds. These records do not contain the wages of those unskilled laborers who were employed in the shop itself; such payments were recorded in a separate "book of the workers." But the salaries of overseers, factors, and apprentices are registered in this ledger; for example, the payment of 8 florins to Giovanni di Neri, "a boy in the shop," and 1 florin to Antonio di Bonsignore, "the apprentice in charge of the laborers."

While our knowledge of the manufacturing companies is quite extensive, we know very little about the subcontractors, and even less about the hired workers whose economic activities are rarely mentioned in the sources. One ledger belonging to a firm of subcontractors has survived; it contains valuable information about the activities of this segment of the Florentine business community.

In the 1370s, the partnership of Lippo di Dino and Francesco di Vanni was formed to engage in the manufacture of loom reeds (*pettini*), which were used in preparing the wool for the looms. Most frequently recorded in the firm's account book are the sale of these instruments to operatives in the industry. Nearly all of these *pettini* were sold locally, but in 1377, one of the partners traveled to Pisa to sell a consignment. Apparently, goats' horns were used in the manufacture of these instruments, or in other combs, for the partners bought several hundred pairs from Ser Simone, a priest of S. Miniato al Monte, and employed a worker to clean the horns. The most noteworthy feature of this business partnership was its diversity; Lippo and Francesco had their fingers in several economic pies. They bought, sold, and exchanged cloth, even though they were not matriculated in the Lana guild, or indeed in any other corporation. On one occasion, they received a load of apples and honey from a business associate in Pisa, which they sold. They also operated a loan business, lending small sums at interest. Their customers included a blacksmith from Pistoia named Guccio di Grazino, an impecunious physician, Maestro Francesco, and the factor of a large cloth *bottega*, Vieri di Masino. The business operations of these petty entrepreneurs were quite as varied and flexible, and apparently as untrammeled by guild restrictions, as those of international financiers.

Providing some unity and order for this large, decentralized industrial complex was the Lana guild, the association of cloth manufacturers. Although the guild had jurisdiction over the personnel of the entire industry, its membership was limited to the *lanaiuoli*, while the subcontractors and salaried laborers were rigorously excluded. The guild had many functions. It possessed a broad mandate to promote the industry's welfare, and this might prompt the consuls to agitate for favorable legislation in the commune or to arrange for the bulk purchase of such essential commodities as oil and woad. To serve the needs of its members, it also owned and operated dye shops and stretching sheds. Its regulatory activities were numerous and varied. Aware that the high quality of the industry's produce was a major asset, the guild inspected all cloth produced in Florence to ensure conformity to its high standards. Normally, it imposed no restrictions upon output, but in moments of crisis, it was prepared to interfere directly in the internal operations of the *botteghe*, to place limits upon production, or to distribute the labor force equitably among the *lanaiuoli*. Guild consuls devoted much of their time to the adjudication of differences between members and subordinates (*sottoposti*): disputes over debts, partnership agreements, labor contracts. An important dimension of guild activity was disciplinary. The foreign official of the corporation meted out fines and other penalties, including expulsion from the guild, to violators of the statutes and regulations. Most frequently penalized were the dyers and other subcontractors, and the wage laborers, who were not represented in the guild, and had no legal recourse to the exactions imposed by the foreign official.

Students of the Lana guild have emphasized that this organization was a monopoly of the manufacturers, who employed it to control the industry and to exploit the subordinate personnel. They have pointed out, too, that the guild's authority over *lanaiuoli* and *sottoposti* was complete and absolute, and that it extended to the most minute details of the production process. While these two propositions are generally valid, each requires some qualification.

The statutes and decrees of the guild have provided the evidence for this picture of comprehensive surveillance and rigid control. These records describe a system in which every phase of production, from the initial stages to the final mending, was closely scrutinized and controlled by guild officials. Wages, working conditions, financial transactions, relations between *lanaiuoli* and subordinates, were all subject to regulation. Such was the ideal articulated in the statutes; the realities were different. The frequency of the penalties inflicted by the guild upon its recalcitrant members and subordinates suggests that the rules were often, perhaps systematically, evaded by manufacturers, subcontractors and workers. The remarkable range of these "crimes" reveal the difficulties in controlling a large, decentralized industry. *Lanaiuoli* were regularly penalized for producing cloth in the *contado* to evade guild controls, for manufacturing more than their assigned quotas, and for selling cloth in pieces instead of in bolts. When labor was in short supply, they sought to entice workers away from competitors by paying their debts and offering them higher salaries, above the scale fixed by the guild. During periods of depression, on the other hand, unscrupulous manufacturers paid off their employees in counterfeit coin, or in cloth, practices prohibited by guild statute. Fines levied against subcontractors usually concerned some violation of production standards. Wool washers were penalized for skimping on soap, dyers for mixing inferior materials in their vats, weavers for stealing yarn which had been delivered to them or for producing inferior cloth.

The guild may have contributed to the perennial violation of its rules by lax enforcement, and by its policy of systematically reducing the penalties fixed by its foreign official. By their decisions, the consuls implicitly recognized the impossibility, or even the desirability, of exercising the totality of control stipulated in the statutes. Sentences of foreign officials who adhered strictly to the letter of the guild regulations were frequently quashed by the consuls, who were also very susceptible to appeals by poverty-stricken offenders for the cancellation of their penalties. Thus, behind the façade of massive regulation and control, existed a relatively free industrial enterprise, whose economic functions were determined as much by the requirements and pressures of the market as by the authoritarian dictates of the guild consuls.

If its controls over cloth production was less than absolute, the Lana guild remained a powerful instrument in the hands of the manufacturers over the inferior categories in the industry. As one means of maintaining its authority, it refused to allow these subordinate groups to matriculate, nor were they permitted to form their own independent organization. Necessity, however, forced the guild to make minor, temporary concessions, particularly to the subcontractors (dyers, stretchers, fullers, menders) who operated their own shops as independent enterprises. To pacify the more ambitious of these craftsmen, the guild permitted a small number of *sottoposti* to matriculate into the guild, to become *lanaiuoli*. During the middle decades of the fourteenth century, the dyers, who were the most militant of the *sottoposti*, were represented in the guild consulate. Guild records also reveal that the consuls were occasionally prepared to negotiate with the subcontractors over prices and other problems of mutual concern. At certain times, however, the economic differences between the *lanaiuoli* and their subordinates could not be reconciled. In 1370, the dyers refused to accept the rate schedule for coloring cloth offered by the *lanaiuoli;* they went on strike. Manufacturers denounced these tactics, but they finally negotiated a settlement. In 1378, the *sottoposti* profited from political disturbances in the city to break away from the guild's domination, and for three years they maintained a precarious, independent existence. But another political upheaval in 1382 ended that brief interlude of freedom, and thereafter they remained firmly under the control of the manufacturers.

The *lanaiuoli* demonstrated little solicitude for the thousands of unskilled or semiskilled wage laborers who performed the menial tasks of beating and carding wool in their shops. Unlike the dyers, fullers, and menders, who possessed a small economic stake in the society, these workers were propertyless. They earned a bare subsistence from their labor and were extremely vulnerable to the economic vicissitudes which plagued the industry. They possessed no economic power, no lever with which to bargain; but their numbers (perhaps 15,000 in the 1370s and 1380s) made them a permanent threat to the industry and to the city's security. Guild and commune cooperated to feed this laboring mass in times of famine, and also to suppress any movement to organize the workers. Religious confraternities, so popular among other levels of society, were strictly prohibited among operatives in the cloth shops. In 1345, an attempt by a wool carder named Ciuto Brandini to organize an association of his fellow workers was crushed by the authorities, and Brandini himself was executed. The judicial sentence described him as a man "hated by all for his condition, activities and bad reputation"; he was specifically charged with urging workers to join his union and with soliciting funds from his comrades "in order that they might more strongly resist" their masters. This movement failed, but thirty years later the cloth workers organized a massive attack against their masters during the Ciompi revolution of 1378. This famous revolt marked the high point of labor agitation in Florence. It has been considered by some historians as the most significant episode of urban social conflict in Europe during the Middle Ages.

This revolution was not simply a revolt of the cloth workers; it had several other dimensions. It was the culmination of a lengthy period of discord between opposing factions within the ruling group. Joining in the struggle were discontented groups of artisans from the lower guilds, who wanted a greater share of offices for themselves. The rebellious elements in the cloth industry were divided into two main groups: the subcontractors, brokers, and factors who possessed some limited economic and social status; and the large mass of destitute, propertyless laborers, with no stake in society and little hope of ever escaping from their depressed condition. All of these disgruntled elements cooperated to bring down the communal regime in July 1378, and to establish a more egalitarian political order in which merchants, artisans, and workers were assigned a fixed proportion of offices and a guaranteed share of political power. This popular regime, however, did not survive. The alliance between these disparate groups quickly dissolved, a process which was hastened by the lockout of the *lanaiuoli*, who closed their shops to prevent the workers from earning their bread. By the end of August, discontented laborers again rose in revolt, but they were suppressed by a hastily organized coalition of merchants, industrialists and artisans, all of whom feared and distrusted these hungry, desperate throngs of carders and beaters. The laborers' guild was dissolved, and the workers were again placed under the jurisdiction of their employers.

Marxist historians have interpreted this revolutionary episode as a highly significant, although precocious and premature manifestation of conflict between two new classes, the bourgeoisie and the industrial proletariat. In their analysis, the Ciompi upheaval was a portent of the bitter struggles involving capitalists and workers that erupted during the Industrial Revolution. These scholars point to the "modern" conditions in the woolen cloth industry which produced the upheaval: the ownership and operation of large factories by capitalistic entrepreneurs intent upon large profits, a regimented and exploited labor force living on subsistence wages and continually being threatened by unemployment and starvation. Marxists have also been impressed by the revolutionary program of the Ciompi. Like their counterparts in the nineteenth century, these workers demanded the right to organize, to form their own guild or union. Moreover, they wanted a share of offices in the communal government and the implementation of a legislative program favorable to their interests. This included tax reform, the abolition of financial privileges traditionally enjoyed by the rich, a two-year moratorium on small debts, and restraints upon the punitive powers of the judicial authorities.

A close scrutiny of this revolution's course suggests the need to qualify the Marxist analysis. The Florentine cloth industry was not a prototype of the modern factory system; its basic unit of production was the small *bottega* employing a handful of men, not the large plant operated by a throng of regimented workers. This labor force was not a monolithic group; it comprised several distinct categories, with quite varied interests. Those entrepreneurs who operated small shops, and who were capitalists on a modest scale, had little in common with the salaried laborers and, indeed, finally turned against them in the last days of the revolution. These *sottoposti* were a conservative, stabilizing element in the economy and the society. Had the cloth industry been more centralized, had the gulf between *lanaiuolo* and laborer not been partially filled by these intermediate groups, Florence would have experienced more frequent and more intense periods of social unrest.

Nor was the workers' program as revolutionary as some writers have suggested. They did not demand communal ownership of the cloth factories, the redistribution of wealth, or the abolition of private property. Insofar as they had an economic program, it was based upon a resurrection of a guild ideal, of a return to that period in the past when guilds were stronger, and when they protected the economic interests of their members more effectively. The Ciompi also believed that they could live and work in harmony with their former masters and that the revolution would bring about a dramatic rise in their economic conditions. None of these naive hopes were realized, and the disillusionment which spread through workers' ranks after the collapse of the Ciompi regime was a factor in the decline of labor unrest within the Florentine cloth industry.

THE WORLD OF THE INTERNATIONAL MERCHANT

Despite its complexity, the economic world of the *lanaiuolo* and the sedentary merchant was in some ways a stable and secure environment. It was molded by the traditions, customs, and working habits of Tuscan society, and was theoretically subject to the regulations of the commune and the guilds. In sharp contrast to this solidly anchored order was the exotic milieu of the international trader and financier. These merchants formed the elite corps of the Florentine business community. They had lived and worked abroad: in Rome and Venice, in Paris and London, in Constantinople and Damascus. Compared with their domestic counterparts, the business activities of these entrepreneurs were more varied, the opportunities for profit greater, the risks more numerous and more perilous.

For the young beginner, aspiring to become a foreign merchant, a lengthy training period was mandatory. The first step was the grammar school where the fundamentals of reading and writing were taught. At the age of ten, the boy was sent to a special school for mathematical instruction. Here he learned simple arithmetic, and also was trained to do fractions, to calculate interest, and to keep accounts. There followed a period of apprenticeship in the office of a merchant or banker, where the youth would run errands and learn the complex details of the trade. Thus Donato Velluti (d. 1370) described the training of his son, who died at the beginning of a promising mercantile career: "I sent him to school. Having learned how to read, and possessing good intelligence, memory and talent, as well as sound ability in speech, he applied himself and made good progress. Then I sent him to learn mathematics and in a short time, he became proficient. I withdrew him from school and sent him to Ciore Pitti's shop, then to Manente Amidei's. . . . He was given an account book of debits and credits, and managed it as though he were a man of forty."

The training of the young merchant was not complete until he had lived and worked abroad. Frequently, he would be sent to a foreign branch of a Florentine firm, employed as a factor or agent, usually under the supervision of an older employee. Such was the experience of Remigio Lanfredini, who had a lengthy apprenticeship with several business firms abroad. He had worked for Giovanni de' Medici in Venice, for another Florentine merchant in Genoa, then with a Pisan organization, before returning to Florence to take a post in the mercantile company of Rodolfo Peruzzi. Some apprentices, however, embarked upon more exciting travels. Buonaccorso Pitti described his first foreign sojourn when, "being young, inexperienced, and eager to see something of the world," he accompanied an experienced trader, Matteo Tinghi, on two trips across the Alps. The first journey took him to Genoa, Nice, and Avignon, where he and

his companion were thrown into a papal prison. His thirst for
adventure unquenched by this episode, Pitti accompanied Tinghi
on another business voyage, taking a load of saffron to Buda
in Hungary by way of Venice and Zagreb.

During this long apprenticeship, and throughout his business
career, the merchant absorbed a vast store of information essential for success in his trade. This would include fluency in one
or more foreign languages and a thorough acquaintance with
coinage and tariff systems, weights and measures, and market
conditions in those areas where his business interests were cen-
tered. The successful merchant would also establish contacts
with other businessmen, both native and foreign, who traded in
his zone of operations. In his mind, if not on paper, would be
catalogued information about their economic status, their honesty and trustworthiness, their shrewdness and intelligence. The
merchant's circle of acquaintances would also include the governor, tax collectors, and judges in his place of residence. The
friendship of these men would always be useful and, in the
event of a crisis, might be of great value.

The few surviving copies of mercantile manuals reveal the
scope and complexity of the knowledge needed by merchants
engaged in international trade. Francesco Pegolotti, who had
served for three decades in the Bardi company in the early
fourteenth century, compiled one handbook of practical information which enjoyed wide circulation. The Bardi firm was
active throughout the Mediterranean world, as well as in conti-
nental Europe west of the Rhine. Thus the book is a vast com-
pendium of information required by a merchant if he were
engaged in trade with the Levant, in the Black Sea area, along
the African coast, or in Spain, France, England, or Scandinavia.
The author gives accurate tables of coinage values, weights and
measures, customs duties, commodities, and also general trade
conditions and opportunities. In perusing this manual, one becomes aware of the incredible variety of standards, changing
from city to city and from region to region, which bedeviled the
merchant and sharpened his wits. Pegolotti lists 288 different
commodities (or their varieties) in the Levant trade, from anise
and ambergris to tin and turpentine. He furnished an analysis,
accurate to the last penny, of the costs of transporting a sack

of wool from London to the Provençal port of Aigues-Mortes. One of the most interesting passages in the work is the description of the trade route to China which had been followed by Marco Polo and other intrepid merchants in search of profit, and by a handful of missionaries eager to win converts to Christianity. Pegolotti reported that "the road leading from Tana [in the Caucasus] to Cathay is quite safe both by day and by night, according to what the merchants report who have used it." Although he had never made this arduous journey himself, his account suggests that the international business community, of which he was a member, did not consider this trip a Herculean feat.

Business correspondence provides some of the most valuable information about international traders and the world in which they lived and worked. These letters are invariably filled with accounts of transactions, consignments of commodities, current exchange rates. But they occasionally contain important references to political events and personalities, to natural calamities, and to the attitudes and opinions of the correspondent.

The richest repository of source material on medieval economic history, the Datini archive in Prato, contains over 100,000 letters of this genre. A random sampling of these missives sent to Francesco Datini (d. 1410) by his business associates abroad will illustrate the contents of this source. Accounts of ship movements were automatically included in letters from foreign ports. Thus a letter of 1400 from his agents in London informed Datini that three Genoese ships had left Southampton with 1200 sacks of his wool and 271 bales of English cloth. From Bruges, Datini's agents wrote that they had dispatched to Paris 32 pieces of cloth made in Malines, which would then be sent on to Montpellier for consignment by sea to Pisa and thence to Prato. It was also customary for agents to quote exchange rates of the leading European currencies. A Lucca correspondent of the Datini firm sent the exchange rate (in Lucchese money) of the florins of Florence, Genoa, Bologna, Pisa, as well as the *écu* of Bruges, the *livre* of Paris, and the ducat of Venice. Frequently, letters contained information about alternative trade routes, a comparison of transport costs, custom duties, and the risks from bandits and pirates. On rare occasions, the correspondent moved beyond the minutiae of business detail to describe the broader economic scene. Thus Datini's representative in Avignon wrote him in 1396 about his views of the Milanese market: "Some time ago . . . I wrote you that . . . if war does not break out between us and the Count [Giangaleazzo Visconti, lord of Milan], that it appeared to me that Milan was a good city for trade. For in that territory we can obtain more commodities and make more profits than in any other city where we might establish ourselves. Milan trades heavily with Genoa, Venice, Florence and Pisa, so that we can make a very reasonable profit from our buying and selling." The agent then suggested that 1000 florins might profitably be invested in trading ventures in Milan, particularly in arms and fustian cloth.

These sources document the characteristic features of the international merchant's career: the wide range of business activities and interests, the great variety of opportunity for investment and profit. The foreign trader dealt in every commodity which served human needs, from precious jewels and slave girls to such prosaic commodities as alum, hides, and wool. He could plan to live and trade among the infidels, as did Remigio Lanfredini, who wrote from Ancona to his brother in Florence in 1408: "I have decided to join with some great merchants, either Genoese or Catalan or Venetian, and travel to Romania or Alexandria, or in Syria or Pera or Acre or Constantinople or Caffa."

Perhaps the most unusual business career of which we have record is that of Buonaccorso Pitti, who described his experiences in a lively and dramatic chronicle. After his first trips abroad with Matteo Tinghi, Pitti set out to trade on his own account. He became a professional gambler, matching his skill and luck at cards and dice with French viscounts and barons, and also with other merchants. He invested his winnings in speculative commodities, such as horses or wine, or in loans to embarrassed nobles who had not been successful at the gaming tables. This form of mercantile enterprise was risky. Pitti never recovered a large loan which he had made to the count of Savoy, and he came perilously close to fighting a duel with a French nobleman, who had been incensed by the Florentine's phenomenal luck with the dice. But the profits were also substantial, and by 1400, Pitti could afford to eschew gambling and invest his money in less dangerous enterprises. In his later years, he stayed in Florence and placed his capital in a cloth factory; he traveled abroad only on government business. But before he finally abandoned his ambulatory career, he had made fourteen journeys outside of Italy, including ten trips to Paris, two to London, and two into Germany.

Occasionally, adverse business conditions or personal misfortune induced the international merchant to pursue unaccustomed paths in search of gain. Such was the fate of Francesco Davizzi, who had been stranded in France during the three-sided struggle between the English army, the forces of the French dauphin, and the Burgundians at the time of Joan of Arc. In a letter written in December 1431 (six months after Joan's martyrdom), he described the bleak economic situation which then prevailed in France. He noted that the English had reconquered some of the territory lost "at the time of the maid" but this had been an expensive operation, involving an expenditure of more than one million pounds. "If the English do not abandon this land," he predicted, "they will destroy their own country irretrivably." His own business prospects were unpromising. There was no opportunity to lend money, "because the king [Charles VII] and all of the lords are penurious on account of the war." But Davizzi then demonstrated how an astute merchant could prosper even in the midst of poverty and devastation, for he wrote that the king had granted to him and an associate the office of master of the mint of Pont Saint-Esprit. Although half of the revenue accruing to this office belonged to the count of Vendôme, there remained enough profit to support the two Florentines. Davizzi had some hope for better times, "if this kingdom does not fall into worse condition."

Some merchants, like Davizzi, operated independently abroad, trading on their own account, lending their capital, and also accepting commissions from other merchants. But a substantial part of the business community in foreign parts worked in branches of firms with headquarters in Florence. The greatest opportunities for profit naturally belonged to these organizations with bases in several cities, for example, those mercantile empires created by Francesco Datini and Giovanni de' Medici. From a very modest beginning as a retail merchant in Avignon, Datini established himself in Tuscany and then created branches in Pisa, Genoa, Valencia, and Majorca. Although he possessed a bank and a cloth factory, the lion's share of his wealth came from trading profits. On his death in 1410, his fortune was valued at 70,000 florins ($300,000). Even more spectacular was the burgeoning fortune of Giovanni di Bicci de' Medici, whose father had eked out a living from a modest patrimony and from the interest on small loans to peasants in the *contado*. Beginning his career as an employee of a distant cousin, Giovanni soon established his own company, first in Rome and Florence, and later in Venice and Naples. Most of Giovanni's profits came from moneylending; trade and cloth manufacture were minor sources of gain. Upon his death in 1429, his estate was valued at 180,000 florins (over $700,000).

The annals of Florentine business enterprise are studded with the names and exploits of merchants and bankers who built vast fortunes. Observing their careers, one might be tempted to conclude that business success was automatic, and that all Florentines possessed the Midas touch. The sources indicate, however, that economic losses and business failures occurred with depressing frequency. It is true that spectacular bankruptcies of giant companies were less common in the fifteenth century than earlier; there were no failures to rival the catastrophic downfall of the Bardi and Peruzzi organizations in the 1340s. But court records do show that each year a score of merchants were declared bankrupt, their assets seized to pay their creditors. Not untypical was the fate of Jacopo Guidalotti, who had languished in jail for two years before his creditors, finally reconciled to their losses, agreed to his release. His petition for tax relief stated that "no property remained to him in the world, and he has nothing upon which to live." Since the merchant's liability was unlimited, all of his assets, if found, could be sold to pay his debts.

A steep rise in the incidence of bankruptcy was a sign of economic difficulty, and a graphic reminder of the perils that surrounded the mercantile career. Some element of risk was involved in every mercantile transaction; business letters are replete with descriptions of shipwrecks, losses by pirates and bandits, broken agreements, larceny. Florentine merchants endeavored to minimize these losses by purchasing insurance, by sending goods by different routes, and by dealing only with trustworthy business-men. Bad judgment accounted for some losses, as was admitted by one chastened entrepreneur, Marco Pagnini, who had mis-managed the affairs of his company's branch in Genoa, not with intent to commit fraud but "on account of his youth and inexperience." Youthful indiscretion was also responsible for an-other crisis which shook the business community in 1387. A group of Florentine factors and employees in Venice were gambling for high stakes and quickly lost all of their cash. So that the game might continue, it was proposed that the players gamble with letters of credit drawn upon the home offices of their firms in Florence. Within a short time, the factor of the Pecora com-pany had written out bank drafts totaling 1500 florins and had seriously compromised the economic position of his employers. Merchants denounced this ingenious form of embezzlement in the most extreme terms. From Venice, Goro Albizzi wrote a Florentine associate that "all honest men and merchants every-where should act together to drive from the [business] world these men who have been responsible for the destruction of this company, which has always been one of the best in this city."

Businessmen who experienced difficulties were rarely given an opportunity to recoup their fortunes; their creditors usually began to clamor for their money at the first sign of difficulty. Often a merchant's death precipitated a massive rush of his creditors to collect from his embattled heirs, as the experience of Domenico Lanfredini testified. Upon his father's death, he was prosecuted by the bishop's court, which claimed that the de-ceased was a usurer. In addition to this attack, he also had to meet the demands of creditors, "who with letters and documents demand so much of me that only a little [of the inheritance] will be left."

Uncollectable debts were probably the greatest source of busi-ness difficulties. Extant account books of mercantile firms reveal how heavy was this charge upon the balance sheet, and how perilous was the life of a merchant in an economic system which, in many respects, was still quite primitive. Business man-uals and correspondence are filled with warnings against making loans to dubious risks, but either these admonitions were not followed or the character of economic enterprise necessitated the advancement of credit on a broad scale. The tax declaration of one international merchant, Andrea Lamberteschi, illustrates this problem, for he listed all of his debtors and commented on the likelihood of repayment. He calculated the total of his potentially bad debts at 1082 florins. The heirs of a Ferrara merchant, Luigi Manticho, owed him 52 florins, and he did not expect to collect more than half, "for they are wicked and without shame." Several debts were written off as lost: 74 florins owed by Taddeo di Piero, deceased; 67 florins by Michele Bonichi, bankrupt; and other small sums owed by poor cloth workers, which were uncollectable. Jacopo di Bartolomeo da Carmignano, who lived in Hungary, had refused to settle a debt of 150 florins. A yarn broker, Daddo d'Ippolito, owed Lamberteschi 83 florins; he avoided payment by running away. Among his other debtors were Francesco di Bindo da Carmignano, "who lives in Bulgaria and won't pay," and a Venetian nobleman, Giacomo Dandolo, whose debt of 350 *lire* was considered lost. Lamberteschi's two sons had borrowed 5000 florins from him to trade in Hungary, and refused to acknowledge any obligation. The formal, stilted language of the tax declaration does not disguise the father's bitterness and anger toward his ungrateful offspring, "who have rebelled against him . . . and give him no respect, nor can he expect any help from them."

Political vicissitudes also menaced the entrepreneur who traded in foreign parts. The sudden outbreak of war, the imposition of an ecclesiastical interdict, or commercial reprisals could result in the imprisonment of foreign merchants and the loss of their goods. During Florence's war with Pope Gregory XI (1375-1378), her citizens throughout Latin Christendom were declared outlaws; their property was subject to confiscation, their persons to imprisonment or expulsion. Forty years later, the commune became imbroiled in a conflict with King Ladislaus of Naples, and the city's large business community in southern Italy and in Rome suffered serious losses. The most permanent threat to Florence's position as an international trading center, however, came from the East. This peril was described in a letter written in 1396 by Rosso Orlandi to a business associate in the Levant after the disaster of Nicopolis, when the Ottoman Turks crushed an invading crusader army and thus opened the war for the ultimate conquest of the Byzantine Empire. The writer commented that the battle was the worst possible news, and speculated whether Florentine merchants in Dalmatia might not be forced to abandon their posts before the inexorable Turkish advance.

The dangers which confronted these merchants and threatened their security were sometimes precipitate, of brief duration, and sometimes slow and gradual in their formation and impact. An example of the first type is contained in a judicial process recorded in the protocols of the Merchants' court, which describes the tribulations of two Florentines operating a business in the Emilian city of Faenza in 1376. As part of the Papal States, Faenza was then ruled by a French cleric, with whom the merchants Bartolomeo Petriboni and Francesco Bernardetti maintained amicable ties. This official had delivered a sack of coins to the merchants for safekeeping, but when Faenza was besieged by a Florentine army (the republic being then at war with the papacy), they wished to return the money to the governor. "You are the *signore*," they said, "and you have a thousand ways to save this money which are not available to us." But the French official refused to receive the hoard, and told the Florentines that the papal *condottiere*, John Hawkwood, was advancing to lift the siege and save the city. Hawkwood did enter Faenza, but he brought an unusual form of salvation. His troops sacked the city and killed several merchants, including the factor of the two Florentine partners. All of their merchandise was confiscated, and they were both imprisoned. Petriboni was accused of spying for Florence, and Hawkwood ordered his transfer to Bologna for trial. He escaped this fate, probably by means of a bribe, and made his way back to his native city. Bernardetti's house was searched and ransacked, and according to his account, "there remained neither garden nor stable nor orchard nor cistern nor wardrobe in the house or its environs which was not dug up or broken into." The searchers found the money belonging to the Frenchman, and they also discovered Bernardetti's personal hoard. The protocols describe a touching scene in Faenza's main square, when Bernardetti's wife fell on her knees before the governor and begged him to intercede with Hawkwood on her husband's behalf. According to this account, the governor began to weep; he ordered the woman to rise and promised her that "all of the losses which Cecco [Francesco] has suffered I will bear myself." Bernardetti did manage to escape from prison and, with the governor's connivance, eluded his captors and returned to Florence. But the French official quickly forgot his promise to the merchant's wife, for three years later he brought suit against the partners for the recovery of the funds which he had left in their safekeeping.

Quite as perilous as the sudden, precipitate blow of fortune which had struck the two merchants in Faenza were the permanent dangers to which every entrepreneur living abroad was exposed. For thirty years, Bernardo Davanzati had traded in the Dalmatian port city of Spalato (Split). One of his friends, Rosso Orlandi, described his dilemma in a letter written to his son Piero, in Venice. According to Orlandi, the most pressing danger confronting Davanzati was the hostility of the local populace, and particularly the Slavic gentry in the hinterland, to whom Davanzati had advanced loans. Orlandi was convinced that Davanzati would not be permitted to leave Spalato with his possessions. "One should not be surprised if they adopt this attitude," he wrote, "for in nearly every country, the natives, and particularly the powerful citizens . . . are opposed to the merchant taking his gains elsewhere, and if they can, they will impede him and willingly take it from him." Orlandi's fears were never fully realized, perhaps because Davanzati elected to remain in Spalato until his death in 1412. But fifteen years later, his grandson Rinieri was forced to write off his Dalmatian inheritance as a business loss. He informed the Florentine tax officials that he could not sell his real estate in Spalato because of the poverty of the inhabitants. Furthermore, he had tried to recover some of the debts owed to his grandfather, with no success. Several of these defalcating debtors, he wrote, "are lords and counts in these regions and have no superiors, and whoever ventures there does so at great risk, and instead of repayment, he may receive blows and be robbed and killed, as has happened to others."

PATTERNS OF ECONOMIC CHANGE, 1380–1450

Although Florentine economic activity was characterized by great variety and flexibility, it was very sensitive to external influences and conditions, and subject to sharp fluctuations. Short-term phases of burgeoning productivity and prosperity alternated with periods of stagnation, for the city's economy was immediately affected by changing market conditions in Europe and the Levant, as well as by such calamities as famine, plague, and war.

In 1380, Florence was in the midst of a serious depression. Natural disasters of unusual frequency and intensity contributed to, and aggravated, social and political unrest in the city, which in turn reacted negatively upon trade and industry. A plague in 1374 was followed by famine in 1375, a year in which the republic had embarked upon a long and exhausting war with the papacy. The settlement of this conflict in 1378 precipitated the Ciompi revolution, with its explosion of proletarian unrest. The years immediately following this revolt were extremely difficult for the woolen industry; the market for cloth was so depressed that production fell to 20,000 bolts in 1380 (compared to 90,000 in 1338). The Lana records for this period are filled with laments about the poor state of the guild, and with references to quarrels between manufacturers and their subcontractors. Contributing to the business malaise were the unsettled political conditions in Florence. The popular regime which governed the city from 1378 to 1382 was under attack from radical worker groups driven into exile after the Ciompi revolt, and also from disgruntled patrician elements. These were years of intensive operations by the military companies which ravaged large sections of the peninsula, and forced Italian states to hire troops for defense, or pay ransom. The establishment of a more conservative government in 1382 did not signify a change in the city's fortunes, for in the subsequent year, another plague swept through the city and claimed thousands of victims.

By contrast, the late 1380s were relatively quiet and prosperous. The republic achieved a measure of internal stability, and those parts of Europe most frequently traveled by Floren-

tine merchants (Lombardy, Venetia, France, the Low Countries)
enjoyed a brief respite from civil war and foreign invasion.
The acquisition of Arezzo and its *contado* in 1384 was a boon to
Florentine entrepreneurs, who could exploit this market under
the secure protection of their government. These were years of
unprecedented profits for Francesco Datini's mercantile companies. His branches in Avignon and Pisa recorded gains which
averaged over 20 percent annually on capital investment.

In the 1390s, every part of the Florentine community was
directly affected by the republic's relations with Giangaleazzo
Visconti, lord of Milan. The despot's expansionist policies led
him into conflict with Florence. By 1400, the two states were
locked in a ferocious struggle for survival which taxed their
resources to the utmost. Although some Florentines—soldiers,
swordmakers, builders of fortresses—profited from this decade
of armed conflict, most categories of economic activity suffered
from the ravaging of farms, the blockade of trade routes, and
the diversion of capital from commerce and industry to military
expenditure. Through his innovations in diplomatic and military strategy, Giangaleazzo raised Italian warfare to a more
sophisticated level. Probing for vulnerable spots in Florence's
economy, he caused serious damage to her cloth industry by
prohibiting the export of wire used to make instruments for
carding wool. And by an astute combination of diplomatic and
military pressure, the Milanese lord isolated and surrounded
Florence in 1402. But the threat of economic strangulation disappeared with Giangaleazzo's unexpected death in September
1402 and the disintegration of his Lombard state.

Merchants' letters in the Datini archives describe the progressive deterioration of the Florentine economy during the course
of this war. The crisis became particularly acute at the turn of
the century, when a recurrence of the plague depressed further an economy laboring under heavy military burdens. Pisa
was occupied by Visconti troops in 1398, and Florentine merchants could no longer utilize that port. In a letter of February
1400, Francesco Datini wrote: "We are in very poor condition,
for we are paying heavy taxes and there is no trade on account
of the plague." Two years later, in January 1402, he wrote: "Here
there is no business; everything is dead." Although Giangaleazzo's

demise a few months later lessened the immediate threat to Florence's security, the war with Milan continued, and the economic situation did not improve appreciably. Frustrations bred by the prolongation of conflict are reflected in a Datini letter of February 1404: "God grant us peace soon, so that merchandise can again come and go as it should; it seems like a thousand years [that we have been at war]!"

Peace with Milan was signed in the following year, but this brought no permanent end to war and its negative effect upon economic activity. A new threat to Florentine security loomed from the south in the person of Ladislaus, king of Naples. Having established himself securely in his own domain, Ladislaus turned his attention northward, toward the vulnerable Papal States and toward Tuscany. War between the king and the Florentine republic broke out in 1408, after Neapolitan troops had occupied Rome. A truce was signed in January 1411, but Ladislaus did not abandon his expansionist dreams. His career, and his threat to Florence, ended with his sudden death in 1414, a few weeks after he had concluded another peace agreement with the republic.

In some respects, this conflict with Ladislaus was more destructive to the city's economy than the Milanese war. Since the thirteenth century, Florentine merchants had been active in mercantile and banking enterprises in Naples, Taranto, Bari and other cities of the Angevin kingdom. Southern Italy had always been an important market for Tuscan cloth. When friction first developed between Ladislaus and Florence, the government complained to the king about the maltreatment of her merchants: arbitary tax levies, confiscation of goods, and even imprisonment. When Ladislaus reoccupied Rome in 1413, he ordered the seizure of all Florentine property there. The losses suffered by the city's merchants in Rome can be estimated from the large number of petitions for tax reductions presented to the Signoria by citizens whose property had been confiscated. Equally detrimental to the economy was the blockade of Pisa by Neapolitan and Genoese galleys in 1409. These fleets seized Florentine merchandise valued at 80,000 florins. Moreover, by cutting off supplies of Sicilian grain and English wool, the blockade raised food prices in the city and created unemployment in the cloth industry. During a particularly bleak phase of this conflict (October and November 1410), Rinaldo Rondinelli asserted that "our people are totally exhausted and [their resources] depleted, for no one is earning anything and business is at a standstill."

The death of Ladislaus and the end of the Genoese war marked the beginning of a decade of peace and prosperity. Not since the 1350s had Florence enjoyed such lengthy respite from war and the heavy tax burdens of military involvement. An incursion of the plague in 1417 temporarily disrupted the economy, but this was the only calamity of its kind. Although the expanding power of the Milanese despot, Filippo Maria Visconti, caused some concern, the republic maintained a tenuous peace with its northern rival. In later years, men looked back upon this decade as a golden age. The merchant Giovanni Rucellai estimated that, in 1423, Florentine merchants possessed some two million florins in cash and merchandise, not counting their investments in real estate or communal bonds. This prosperity, Rucellai claimed, was due entirely to the cessation of war. "From 1413 until 1423, for ten years, we joined a tranquil peace, without any fear; the commune had few expenses for troops, and few taxes were levied, so that the region became wealthy."

This interlude of peace came to an end in 1424. In that year, war again broke out with Milan. Although interspersed by numerous truces, the struggle did not finally terminate until the death of Filippo Maria Visconti, the ruler of Milan, in 1447. But the early phases of this conflict were particularly damaging to Florence. Tax burdens increased enormously. Many parts of the Florentine dominion were ravaged by enemy troops, and subject populations became restive and rebellious. Speakers in council meetings lamented that the purses of the citizenry were empty, that the fiscal requirements of the war (nearly 100,000 florins monthly) were too heavy to bear. From 1429 on, communal records reveal a significant rise in the incidence of bankruptcy. And, in a particularly desperate moment in 1431, the shortage of currency in the city inspired a proposal to allow Jews to establish themselves as moneylenders in the city. This was a dramatic reversal of traditional policy, for the commune had steadfastly refused to authorize Jews to live and trade in Florence.

Additional evidence of economic crisis is found in a series of provisions beginning in 1424, and repeated regularly thereafter. A law of that year provided a twenty-five year exemption from taxes and personal debts to agricultural laborers in the *contado* who had emigrated from Florentine territory, if they returned to till the soil. This provision was repeated in 1427 and again in 1431. In 1431, the benefits of these exemptions were extended to all residents of the *contado* and district, whether or not they worked on the land. And this was followed by another law granting tax exemptions for twenty years to all foreigners who immigrated into the city. These provisions attest to a general labor shortage in these years, most severe in the countryside, but also noticeable in the towns. Depopulation was the result of several factors: visitations of the plague, the exodus of peasants from areas ravaged by armies, or who suffered from heavy tax burdens. The labor shortage was a serious impediment to Florence's prosperity, and may have been the most important factor in the depressed conditions which prevailed in the middle decades of the fifteenth century.

First compiled in 1427 and then revised in 1430 and 1433, the *catasto* records provide the most concrete evidence of this crisis. In the first set of returns, for 1427, there are only scattered references to business losses suffered by Florentine merchants. Most of these reverses occurred in southern Italy. For example, Jacopo di Vannozzo de' Bardi had invested nearly 7000 florins in his trading company in L'Aquila, but he wrote off one-third of that amount as a business loss, "on account of the depressed conditions of the region." Another merchant, Jacopi de' Ruote, claimed losses of 3200 florins in bad debts from his Apulia enterprises. A partnership headed by Maestro Francesco di Ridolfo lost 4800 florins from operations in Naples and Apulia, when the firm's cargo of grain was confiscated by royal officials. Returns submitted to tax authorities in 1430 contain more frequent references to "bad times," but three years later, when the city had been at war for nearly a decade, the signs of economic difficulties in the *catasto* volumes are very clear.

Claims of economic loss in tax declarations must always be viewed with caution, but the evidence in these records is so detailed and abundant that it cannot be discounted. Reporting on his investment in a cloth factory operated by the Alessandri family, Guidetto Monaldi stated that this firm had incurred heavy losses instead of profits, "due to the bad times." Tommaso Popolani, who owned a string of four shops used by bankers and moneychangers, informed the tax officials that only one of these shops had been rented. Silk manufacturers were more active and prosperous than other cloth producers in these years, but Francesco della Luna asserted that his factory had not been operating, and that he was unable to sell cloth in foreign markets. From every quarter abroad, merchants complained about sluggish trade conditions and meager profits. Reporting on his business in Bruges, Benedetto Alberti stated that depressed trade conditions in Flanders excluded any possibility of profit. Two brothers, Niccolò and Bernardo Giugni, described a similar situation in their trade with Palermo and Syracuse, where they suffered losses of 2500 florins. Ridolfo Bardi was involved in commerce with Catalonia, but he lost 3000 florins when a cargo of merchandise was seized and confiscated by the Genoese. Southern France was a merchant's graveyard, according to Bernardo Venture, who had invested 1000 florins in a Montpellier firm which then went bankrupt. Other merchants operating in Avignon and Narbonne reported similar losses, and blamed them on the depressed state of the region. In only two centers, Venice and Rome, were business conditions and opportunities for profit still normal.

It is a relatively simple task to chart the pattern of these short-term business fluctuations, the expansions and contractions of the economy influenced by such immediate stimuli as war and pestilence. More complex, and more difficult to describe, are the long-term changes, the gradual shifts and transformations of economic activity. Our knowledge of the Florentine economy in the fifteenth century is still rudimentary, and until we know more about the subject, we must limit ourselves to a formulation of problems, and to cautious surmises based on limited evidence.

Since the late fourteenth century, significant changes had occurred in the composition of the entrepreneurial class. Some mercantile families died out; others went bankrupt or were persuaded by adverse circumstances to retire from the management of commercial and industrial companies. Of the prominent families in the front rank of Florence's business community in 1380 (Albizzi, Ricci, Strozzi, Alberti, Guasconi, Rinuccini, Del Palagio), only the Albizzi and the Strozzi were still heavily involved in trade, banking, and industry in 1430. The Rinuccini and the Alberti had suffered political reprisals at the hands of the dominant political faction, and many of the Alberti lived in exile, pursuing their commercial interests in Venice, Bruges, and London. Other families, like the Medici and the Corbinelli, had returned to entrepreneurial activity after a period of withdrawal. The Pazzi made a spectacular entrée into the business world in these years. Prior to 1400, no member of this ancient noble house had pursued a mercantile career; in 1450, the Pazzi ranked second only to the Medici among the city's banking families. Competing with these native merchants were men from neighboring towns who established themselves in Florence. Among the more prosperous of these immigrant families were the Panciatichi of Pistoia and the Borromei of Pisa, both enormously wealthy in the 1430s, as the *catasto* records prove. The route still lay open for the talented and aggressive individual, without family or fortune, to enter the entrepreneurial class. The *catasto* records identify those men with obscure antecedents, like Gregorio Dati and Lorenzo Lenzi, who acquired substantial fortunes in these years.

A significant economic development of the fifteenth century was the rapid expansion of the silk cloth industry, and the decline of woolen cloth production. Since neither of these industries has been studied carefully and systematically, they cannot be compared in terms of size, capital investment, labor force, and output. But the evidence points to a growing market for silks and brocades, while the demand for Florence's staple industrial product, woolen cloth, shrank steadily. On this problem, as on so many others, the *catasto* records yield useful data. They reveal, for example, that scores of woolen cloth factories were not rented in the 1420s and that their owners could not find tenants "at any price." This was not a temporary condition; many property owners submitted reports like that of Jacopo Acciaiuoli in 1427, who informed the tax authorities that three of his four cloth factories "are locked up and unrented, and for more than eight years, I have received no income from them." Even with factories closed and output reduced, the manufacturers were operating with meager profit margins, as low as 3 or 4 florins per bolt. The *catasto* return of one entrepreneurial family, the Fortini, provides a basis for a rough comparison of the two industries in the 1420s. Andrea Fortini had invested nearly 6000 florins in a woolen cloth factory in 1417. After ten years, his net profit was 2467 florins, or just under 4 percent on his original investment. Andrea's nephew Bartolomeo was a partner in a silk firm; his capital amounted to 2200 florins. After two years and four months, his share of the profits was 600 florins, or nearly 12 percent annual return on his investment.

The sharp contrasting fortunes of these two industries reflect trends in the international market, over which Florentine entrepreneurs had no control. The decrees enacted by the Lana guild in the fifteenth century reflect its preoccupation with competition, its frenetic attempts to defend its interests by restricting or prohibiting cloth production in the Florentine dominion. But serious competition came not only from Italy, but also from the burgeoning industries in England and Spain. A provision of 1472 stated that Perpignan cloth to the value of 40,000 florins was sold each year in Florentine territory. The silk industry was not troubled by restricted demands. Its sumptuous brocades and silks decorated with gold thread found a ready market in the princely courts of Italy, France, the Low Countries, and England, and also in more distant regions where a small but wealthy ruling class could afford such luxuries. The ebullient spirit of this industry is reflected in legislation affecting it, so different in tone from the Lana decrees, with their forebodings of economic decline and their attempts to preserve a crumbling monopoly. Typical is the provision of 1429 which granted tax immunities and a debt moratorium to silk workers who returned to the city. The law was designed, so the preamble stated, to promote the welfare of "this most singular and excellent guild, ranked by merit among the first of our city, which manufactures silk cloth with marvellous skill, finer and more precious than any produced elsewhere . . . ."

Another major development in the Florentine economy was the city's emergence as a maritime power. With the capture of Pisa in 1406, Florence had direct access to the sea for the first time in her history. Both political and economic factors influenced the republic's decision to become a maritime power. Florentines never forgot the strategy of the Milanese ruler Giangaleazzo Visconti, who surrounded them in 1402 and planned to subdue the city through the blockade of her trade routes. The republic's campaign to conquer Pisa was a manifestation of her determination to establish a permanent sea base. In the 1420s, Florence began to construct a fleet, and sent galleys to Flanders and England, and also to Alexandria and Beirut in the Levant. These enterprises did guarantee a regular supply of wool for the city's cloth industry and a more secure access to foreign markets, but they also inspired resentment and hostility, particularly among the Genoese, who feared Tuscan competition in maritime transport. It would be difficult to prove that Florence obtained a substantial economic advantage from her maritime enterprises, which were expensive to establish and costly to defend and maintain. The Florentines, however, viewed this expenditure as an investment in their security, not as a profit-making enterprise.

The balance sheet of the city's economy in the middle decades of the fifteenth century was a peculiar blend of light and shadow, of positive and negative factors. Her economic assets were formidable: a large and industrious population; a massive industrial plant; entrepreneurial expertise; a vast commercial and financial network. By the standards of the age, Florence was a wealthy city. With fortunes in excess of 100,000 florins, Cosimo de' Medici and Giovanni Rucellai were two of the richest men in Europe. Beneath these Midas figures was a more numerous category of perhaps 200 citizens, the medium rich, men of substantial wealth, which permitted a comfortable if not a lavish style of living. One of Florence's most valuable assets was her craft tradition. From the workshops of her goldsmiths, embroiderers, sculptors, and painters came some of the finest products of European craftsmanship. The skills and reputation of these artisans earned substantial incomes for themselves and increments to the city's resources.

But this evidence of wealth and prosperity, so impressive to the visiting foreigner, disguised some serious weaknesses. The most significant fact about the economy was that, like the city's population, it had ceased to grow. Brief periods of prosperity and economic expansion in the early 1420s and in the 1460s did not alter this pattern of economic stasis. Shrinking markets explain many, if not all of the difficulties that plagued the mercantile community. In many regions where Florentines—and other Italians—had enjoyed a near-monopoly of banking and international trade, local merchants and financiers were now replacing the foreigners; the products of local industry, particularly cloth, were outselling Italian wares. In England and the Low Countries, in Spain and the Levant, competition was more intense, the opportunities for profit fewer. Succeeding chapters of this book will discuss certain occupational trends which are partially explained by this troubled economic scene: a lack of enthusiasm for entrepreneurial activity; a preference for the life of the rentier and the country gentleman; the enhanced attraction of legal or humanistic training, and a bureaucratic career.

THREE

The Patriciate

THE STRUCTURE OF PATRICIAN SOCIETY

The preceding analysis of the Florentine economy has focused particularly upon the activities of those merchants and industrialists who owned a major portion of the city's capital resources and who controlled the large business firms. This concentration on "big business" has neglected other important dimensions of the economy: the small, local enterprises of retailers and artisans, the activities of workers in cloth factories and building projects, the unremitting toil of the peasantry upon whose labor the city's existence and survival literally depended. To justify this emphasis, it is not sufficient to claim that the activities of rich bankers and merchants are more fully documented (although this is true), or more varied and interesting than those of a pork butcher or a cloth shearer. It can be argued, however, that the scale and magnitude of Florence's international trade and banking, and of her cloth production, was a distinctive feature of this economy, which set the city apart from smaller towns like Pistoia or Parma or Forlì. A similar argument is used to justify the focus of this chapter upon the social behavior and values of those families that constituted Florence's patriciate, her aristocracy. By virtue of their wealth, pedigree, and prestige, these houses formed the most powerful and influential "class" in the community. Moreover, they possessed certain distinctive qualities and traits, a particular outlook, which distinguished them from the rest of Florentine society and, to a certain degree, from the aristocracies of other major Italian cities. In a literal sense, these patricians were the creators of the Renaissance: its style of life, its values, its modes of thought and perception. The remaining chapters of this book are devoted to the analysis of this new style and these values: in politics, religion, education, and art.

Two important attributes of this social order were the critical importance of wealth as a determinant of status, and the survival, from the city's medieval past, of a corporate structure and ethos. These qualities, which were blended in the Florentine crucible, were fundamentally irreconcilable. A capitalistic economic order is characterized by risk, uncertainty, flexibility, and sharp fluctuations. It fosters individualism and contributes to social mobility and dislocation through perpetual redistribution of wealth. Conversely, a corporate social order stresses group action; its goals are stability, security, conformity. It gives its members a sense of identity, of "belonging"; it teaches them to accept the principles of a hierarchic social structure, a sense of social place. It is instructive to visualize Florentine history during its most dynamic period as a perpetual conflict between these two contradictory elements. The tension created by their juxtaposition may have been a source of vitality and creativity. It also explains some peculiar features of this society in the early Renaissance: the coexistence of cosmopolitanism, a byproduct of Florence's international economic and political role, and of parochialism, an attitude encouraged by the corporate social order.

The family constituted the basic nucleus of Florentine social life throughout the Renaissance, and the bond existing between family members was the strongest cement in the city's social structure. One of its sources of vitality was tradition, the collective memory of a past when family members were forced to unite and act as a group in order to survive. The strong kinship sense of such prominent families as the Cavalcanti and the Buondelmonti was nourished by memories of the roles these houses had played in the city's history—the street fights against rival clans, the exploits of their ancestors in battles against Florence's enemies. Physical evidence of this cohesiveness was the concentration of a family's households in one district, along a single street, or surrounding a square. Other kinds of evidence survive in written form: in the list of offices and dignities held by members of a family, in the proud claims to family antiquity and distinction recorded in private diaries. As early as 1350, a member of one prominent mercantile house, the Alberti, commissioned an agent to search for documents which would throw light upon his family's origins. Sixty-five years later, Doffo Spini expressed surprise that no member of his family had ever written about their ancestors; he then recorded all of the data he could recall pertaining to the early Spini. Most diarists had rather inflated views of the wealth and social status of their ancestors; few were as modest as the merchant Giovanni Morelli who wrote in 1400 that his forebears were poor but honorable folk who had migrated into Florence from the countryside in the thirteenth century. Morelli justified the composition of his family history by stating that he wished to instruct his sons concerning their past, and he added: "For everyone today pretends a family background of great antiquity, and I want to establish the truth about ours." No genealogical tree, however, was so fanciful as that created for the Medici by a court historian of the sixteenth century, who traced that family's origins to one of Charlemagne's captains who had accompanied the emperor into Italy in the eighth century.

It was to the family that the individual owed his primary obligation; the rank and condition of the family largely determined the course which his own life was to take. The family's status (and this was carefully weighed and measured) established the individual's position in society. The family provided wealth, business and political connections, the opportunity for public office. Not only was a man's bride normally chosen by his father but the paternal choice was limited to those houses similar in rank to his own. Even after a son was legally emancipated from his father, he was bound to his relatives by many ties. A head of a household who planned to marry his daughter would invariably consult with his kin about the choice of son-in-law. Any important decision—the purchase of land, a marriage contract, the making of a will—was made with the advice and consent of father, uncles, cousins. From this system, which restricted the individual's actions, he received certain positive benefits. He could normally expect his relatives to assist him in case of grave financial need, and to give him support in lawsuits. Although the vendetta was slowly disappearing as a social institution, a scion of a large and powerful family could be secure in the knowledge that only a very bold man would deliberately court the hostility of his kin by attacking him.

In a society thus organized around the family, the marriage contract was a document of supreme significance. First, it was an important financial transaction. The size of the dowry was an indication of the economic status of the contracting parties. In 1400, a dowry of 1000 florins was common in patrician marriages. In his account book, the silk merchant Gregorio Dati described how he invested dowry money in business enterprises and received substantial profits from his wife's capital. Marriage connections also had political implications. It was customary for families belonging to the same party or faction to intermarry. Conversely, an alliance contracted with a family in political disfavor was a dangerous and foolhardy enterprise.

Marriages were also indices of social status, and of the rise and decline of particular families. In 1396 a merchant from a family of middling rank, Francesco Davanzati, wrote to his father in Venice of a marriage arranged with the socially prominent Peruzzi: "Bartolomeo has taken a bride and has made a great and noble marriage alliance . . . . Truly none of our ancestors have ever made so honorable a marriage." But families which had suffered misfortune were often forced to marry beneath them. One of the city's most prominent houses, the Strozzi, lost influence and status in 1434 when their political enemies, the Medici, came to power. In 1448 Alessandra Strozzi wrote to her exiled son in Naples about a marriage which she had negotiated between her daughter and a young silk manufacturer named Giovanni Parenti who (she wrote) "possessed a little status." The phrase contains a hint of irony, for Parenti's grandfather had been an artisan. Giovanni's marriage with a Strozzi was a clear sign that the Parenti had "arrived," and also that the fortunes of one Strozzi household had declined.

The accounts of births, deaths, and marriages bulk large in the private records of any society, but the space devoted to marriage negotiations in Florentine letters and diaries is conclusive evidence of the importance of this activity in patrician circles. The archives of the Del Bene family contain a series of letters written in 1381 by Giovanni del Bene to his cousin Francesco, describing the complex negotiations which he had pursued to arrange marriages for his niece Caterina and his nephew Amerigo. He recounted the lengthy and detailed discussions that took place within each family circle, and then between the families on a broad range of issues: the size of the dowry, the selection of the church where the betrothal would be solemnized, the bride's costume, the elaborate protocol of visits and announcements. The conclusion of Amerigo's marriage agreement was postponed when the prospective bride's father objected to the bond of 2000 florins, which he would be required to pay if he broke the agreement. His argument is eloquent testimony of the intimate character of this society: "The rumor which has spread of the large dowry which I have given has ruined me and done great harm with respect to my taxes . . . . Concerning this bond of 2000 florins, everyone will think that I provided a dowry of that size, and this will be my destruction." Caterina's marriage proceeded more smoothly, but this contract aroused the anger of Francesco's wife, Dora, who complained that Caterina was betrothed before her own child, Antonia. Describing this domestic crisis to Dora's husband, Giovanni wrote: "I have always considered Dora a sensible woman, but her behavior in this matter does honor neither to her nor to us. . . . She has become so melancholy and distraught that she does nothing but weep and complain that your daughter will never be married, and that you aren't concerned about it. She says the most shocking things that I have ever heard." Giovanni urged his cousin, who was absent from the city on government service, to write his wife some comforting words.

Together with wealth, antiquity, and the possession of high communal office, marriage connections were the most important criteria for determining social status. And since two of these factors—wealth and political power—were constantly fluctuating in this volatile society, the status of a particular family was never stable and secure. Economic decline was often the prelude to a family's descent in the social hierarchy, for it was usually followed by loss of political influence, and an inability to contract decent marriages. To incur the enmity of the ruling group was even more dangerous, for this involved not only social ostracism and exclusion from office, but the danger of economic loss through property confiscation and discriminatory taxation.

How a combination of economic and political adversity could weaken a powerful family was graphically illustrated by the fortunes of the Castellani. Throughout the fourteenth century, this house, though small in number, had been one of the most important in Florence: wealthy, politically influential, socially prominent. A visual monument to its stature is the imposing Castellani palace which still stands on the bank of the Arno immediately behind the Uffizi. The wealth of this family was based upon the cloth trade, and its members could point to a distinguished tradition of public service over two centuries. The Castellani had filled all of the commune's highest offices; they were so influential that Sienese ambassadors consulted with them, as private citizens, concerning diplomatic problems. Charter members of the ruling coalition which controlled the government after 1382, the Castellani possessed all of the resources and advantages for maintaining their high rank. Their decline from this pinnacle, which began about 1400, was gradual but steady. In 1390 two Castellani households ranked among the first ten in their quarter of S. Croce in the size of their tax assessments. Thirty years later, the wealthiest member of the Castellani was ranked only eleventh, and his relatives were far down on the list, barely ranking among the first 100 households in wealth. We do not know the circumstances of this economic decline; perhaps a combination of poor business judgment and bad luck lay at the root of the Castellani's misfortune. Possibly this generation was less talented in business affairs than its predecessor. Appealing for tax relief in 1396, one of the Castellani blamed his economic ruin on his large family and on business losses due to circumstances beyond his control. The final and most serious miscalculation of this ill-starred house was to join the enemies of the Medici in 1433. From this decision, the family never recovered, and it sank into the oblivion which was the fate of many illustrious houses, whose palaces and coats-of-arms still survive in Florence, mute testimony to the evanescence of worldly fame and fortune.

Displacing families sliding into obscurity were parvenu houses which combined talent, cleverness, and audacity to climb into the ranks of the patriciate. Thus the ruling class was constantly nourished by new blood, although the quantity fluctuated sharply from generation to generation. Typical of these new houses that rose to prominence in the Quattrocento are the Vespucci, whose most famous member, Amerigo, gave his name to the New World. Amerigo's modern biographer, Germain Arciniegas, credited the Vespucci with descent from the feudal nobility, but he has been misled by amateur genealogists with a talent for creating noble ancestry out of servile origins. The Vespucci emigrated to Florence from Peretola, a village six miles from the city, but not until the end of the fourteenth century did they make any substantial mark. The occupation of the first urban Vespucci was wine selling, a lowly profession which conferred neither social distinction nor political influence. Simone Vespucci was the first member of the family to gain wealth, reputation, and modest political stature from his occupation as a silk manufacturer. His descendants prospered, and either through luck or astuteness, they tied their fortunes to the Medici. After 1434, they regularly held high office, and in 1447 a Vespucci occupied the office of standard-bearer of justice, the republic's most exalted position. Amerigo Vespucci's father was a notary of modest means, but through the family's close links with the Medici, Amerigo had access to opportunities which ultimately catapulted his name into the stream of world history.

The patrician's social milieu was not limited to his family, but extended far beyond this nucleus to embrace the city and the surrounding environs, and the world beyond. The quality of these relationships depended upon many factors: the individual's social and economic status, his occupation, and his particular talents. Men of such stature as Niccolò da Uzzano or Cosimo de' Medici would include kings, popes, and cardinals among their acquaintances. Niccolò da Uzzano was a banker who maintained close contacts with Florentine entrepreneurs, and also with merchants and moneylenders from other European marts. As one of the city's leading statesmen, he knew personally and intimately most of the politically active citizens who gathered in the Palazzo Vecchio to deliberate on the republic's affairs. Service as an ambassador took him to Rome, Bologna, and Venice, where he met the spiritual and temporal leaders of Christian Europe. Elected as governor or judge of commu-

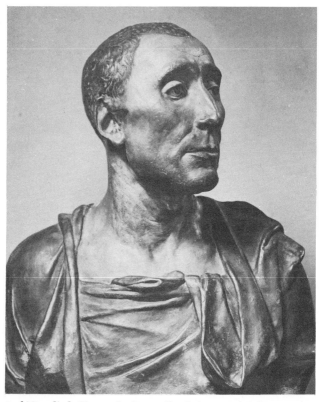

Bust of Niccolò da Uzzano by Donatello. (Alinari-Art Reference Bureau)

nities within the Florentine domain, his circle of acquaintances also included the prominent citizens of these localities. On a lower but still important level, he was on intimate terms with the peasants who farmed his land in the *contado*, with the artisans who repaired his houses, and with the druggists, winesellers and retail cloth dealers who traded with him, and whose friendship and support contributed to his power and influence in the Palazzo Vecchio.

The social world of the Florentine patriciate represented a balance between two contrasting principles: the aristocratic and the egalitarian. The egalitarian strain was fostered by the open, flexible character of the society, by the constant fluctuations of fortune and status, and also by the political structure.

Since 1293, powerful magnate families had been excluded from the commune's highest offices, and after 1343 lower guildsmen were guaranteed a share of these offices. In the street and in the council hall, the patrician rubbed shoulders with artisans and shopkeepers, whose votes and opinions were not without significance in politics, and whose economic activities and interests touched his own at a hundred points. Cosmopolitanism also contributed to this tendency. On a given day, a Florentine merchant might lend money to an impoverished English soldier, honor a letter of credit sent by an Arab trader in Algiers, and listen to a French cardinal of noble birth present an address to the communal council. But even though Florentine society was not hierarchical (in an institutional sense), its patrician elements did exhibit strong aristocratic and élitist impulses. The social ideals and pretensions of Europe's nobility, which were accepted by Tuscany's feudal families, never died out completely in this urban milieu, and in the fifteenth century, they experienced a remarkable revival.

The persistence of a sense of rank and hierarchy in Florence also encouraged a new phenomenon, the proliferation of patron-client relationships. These neofeudal bonds became particularly frequent in the period of "oligarchic" government after 1382. In one sense, they represent a continuation and extension of the old feudal relationship between lord and *fedelis* which never disappeared in the city, and remained quite strong in the rural regions. This survival can be seen in the maintenance of bands of retainers, the ancestors of the *bravi* in Manzoni's *I promessi sposi*, who were fed, clothed and armed by prominent citizens for protection and defense, and also for less respectable purposes. The assembly of these gangs of toughs, normally recruited from the *contado*, was a common phenomenon in times of political unrest.

More important than this anachronistic survival for the development of patron-client relationships was the slow disintegration of the corporate structure of Florentine society. In the past, the individual had received status and security not only from his family but also through membership in, and identification with, one or more of the city's corporate bodies. Of central importance was his guild, which both protected him and defined his economic relationships with others. As a guildsman, he was automatically a member of the commune, the organ that governed the city and its territory. But he could also identify himself more specifically with a political organization, the Parte Guelfa, and with the residents of his district or *gonfalone*, organized originally into military companies, and still mustered on rare occasions to defend the city in times of crisis. To give expression to his pious impulses, he might join a religious confraternity, such as the *Misericordia*, which took care of the sick, or perhaps one of the societies which met periodically to recite prayers or engage in devotional practices.

By the end of the fourteenth century, these corporate groups were declining in strength and vitality, and were playing a less important role in Florentine life. The communal government had steadily whittled away the rights, privileges and immunities of the guilds. The once-powerful Parte Guelfa also grew weaker, as a result of the indifference of the citizenry and the jealousy of the communal government. While these corporate organs were losing power and prestige, the family bond was also weakening. In the Quattrocento, families did not constitute such unified and solid blocs as in the previous century, when survival depended upon unity. Adherence to rival political factions split some families, as did too the disparity in wealth among the households of a clan. Illustrating a type of petition presented with increasing frequency to the communal executive is that of Andrea Salterelli, who described himself as a "young man of quiet and peaceful temperament and condition, who is in the wool trade and desires to live in harmony with his neighbors." He appealed to the Signoria to be legally separated from his relatives "who belong to a different rank and who lead less honorable lives and are not engaged in any trade." This petition reflects a significant change in the Florentine patrician mentality; men now sought identification and status on their own merits, and did not wish to be judged by the condition and behavior of their kin. The strongest incentive for familial division existed within magnate ranks, whose members could be fined for the misdeeds of their relatives. To escape these economic penalties, and to obtain the right to hold important offices, many magnates requested the commune's permission to change their names, and thus to cut their ancestral ties.

In this society in which corporate groups had lost much of their power and cohesiveness, the individual was extremely vulnerable. He was no longer protected, to the same degree as before, by family or guild connections. To defend himself against the dangers and threats which now confronted him, he sought the support and friendship of men more powerful and influential than himself. He did not neglect marriage alliances, and he continued to join a guild, the Parte Guelfa, or a religious association. But he now placed greater reliance upon these personal connections with important men, which counted for more than membership in corporate groups. This phenomenon was well described by Giovanni Morelli, who gave this advice to his son:

Connect yourself by marriage with those who are in power . . . and if you cannot arrange this, then make him [the man of influence] your friend by speaking well of him, by serving him in whatever way you can. . . . Seek his advice. . . . Show him your trust and friendship; invite him to your house, and act in ways that you think will please him, and will dispose him benevolently toward you. Always keep on good terms with those in power: obey and follow their will and their commands; never speak ill of them and their activities, even if they are evil. Keep silent and do not speak unless in commendation.

The character of this network of relationships can be seen more clearly by studying the bonds which linked one patron to his clients. A good example is Forese Sacchetti, a figure of middling status and importance in Florentine life during the first quarter of the fifteenth century. While not one of the most powerful men in the city, Sacchetti belonged to that second echelon of influential citizens who regularly held office in the republic. Sacchetti's correspondence, a part of which has been preserved in the archives of the *Conventi Soppressi*, reveals that his circle of *raccomandati*, of men who made claims upon him, was quite large, that it includes residents of both the city and the *cortado*. These clients petitioned Sacchetti for tax relief; they were seeking a government post, or an ecclesiastical benefice, or (in one case) a university chair in Perugia. They sought release from prison, or they merely wanted to receive Sacchetti's assurance that he would protect their interests.

But more significant than the nature of the request is the bond of obligation upon which the appeal rested. One petitioner wrote: "I know of no one, my lord, to whom I can turn in my hour of need with more security and trust than you, who are both able and willing to help your friends and servants." Several correspondents made the point that they regarded Sacchetti *in loco parentis;* for example, in this appeal: "I have always considered you as my father, since I have never recognized any other father in the world except Forese Sacchetti." Frequently, petitioners wrote to him on behalf of someone else, as did one man who sought to obtain the release from jail of a prisoner "to whom I act as a son should act for his father, and who has always treated me as his son." Some writers based their appeal strictly upon friendship, whereas others emphasized the service which the petitioner was prepared to do for his patron. A native of S. Miniato wrote to Sacchetti that "the people of this town know that I am your servant, and therefore I must write to you on their behalf." One poor suppliant, however, stated the bleak and unvarnished truth when he wrote: "You see how much faith I have in you; I hope that you are content with that. I can do nothing for you, except to live in accordance with the dictates of my conscience." Such candor is refreshing, and it suggests that in many cases the patron expected only gratitude in payment for benefits, aware that his generosity would become common knowledge, and that his influence would be increased by evidence of its efficacy.

In his description of social change in the Renaissance, Jacob Burckhardt argued that the individual had become emancipated from the corporate bonds of the medieval world, that he had become a free man in a free social order. The Florentine experience does not corroborate these conclusions of the Swiss historian. It is true that collective restraints upon the individual had weakened, although they never entirely disappeared. In particular, the vitality of family bonds and commitments remained much greater than Burckhardt suggested. But contradicting the vision of Renaissance man joyfully breaking his traditional bonds and exulting in his liberty is the picture of the Florentine who desperately sought new sources of security and identity to replace those which had disappeared. He forged bonds of friendship and obligation with protectors and benefactors, who would defend him against his enemies, and also against the burgeoning power of the state. Nor was the powerful citizen, the patron, really free. He too was enmeshed in a network of obligations and commitments, which limited and controlled his freedom of action. He could not release himself from these obligations without incurring loss of social prestige and political influence. The social freedom of the Renaissance man postulated by Burckhardt and elaborated by his followers is, in fifteenth-century Florence at least, a myth.

SOCIAL VALUES AND THEIR INNER CONTRADICTIONS

The behavior patterns and values of the Florentine patriciate represented a blend of four distinct traditions, often incompatible and frequently irreconcilable. In order of antiquity but not necessarily of vitality, these traditions were Christian, feudal, mercantile, and communal. In his behavior and his ideals, each patrician was a composite of these traditions. Frequently, one element predominated over the others, and gave a distinctive and unique cast to the individual's personality. No one escaped the tensions and contradictions of this pluralistic social heritage.

The discords of these traditions are significant. Like all Europeans, the Florentine's values were influenced by his religious beliefs. From childhood he was instructed in the Christian virtues of love, charity, humility, and poverty. In sermons and devotional literature, he was warned against the sins of pride and avarice, of gluttony and lechery. He was taught to shun wealth, to be content with his lot in this vale of tears, to be humble in his demeanor, and to turn the other cheek to his enemy. The values which he inherited from the feudal past were quite different. These were largely the ideals of Europe's warrior nobility; they emphasized such qualities as honor, pride, glory, and generosity, and such bellicose military virtues as aggressiveness and valor. At variance with both of these traditions, the Christian and the feudal, were the values derived from those business pursuits upon which the city's wealth and power were established. Finally, the civic values derived from membership in, and loyalty to, the political community often conflicted with these older traditions. The tensions arising from this particular category of disharmony will be examined in the next chapter, which focuses upon politics.

Some of these value conflicts are revealed by Florentine attitudes concerning occupations. The two most respected professions in the city were the law and international trade. Lawyers enjoyed the high prestige which Florentines (and all Europeans) accorded to men with university degrees. But knowledge of the law was particularly valued in Florence, where social and economic relations were governed by a complex and sophisticated legal code, and where the lawyer's talents were useful in politics. The prominent status granted to the international merchant distinguished Florence from other cities which did not engage so extensively in European commerce. Gregorio Dati was stating a commonly held opinion when he wrote: "A Florentine who is not a merchant, who has not traveled through the world, seeing foreign nations and peoples and then returned to Florence with some wealth, is a man who enjoys no esteem whatsoever."

This exaltation of the merchant was not the simplistic approbation of a commercial society for the activity from which it derived much of its wealth. The attitude was more complex, and it reflects the evolution of the city's social structure. Gregorio Dati was probably correct in his claim (made in 1410) that the international merchant was universally respected, but his statement would not have been so valid a half-century earlier, when there still survived among the families which descended (or pretended to descend) from feudal nobility a conviction that commerce was an unworthy and degrading occupation. Luca da Panzano, a descendant of an old noble house which had received a baronial title in the twelfth century from the Holy Roman Emperor, commented on his selection to the Merchants' court that "since we were old nobility, no one from our house . . . ever held this office, since they were not merchants." A scion of another noble family, Bernardo da Castiglionchio, drew a finer distinction between the categories of mercantile pursuits. He noted with pride that no member of his family had been forced by poverty to engage in a lowly trade or occupation. Some of his ancestors had been merchants, he admitted, but they had engaged in "noble and honest not base merchandise, voyaging to France and England and trading in cloth and wool as do all the greater and better men of the city."

In the professional hierarchy established by Florentine preferences and prejudices, cloth manufacturers and bankers ranked immediately below the lawyers and international merchants. As late as 1400, the stigma of usury—illegal gain—still attached to the banking profession. The Prato merchant Francesco Datini was advised in 1398 to abandon his plan to establish a bank by one of his associates on the grounds that banking was less profitable, less honorable and less pleasing to God, "for there is not one [banker] who does not make usurious contracts." Farther down on the scale were businessmen who participated in local trade (druggists, goldsmiths, used-clothes dealers), and then the petty shopkeepers and artisans: masons, carpenters, winesellers, blacksmiths, and bakers. Physicians occupied a median position in this hierarchy, below the great merchants and industrialists but above the shopkeepers. University professors were accorded respect and deference, as were the humanist scholars who dominated Florentine intellectual life in the fifteenth century. But grammar school teachers possessed as little social status and wealth as their modern counterparts. The tax assessments of *maestri di grammatica* were among the lowest in the city, and they were not permitted to organize into a guild and thus be eligible for public office.

A lucid exposition of the social values of the Florentine patriciate is found in the memoirs of Giovanni Morelli, written between 1393 and 1421. Morelli was a wealthy merchant of solidly respectable (but not distinguished) lineage. His memoirs reflect his mercantile background and orientation, and his ethics are essentially those of the successful business entrepreneur. Thrift, sobriety, caution, restraint are the supreme virtues. Morelli considered the conservation of the family patrimony to be a primary goal of life. So fearful was he of business failure that he advised his sons to operate alone, and never to employ factors or agents. He warned against the practice of usury less through fear of divine retribution than for concern about legal penalties. Recognizing that business talent was not inherited by everyone, he counseled those without it to abandon trade, to invest their money in land and live as rentiers. He repeatedly warned his sons to trust no one, not business associates, peasants, or factors and employees in one's shop. This obsessive fear of betrayal might seem to be a manifestation of Morelli's paranoid personality, but similar sentiments were expressed by several of his fellow-citizens. He was articulating the economic insecurity of the whole society.

Morelli's values are expressed with greatest clarity in his judgment of others. His father Paolo was a man of supreme talent and worth (in his son's opinion), who triumphed over many obstacles and difficulties to achieve success. He had been tricked out of part of his inheritance by his brothers, but rather than harbor resentment he continued to treat them with Christian affection. "He maintained close relations with them, demonstrating his great love by helping them as much as possible, by advising them on their affairs, and thus demonstrating his faith and hope in them." Disaster struck the family in 1363, when the plague killed his brother, and Paolo was forced to work hard to save the family patrimony. Then he too died of the plague in 1374, when he was forty. Had he lived another ten years, Giovanni wrote, "he would have achieved a great fortune of 50,000 florins.

The qualities stressed in this biography are astuteness in economic affairs, family loyalty, and sociability. These traits were also lauded in Morelli's description of his cousin, Giovanni di Bartolomeo. As a young man, Giovanni was "very obliging, almost prodigal, so that his expenditures were frivolous and not very honorable." But marriage sobered him: "He became the most thrifty man in the world and an excellent administrator of his property." Morelli also wrote approvingly of his cousin's social demeanor: "He was an agreeable man, very lighthearted, eager to converse, astute, affectionate, friendly, a fine storyteller." From other sources, it is clear that these gregarious qualities, the ability to forge warm and intimate human relationships, was a prized asset in Florence, and one that did not derive from the business ethic. Another trait which Morelli praised was liberality. Of his father Paolo he wrote: "He was a great giver of alms, and he never refused anything asked of him by rich or poor, and particularly money." Yet Morelli also emphasized the virtues of parsimony and austerity in living habits. Unconsciously, he was expressing a conflict between the burgher impulse toward thrift and the aristocratic trait of open-handed generosity.

This conflict between mercantile and noble values was also reflected in other dimensions of social behavior. In the distant past, the Florentine bourgeoisie had created an image of the feudal magnate as a violent, lawless figure, who habitually exploited and maltreated peaceful merchants and artisans. As the old feudal nobility became domesticated and practically indistinguishable from the urban bourgeoisie, this image bore less relation to reality. Yet the myth persisted into the fifteenth century. It found expression in countless accusations against members of magnate families, who were described as *grandi e possenti,* as in this secret denunciation delivered to a judge in 1394: "You should know that the Bardi are a great and arrogant family and they have no concern for anyone, and every day they use violence against everyone [whom they encounter]." This sentiment also was articulated in the petitions for family divisions, in which the appellants invariably characterized themselves (as did the Velluti family in 1395) as "pacific and tranquil men who seek to maintain peaceful relations with everyone," and who described their relatives as men "who seek to offend others and who do not pursue peaceful ways." Yet the manners of the feudal nobility were not universally despised, even by the peace-loving merchants. Displays of strength and force, even aggressive and arrogant manifestations of power, still commanded respect, fear, and admiration.

The Florentine patrician was very troubled by the gulf between Christian norms and the realities of social behavior. In three particular areas, the conflict was acute: in the conception of "honor," in sexual mores, and in the problem of wealth. The stress upon honor, derived in large part from the chivalric code of the feudal nobility, permeated the whole system of patrician values. To live honorably meant to act according to the standards of one's class, and to be imbued with a sense of personal dignity and responsibility. Dishonorable behavior comprised any act that lowered or demeaned the status and prestige of the individual or his family. In a capsule biography of a distant relative, Piero di Ciore Pitti, the lawyer Donato Velluti (d. 1370) described a man who had plumbed the depths of dishonor. After wasting his paternal inheritance, Pitti earned his livelihood as a soldier and then as a day laborer in a cloth factory. "He was wounded by one of the Machiavelli and never engaged in a vendetta. He took for a wife Monna Bartolomea, the grand-daughter of Bongianni, the wine seller, who had been the whore of other men, and with whom he lived in a miserable state." When Pitti died in a hovel near the church of S. Giorgio, none of his relatives attended his funeral. Florentines displayed little charity or pity for the fallen, even those who were not wholly responsible for their fate. One unfortunate member of a prominent family, Giovanni Corsini, was described by a chronicler as "so immersed in a brimming expanse of misery and poverty that . . . he was even despised by his own relatives." The church's exaltation of humility, its denunciation of pride, made very little impression upon the Florentine patriciate.

The sexual mores of the upper class coincided with the Christian ethic in a single respect: in the universal concern for the chastity of its women, before and after marriage. Women of good family were closely guarded from contacts with strange men; they left their houses rarely, and then to go to mass or to family celebrations. The intimate relations between young men and women which Boccaccio describes in his *Decameron* are fictional; even the crisis of the Black Death would not have led to such free contact between the sexes. Boccaccio certainly exaggerated the extent of illicit love and infidelity within the patriciate, but his descriptions of licentious behavior had some basis in fact. Paolo Sassetti, a merchant of respectable family, recorded in his diary the fallen state of his cousin Letta, the daughter of Federigo Sassetti, who died in 1383 in the house of her paramour, Giovanni Porcellini. "May the devil take her soul, for she has brought shame and dishonor to our house." Sassetti reconciled himself to this situation by commenting that men could not repair what God had decreed in punishment

for their sins, but then he added: "We will launch such a vendetta [against Porcellini] that our pride will be assuaged."

No social stigma attached to the male for sexual relations with
other women, so long as he did not bring dishonor to his family
by marrying a mistress of lowly birth. Florentine men took
their pleasure with women whenever opportunity and inclination permitted, and this was not infrequent. Common targets
of their affection were the domestic servants and slaves of the
household, although it was not unusual for alliances to be formed
with women of the lower classes in city and countryside. Giovanni
Morelli's account of his cousin's extramarital relations is not
untypical. "He had no children from his wife Simona, although
he did have several illegitimate offspring, some from a woman
of good family, and some from a slave who was very beautiful,
and whom he later married to someone from the Mugello."
With uncharacteristic reticence, he added: "I don't wish to name
her husband, since it would not be proper [to identify] this
family, for it is of quite good condition." The offspring of these
illicit alliances were not ostracized by society, but they did
suffer discrimination. Normally, they did not inherit a full share
of their father's property, although they frequently received a
monetary bequest. The commune would occasionally approve
petitions to legitimize a bastard child, but only if the father had
no male heirs.

The problem of wealth, its acquisition and its use, created
the sharpest discord in the ethical and moral system of the Florentine patriciate. The traditional Christian hostility to riches
was constantly reiterated in the sermons of friars, in devotional
literature, and in the writings of theologians. Efforts to bridge
the gap between belief and practice, between word and deed,
constitute one of the most significant themes in the history
of this city, and, indeed, in the history of late medieval Europe.
Every Florentine felt some guilt for living in a society whose
material existence conflicted so sharply with its spiritual ideal.

Florentines responded to this dilemma in two ways, either
by admitting guilt and seeking to assuage it, or denying it by
justifying the acquisition of wealth. Evidence for the open and
candid admission of guilt is most abundant in the testaments
of fourteenth-century merchants, who specifically admitted that

their fortunes were increased by usury. The grandfather of Cosimo de' Medici, Bicci (d. 1363), stipulated in his will that 50 *lire* should be set aside to compensate those from whom he had taken money illicitly. Society equated the practice of usury with damnation, and the souls of manifest usurers were believed to be lost irretrievably. They were not allowed to make wills, nor were they given Christian burial. After 1437, only Jews were permitted to operate pawnbroking shops; thus the authorities could not be accused of permitting Christian souls to suffer eternal damnation. Although usury was strictly defined, and strenuous efforts were made to distinguish between licit and illicit gain, the failure of the theologians to agree upon these distinctions sowed doubts in men's minds which were never entirely dispelled. The tacit admission of guilt was usually expressed by large bequests to charitable or religious foundations. Vespasiano da Bisticci was describing the mental state of many businessmen when he noted that Cosimo de' Medici "had prickings of conscience that certain portions of his wealth . . . had not been righteously [i.e., licitly] gained," and Cosimo's decision to rebuild the monastery of S. Marco was one of many similar acts made by troubled men. The artistic creations of medieval and Renaissance Florence are the result, in large part, of the guilt feelings of the patriciate.

Two random examples will illustrate specific ways in which some individuals responded to the tensions between the Christian ideal and the realities of the business world. Donato Velluti described a strange interlude in the life of his cousin Bernardo, who had followed the normal routine of the merchant class by entering a cloth factory as an apprentice, and then establishing a partnership. During Lent in the year 1350, he experienced a religious crisis and fled to the monastery of Certosa. There he spent a year as a novice, rejecting all appeals from his relatives to return to the world, and he remained "as firm as a rock [in his determination] to stay there and die." While settling his temporal affairs before taking final vows, he became involved in a controversy with his uncle over a disputed inheritance. Fearful that his orphaned brothers and sisters would lose their patrimony, he abruptly changed his mind and informed the prior that he was leaving the monastery. Ignoring the monk's pleas and warnings that he was jeopardizing his soul, Bernardo returned to his shop in Florence and picked up the strings of his abandoned mercantile career.

The solution adopted by Gregorio Dati to placate his conscience was less drastic, but no less revealing of the tensions under which the merchant lived and worked. In his "secret book," Dati lamented his failure to abide by the precepts of his religion. "For our sins," he wrote, "we are subjected to many tribulations of spirit and to many bodily passions in this miserable life, and if it were not for the aid of divine grace . . . we would perish daily." He confessed that during his lifetime he had regularly disobeyed God's commandments, and then added: "Since I do not trust myself to reform my habits to their proper state, I must begin slowly, step by step." Dati promised that he would refrain from any business activity on feast days, and that he would not allow others to labor on his behalf "for gain or temporal benefit." But the merchant realized that the flesh was weak, and that circumstances might force him to break his resolution. Thus he promised to give 1 florin to the poor whenever he violated this rule, "and I have written this down to keep it firmly in mind and for my embarrassment, if I contravene it." Dati also sought to protect himself from religious penalties by stipulating that these resolutions were not, strictly speaking, vows, "but I make them to encourage myself to observe these good practices, insofar as it is possible for me." As befits a sensible merchant, he limited his commitments and obligations, and sought to steer a prudent course between the demands of the world and of the spirit. He recognized and accepted the dangers of this temporizing course, which required both courage and faith.

THE QUALITY OF SOCIAL BONDS: FRIENDSHIP AND ENMITY

The form and texture of Florentine social relationships in these years is revealed most clearly in private correspondence, a substantial amount of which has survived. The most distinctive feature of these letters is their intimacy. Men expressed themselves freely and openly, and they displayed a remarkable talent for introspection. They described their sentiments and passions, desires and ideals, loves and hates; and they passed sharp and perceptive judgment on others. Opinions were recorded with a candor that is surprising, when one considers the frequency with which correspondence was intercepted and read by unfriendly eyes. Even business letters, or personal appeals for aid from strangers, bear this stamp of intimacy and involvement. One quality that is absent from Florentine letters (and from the Florentine character) is indifference or detachment.

Through the fortunate survival of several hundred letters sent by the Florentine notary Lapo Mazzei (d. 1412) to the Prato merchant Francesco Datini (d. 1410), it is possible to reconstruct their relationship. From similar humble origins, Mazzei and Datini had followed diverse paths, the former to become a notary of modest wealth and status, the latter to achieve distinction as the richest merchant of Prato. Datini had assisted the young Mazzei when he was a student in Bologna, and this act of generosity was the initial strand of their friendship. Datini often appointed the notary to be his procurator or legal representative in Florence. Mazzei's efforts on behalf of his friend did not go unrewarded, and frequently a barrel of wine or a carton of cheese would be delivered to his home. Datini found a place for Lapo's son in one of his mercantile enterprises and lent money to his friend for the purchase of real estate. But the essence of the bond between the two men was affection, which survived the vicissitudes of time and Datini's acerbic personality. For the merchant was quick to ask friends for help, and equally ready to take offense if it were not immediately forthcoming. Irked by Datini's anger on one occasion, the notary attempted to define their relationship:

Francesco, I am not bound to you as Orestes to Pylades, or Damon to Pythias, who for the sake of friendship sought to die for the other. Nor am I like the men of Sardanapolis, who were friends only for gluttony and profit. But I am not the worst among the lukewarm friends who run around today, and may God protect you from adversity, so that

I be not among the first to forsake you. It is not right that everyone
should satisfy your smallest whim, and then immediately you tell me:
"I have no friends."

For Datini and Lapo Mazzei, friendship signified obligations
and service, the right to make demands upon the other, and
the willingness to share burdens, problems, and responsibilities. Their correspondence describes every dimension of their
lives, both private and professional. Datini asked his friend's
advice on business affairs, and for opinions on the personnel
employed in his companies. He relied heavily upon the notary's
local knowledge, and his acquaintance with influential Florentines. "I know something about the government of this city," Lapo
wrote his friend, "and you can trust my judgment. I have more
dealings with the men who control the state than do many other
notaries here." Acting as Datini's agent, the notary protected
the merchant's interests in lawsuits and pressed his petitions for
tax relief before the fiscal authorities. It was through Lapo's
good offices that Francesco was introduced to such prominent
citizens as Guido del Palagio, Niccolò da Uzzano and Messer
Rinaldo Gianfigliazzi.

The close bond between the two men is demonstrated, too,
by Mazzei's persistent efforts to mediate between Datini and
his wife, Margherita. Relations between the couple were never
smooth; Datini was brusque and impatient, his wife sharp-
tongued, demanding, and shrewish. Contributing to their mari-
tal difficulties was physical separation, for Francesco was often
absent on business. Margherita's inability to have children and
her husband's infidelities, which produced at least two illegitimate children, also imposed strains on their relationship. Mazzei repeatedly urged Datini to show more tolerance toward his
spouse, while in turn Margherita was advised to curb her
tongue and to be more patient of her husband's irascible nature.
In other ages and in other societies, Mazzei's behavior would
have been considered intolerable meddling. But in this relationship, which was certainly not untypical, Lapo's concern was
accepted as proper and legitimate.

In Lapo's judgment, the most troubling aspect of his friend's
life was his excessive preoccupation with worldly matters and

his indifference to the state of his soul. Himself a man of deep piety, Mazzei could not understand the merchant's compulsive need to acquire more wealth, to extend his material interests ever farther. In one letter, Mazzei expressed his doubts and fears with clarity and eloquence:

Francesco, I have considered your state a hundred times, on my walks, and in bed, and in my study. . . . And charity constrains me to tell you the truth, which I think a most precious thing among friends. . . . When I think of the cares of the house you are building, of your warehouses in far-off lands, your banquets and your accounts, . . . they seem to me so far beyond what is needful that I realize it cannot be that you should seize an hour from the world and its snares. Yet God has granted you an abundance of earthly goods, and has given you, too, a thousand warnings, to awaken you. . . . In short, I would you should wind up many of your matters . . . and desist at once from any more building, and give away some of your riches in charity. . . . I ask you not to become a priest or a monk, but I say unto you: put some order in your life.

In another letter written to his friend in 1405, Mazzei described a scene which reveals with particular clarity the intimate nature of Florentine relationships. For months, the notary had been defending Datini in a lawsuit brought by the mother of the merchant's deceased partner, to recover assets which allegedly had belonged to him. The case was lengthy, acrimonious, and complex, and it frequently drove Datini into fits of anger. After the Merchants' court had awarded 1000 florins to Francesco's adversary, Mazzei met the latter's legal representative, Bartolo Pucci, in a church. There the notary recounted all of the trouble which Pucci had caused to Datini and himself, "and how Bartolo disturbed Francesco more with one request, than all of his friends could do in a month." And after complaining that Bartolo's further prosecution of the case would be useless, Mazzei then asked his adversary "a most singular favor in this church, which was that every day of his life, beginning today, he should regard me as his friend." This appeal had the desired effect, and the shaken and remorseful Pucci seized Lapo's right hand "and said words to me that I will not write, for they were excessive, to seal this friendship, thanking me so warmly that

he was almost on the brink of tears." Bartolo then led Mazzei
to the church altar and seized a book, upon which he made the
sign of the cross, and then swore never to offend Francesco or
his associates, and to terminate the legal processes which were
still pending.

This scene was probably not typical, but it reveals the
strength of the impulse to define personal relationships in sharp,
unambiguous terms. If not friendship, then enmity, and Florentines were as preoccupied with their enemies as with their
friends. Hostility was intense, persistent, and universal. It arose
from a multitude of circumstances: economic disputes, political
bickering, ancient family quarrels, personal dislikes and affronts.
Contributing to this atmosphere which bred hatred was the
extremely competitive nature of Florentine economic life. In
this loosely structured, pluralistic society, the opportunities for
disagreement and discord were infinite.

Where personal bonds were closest, as in the family, the
possibility of friction was greatest. Internal family divisions
contributed to the progressive weakening of the blood tie as a
cohesive element in Florentine society. Conflicts arose over the
division of a patrimony, the disposition of a dowry, the management of an orphan's estate. If one believes the testimony of Giovanni Morelli, orphans rarely escaped with more than a tenth
of their original inheritance, the remainder having been stolen
by rapacious guardians. Recorded every year in the judicial
records are cases involving widows who sought to pry loose
their dowries from the clutches of their husbands' families. More
surprising perhaps than the incidence of these family quarrels
is the intensity of the hatred they often provoked. In appealing
to a guild court for a favorable judgment against her son, Baldetta Manetti wrote: "For God's sake, I recommend myself to
you [the consuls of the guild], for you know that poor widows
should be favored, and especially against their evil sons who seek
to rob them." Niccolò Bastari pleaded with his brother in Ragusa
to return to Florence and assist him in settling a property dispute
with their relatives: "We pray you, Giovanni, for God and for the
cross and for the salvation of our family, and for your own interests, to return home. If you don't, we see the minds of others
so full of evil and malice, spreading lies and false stories to such

a degree that we won't find anyone to adjudicate the quarrel. Angelo and I are both prepared to die rather than see my children wrongfully reduced to beggary."

These statements may contain hyperbole, but one cannot ignore or treat casually the poisonous hatred which Remigio Lanfredini poured out against his father Lanfredino, in a letter written from Venice in 1395 to his brother Orsino. Remigio was outraged by his father's decision to make peace with an enemy of the family, without consulting his relatives. Learning of this action, Remigio confronted his father, "who began to cry like Cain, the traitor that he is, and I will never call him my father, but a wicked and evil traitor!" The father defended himself by pleading that he had been ordered to make peace by the marquis of Ferrara, and then added: "Look, Remigio, you are my son and you ought to be content with my action. I did it for the best." But even the poor man's wife joined in the chorus of vituperation: "Lanfredino, betrayer of your own kin! You have brought such shame on your children by making this peace, and telling no one about it. Now you have taken away their goods, their honor, and everything which they possess in this world!" Apparently unable to bear this indignity, Remigio left Ferrara to begin a new life in Venice, changing his name to Bellini. But he could not erase his bitterness from his mind. "We can now see that Lanfredino does not care a fig for us, and thinks neither about honor nor shame . . . If I were to see him cut to pieces in front of me, I would not rise from my seat!"

Much of this domestic rancor was dissipated in private grumbling and complaint; its expression in correspondence and conversation doubtless served as a safety valve. But in some instances, hostility took more serious forms and found an outlet in litigation, and occasionally in violence. The court records from this period attest to the quarrelsome and litigious nature of the Florentines. The private memoirs of the merchant Antonio Rustichi, written between 1420 and 1435, contains a description of a series of judicial processes in which he was involved. The frequency of these accounts suggests that Rustichi, like many of his neighbors, thrived on lawsuits. His first recorded dispute (1420) involved a petition presented to the commune by his brother Giovanni, requesting that Antonio be designated as a

magnate, and thus ineligible for high office. According to Antonio, this was done without any cause, "but only to ruin me." This
quarrel originated over property inherited by the brothers, and
the commune endeavored to settle the dispute by appointing
arbiters to study the case and reach a decision. This litigation
dragged on for five years before a settlement was finally reached.
Another conflict of a different character arose from a quarrel
between Antonio and Simone Buonarroti. Rustichi brought a
criminal charge against this ancestor of Michelangelo for attacking him without provocation (so Antonio alleged), while he
was sitting on a bench in front of a neighbor's house. When
Simone appeared before Antonio "in the presence of my relatives and friends" to apologize for his assault, and to explain that
he had been possessed by a devil, Antonio graciously withdrew
the criminal complaint. His legal costs amounted to nearly 1
florin, but this was more than compensated by the balm of Buonarroti's public apology and humiliation.

Antonio was apparently the instigator, as well as the victim, of physical violence, for he was haled before a judge in
1427 to answer charges that he has assaulted a serving woman
named Chiara. The accusation was brought by the woman's
employer, and Antonio was fined 100 *lire* and required to pay
an additional 40 *lire* in court costs. He insisted upon his innocence, and to his description of the case in his diary, he
appended this comment: "I make this record so that I shall not
forget, if ever I have the opportunity to pay them back in the
same coin." A year later, he was back in court, complaining
that he was the victim of a usurious contract. He persuaded
the judge to reduce his obligation by 3 florins, although he
probably spent more for legal fees. In 1431 he was thrown into
prison for a debt of 300 florins, and he won his freedom only
after he swore to pay principal and interest within six months.
Two small cases terminated Rustichi's perpetual struggle for
justice. He won a judgment of 20 *lire* from a carpenter who had
rented a shop from him, and he successfully defended himself
in another suit which alleged that he had cut down trees belonging to his neighbor.

As Antonio Rustichi's career reveals, the patrician's social relations were occasionally tinged with violence—not only the

collective disorder of political turmoil but the private act of hostility. A central theme in Florentine history was the perpetual conflict between the primitive impulse to express anger and frustration through violence, and communal efforts to restrain these outbreaks through legislation, judicial penalties, and peace commissions. Efforts to curb the lawlessness and arrogant behavior of the most powerful clans were institutionalized in the Ordinances of Justice (1293). These statutes required members of designated magnate families to post bond guaranteeing the good behavior of themselves and their kin. Gradually, this combination of harsh judicial penalties and confiscatory fines impressed upon these families the benefits of civilized social behavior. Men who suffered injuries sought recourse in the courts with greater frequency, and they usually obtained more efficient and more equitable justice.

Although not entirely trustworthy, statistics compiled from criminal records tend to substantiate this picture of decreasing violence and disorder within the patrician class. Between 1343 and 1378, members of the Medici family (comprising some fifty adult males) were convicted of twenty crimes of violence, including six murders. From 1378 to 1434, they received only six convictions (all prior to 1396), none of which involved homicide. The incidence of crimes among the Strozzi, the largest family in the city, indicates a similar trend. Nine Strozzi were condemned for assault between 1382 and 1384, but during the next half-century, only ten members of the family were penalized for criminal acts in the Florentine courts. Not all of their peccadilloes were caught in the judicial net, and their political influence and social rank doubtless saved them from some prosecutions. But even with these qualifications, their record indicates that over the span of a century, they had learned to restrain their violent impulses.

The turbulence and disorder so characteristic of social relations in Dante's time had largely subsided by 1400, and the fifteenth century is, on the surface, a more tranquil and civilized age. Street brawls between families or political factions had practically disappeared from the Florentine scene. Crimes of violence committed by patricians were not unknown, but most were unpremeditated, arising from an argument, an accidental wound, a real or imagined insult. Occasionally, a delict described in the judicial records recalls a more primitive and uninhibited past. In his memoirs, Luca da Panzano candidly recounted his visit to Naples in 1420, undertaken for the express purpose of killing Nanni di Ciechi, a "traitor" who had incurred the enmity of the Panzano clan. Nor was murder for pay unknown; the court records of 1396 describe the details of a homicide by a hired assassin employed by Angelo Ricoveri to kill his enemy for 300 florins. But these were rare incidents, and not the everyday occurrences described with such relish in historical novels.

Contributing to the pacification of the Florentine aristocracy was a more efficient system of justice and internal policing. But another important factor was the change which had occurred in the standards of behavior observed by the patriciate. In his memoirs written in the 1320s, the prominent magnate Simone della Tosa described the many crimes committed by his relatives, and the heavy fines which had been levied against them. He gave no hint that he deplored this behavior, although the economic losses suffered by the Tosinghi must have pained him. At the close of the century, the private papers of another patrician, Luigi Guicciardini, reveal a very different outlook. Luigi recorded the misdemeanors of his kinsman Simone, who had petitioned him for help from the communal prison. Simone's criminal career was brief, but impressive in its intensity. He first attacked a fellow apprentice with whom he worked in a silk shop, and was discharged by his employers. There followed a succession of quarrels and altercations, in which Simone demonstrated his versatility with weapons, by using a knife, a club, and his bare hands against his antagonists. He even attacked a mourner at a funeral. Collecting a band of marauders in the *contado*, he so terrorized a Machiavelli household that the father complained that the women of his family did not dare to show themselves at the windows. Imprisoned for assaulting a peasant with a pair of shears, he was later captured in an escape attempt, for which he received a jail sentence of five years. A century earlier, Simone's indiscretions would probably have been condoned by his relatives, who would certainly have tried to obtain his release from prison. In 1396, however, Luigi

Guicciardini sealed the fate of his errant kinsman with the comment: "The abominable activities of this man are infinite."

CHANGING SOCIAL VALUES: FROM TRECENTO TO QUATTROCENTO

Some patrician values and modes of behavior remained stable throughout the Renaissance; others changed quite significantly. A useful technique for measuring these changes is to compare the careers of prominent Florentines in these decades, from the late Trecento to the age of the Medici in the mid-fifteenth century. A worthy representative of the Florentine aristocracy in the last quarter of the fourteenth century is the merchant Guido del Palagio (d. 1399). His career is instructive not because it was typical but because it represented the patriciate at its best. His life can be viewed as the achievement of a social ideal, and also as the embodiment of traditional values and attitudes which were slowly disappearing.

The Del Palagio were an old and respected family, but they did not rank among the most prominent, either in wealth or in antiquity. Guido was a successful cloth manufacturer, but his eminence did not derive from his fortune or his business acumen. Rather, it came from his political talents and his reputation for piety. He was a close friend of Giovanni delle Celle, a hermit who had become the spiritual adviser for a small group of devout Florentines. Guido made the standard gestures expected of a pious Christian, giving alms and restoring a Fiesole monastery which had fallen into ruin. But like his good friend Lapo Mazzei, he also endeavored to live according to the principles of his faith.

Guido's piety did not induce him to withdraw from the world, but it gave a particular color to his public activities. He was perhaps the only prominent statesman of his time who did not become involved in a clique or faction. His independence of partisan politics may explain his universal popularity with the electorate. He was chosen for high office in the regimes which governed Florence before and after the Ciompi revolution. In the scrutiny held in 1391 to select those eligible for the Signoria, Guido received the largest vote of any candidate, 144 of 149 votes cast. Another significant index of his political influence was his frequent election to the Ten on War, a commission appointed in times of crisis to direct the republic's military and diplomatic activities. A modest man, Guido avoided the political limelight, and he spoke rarely in council meetings. But his opinions and judgments were highly respected, for his personal integrity and patriotism were unquestioned.

The testimonies to Guido's reputation are numerous, and his memory remained alive in Florence for decades after his death. The humanist Poggio Bracciolini called him a man "of the greatest sanctity," and a memorialist of the mid-fifteenth century described him in these terms: "a famous Florentine citizen scarcely without equal, and to his prestige there was added goodness and charity, for he was well provided with the things of this world, and was a lavish giver of alms." But the most revealing testimony to Guido's reputation is contained in two letters from Lapo Mazzei to Francesco Datini. On one occasion, Lapo congratulated his friend for his perspicacity, "for in this great city you have chosen this man [Guido] above all others, who will never want or desire anything from you, unless it be for the honor and salvation of your soul and the satisfaction of your person." The second letter was in reply to Datini, who had apparently heard some gossip denigrating Guido and minimizing his standing in the community. "Tell your friend," wrote the angry Lapo, "that either he is vile, and is saying this to trouble you . . . or he has no knowledge of the condition of this city." And he concluded with this tribute to Guido: "Every day he grows in the love of the great, the middling and the small, and I'll tell you more, that both the good and bad [citizens] honor him with words and deeds to a greater degree than ever before. . . . He has the most solid reputation of any citizen of any town in Tuscany!"

Guido del Palagio's reputation was based upon a complex of traditional virtues: honor, integrity, piety, commitment to public service. These qualities are not emphasized in contemporary descriptions of Cosimo de' Medici, the most prominent citizen of the generation which reached manhood in the early fifteenth century. Vespasiano da Bisticci's biography of Cosimo is laudatory and uncritical, but it is an honest evaluation of the man,

Bust of Cosimo de'Medici by Verrocchio. (Staatliche Museum, Berlin)

and depicts him as he was seen by the majority of his fellow-citizens. No modern biographer has succeeded in penetrating the surface of Cosimo's personality, of exposing the man behind the public facade. We can use this facade, however, to measure some of the changes that had occurred in the life style of the patriciate.

Cosimo's authority derived from his great wealth and his leadership of a faction. Vespasiano da Bisticci described a conversation between Cosimo and a political rival, in which the former articulated his political philosophy: "Now it seems to me only just and honest that I should prefer the good name and honor of my house to you: that I should work for my own interest rather than for yours. So you and I will act like two big dogs who, when they meet, smell one another and then, because they both have teeth, go their ways. Wherefore now you can attend to your affairs and I to mine." He demonstrated a particular talent for working behind the scenes, achieving his goals by manipulating others. His instruments were the bonds of obligation by which he tied his supporters to himself. Vespasiano wrote: "He rewarded those who brought him back [from exile], lending to one a good sum of money, and making a gift to another to help marry his daughter or buy lands . . . ." His political enemies were not killed but exiled; the refusal to shed blood was characteristic of this cautious politician who gained his objectives by less flamboyant methods. In one sense, his style represented the triumph of the mercantile mentality. He typified the rational and calculating entrepreneur, the shrewd, tough-minded realist who had banished passion and emotion from politics.

The material dimensions of Cosimo's life also reflect significant innovations in the patrician mode of living. The construction of a massive palace on the Via Larga provided the arena for a more refined and luxurious style of existence, which set the pattern for the Florentine upper class. Although Cosimo deliberately affected the manner of an old-fashioned merchant with simple tastes, his living style signalled the abandonment of such traditional virtues as austerity, thrift, and frugality, and the acceptance of ostentation as a socially desirable trait. The new ethic received political sanction with the repeal or nonenforcement of sumptuary legislation, a characteristic feature of communal policy in earlier times. Seven years after Cosimo's death, his grandson Lorenzo stated that the Medici had spent over 600,000 florins for public purposes since 1434, and he remarked that this expenditure "casts a brilliant light upon our condition in the city." The living standard in the Medici palace was more luxurious than Cosimo's ancestors had ever known. This expenditure for magnificent decor, costly furnishings, and elegant clothing was designed to provide an impressive setting for prominent guests, to create an image of Medici (and Florentine) wealth and taste. Cosimo was host to both the German emperor Frederick III and the Byzantine emperor John Paleologue, as well as other, less distinguished princes of church and state who dined and lodged in the palace on the Via Larga, or in the villas at Careggi and Cafaggiuolo. The Medici were not the only

Wedding scene from Adimari *cassone* in the Galleria Accademia. (Alinari-

Florentine family to dispense lavish hospitality, but the scale and opulence of their entertainments marked them as the city's most illustrious house. A visit to the Medici household was a dazzling experience, as young Galeazzo Maria Sforza, son of the lord of Milan, testified in letters to his father Francesco. This product of a courtly milieu extolled the beauties and charms of the villa at Careggi, and praised the musical and dramatic entertainments which were provided for his amusement.

The trend toward ostentation and luxury which is so apparent in the private lives of the Medici was also visible in their public ceremonies. Both funerals and weddings had become more formal, more elaborate, and more expensive. The temptation to use these occasions to publicize family wealth and status was strong, but in the past, it had been restrained by sumptuary laws and by the characteristic Florentine aversion to wasteful expenditure. In the Quattrocento, these restraints were no longer effective. Chronicles of the Medici family describe the elaborate character of these events, and also their cost: black cloth for the family of the deceased, wax candles and torches, decorations for the bier and for the horses in the funeral procession, food for the mourners. Equally lavish expenditure became standard

Art Reference Bureau)

form at marriage celebrations, as the well-known painting of a
wedding ceremony on the Adimari *cassone* reveals.

Among the more blatant manifestations of patrician extravagance were the jousting tournaments, which became very popular
in the fifteenth century. These atavistic survivals of the chivalric age had no genuine roots in Florence. They were revived
in the last quarter of the fourteenth century by visiting nobles,
among whom were King Peter of Cyprus and Luchino Visconti.
The tournaments were usually held in the square in front of S.
Croce, and they attracted large throngs of spectators. It was
the custom for foreign knights to joust with young men from
patrician families, whose ancestors had fought to defend Florence from the feudal nobility, both foreign and domestic. These
tournaments provided wealthy citizens with the opportunity to
flaunt their riches, for the combatants and their entourages were
dressed in the family colors, mounted upon expensive horses,
and sent into the arena to fight for the glory of the house.

There is no simple explanation for this intensified patrician
impulse to express itself in such material terms as spending
inflated sums on drowries and indulging in conspicuous con-

sumption. It cannot be understood solely in terms of greater prosperity; Medicean Florence was not richer than the Florence of Giotto or Boccaccio. Nor should this phenomenon be seen as a total rejection of traditional values. The penchant for luxury had always existed in patrician society, most strongly among the old magnate clans, but it had been restrained by ascetic impulses, some of which were religious, and some mercantile in origin. This tenuous balance was destroyed in the fifteenth century. By indulging in extravagance and display, patricians were announcing their release from the restraints imposed by egal-itarianism; they were emphasizing their special, exalted place in Florentine society.

Cosimo's career reflects this aristocratic, elitist tendency. His pose as a simple merchant, his pretense of being no greater than any other citizen, deluded no one. He crushed his enemies and exalted his friends and supporters. The artisan or shopkeeper who encountered Cosimo in the street might take pleasure from rubbing shoulders with the great man, but he also knew that the banker could determine his fate. Cosimo's father, Giovanni, had been at home in the streets, the squares, and the churches of the city; he had conducted his business in his shop in the Old Market. Cosimo erected a vast palace which symbol-ized both his power and his separation from his fellow-citizens. There in his private chapel, decorated by Gozzoli with magnif-icent frescoes, he worshipped in isolation. There in his study he made the major decisions which determined the course of Florentine policy. Before his death, Cosimo had created the structure for that esoteric milieu in which his grandson Lorenzo was to flourish.

Cosimo was a taciturn man who habitually kept his thoughts to himself. If he ever reflected upon the political and social changes which had occurred in Florence during his lifetime, he left no record of his opinions. He and his contemporaries were perhaps too intimately involved in these changes to appre-ciate their significance, and to perceive clearly the differences between their style of living and that of their ancestors. The next generation, to which Cosimo's son Piero (d. 1469) belonged, was more accustomed to the aristocratic outlook and values of the age, and less inhibited about describing them. The memoirs of one representative of this generation, Giovanni Rucellai (d. 1481) reflect these elitist modes of thought and behavior, but they also demonstrate the persistence of traditional habits and values.

Rucellai qualifies as a spokesman for the Florentine patriciate of the mid-Quattrocento; his credentials are impeccable. A member of a prominent mercantile family, he pursued a business career and became one of the city's wealthiest men. He was connected by marriage to its leading families; his wife was the daughter of the distinguished statesman and humanist Palla Strozzi; his son Bernardo married Cosimo's granddaughter Nannina. Rucellai emulated Cosimo by building a family palace in the classical style, but he hired Leon Battista Alberti (and not Cosimo's favorite, Michelozzo) to design the structure. His memoirs possess the typically disorganized form of the merchant's diary; much of their content is quite ordinary and conventional. They include fragments of a chronicle, information concerning Rucellai births, deaths, and marriages, and advice to Giovanni's sons, formulated in a very traditional idiom. In a manner reminiscent of Giovanni Morelli, he instructed his heirs about the perpetual threats to their property, particularly heavy taxation, and the hazards and pitfalls of a mercantile career. The model which he describes, and which he urges his sons to emulate, is typically Florentine: the cautious and astute merchant who protects his economic interests by perpetual vigilance; the sober head of a household, solicitous of his family's patrimony and reputation; the conscientious citizen who serves the public welfare when he is called to political office.

Within this thicket of conventional attitudes and viewpoints, the novel elements in Rucellai's value system stand out quite sharply. One of his most remarkable statements (which would have horrified his ancestors) was this comment on wealth: "I think I've done myself more honor by having spent money than by having earned it. Spending gave me a deeper satisfaction . . . ." Noteworthy, too, was his defense of liberality, his opinion that "the rich man must be generous, for liberality is the most noble and attractive virtue which he can possess." He advised his sons to liquidate their mercantile company after his death, unless they were prepared to manage the operations themselves. Particularly instructive are his views on politics. "I would not advise you," he addressed his sons, "to seek or desire offices and political influence. There is nothing which I esteem less, or which seems less honorable, than to be involved in public affairs . . . because of the dangers, the dishonest activities, the injustices . . . and because they are neither stable nor durable. . . ." These statements define and justify an aristocratic mode of life; they reflect a milieu of leisure and enjoyment, and also of withdrawal and disengagement from affairs. There is little trace in this diary of the drives and impulses to action, involvement, and acquisition which marked the careers (and the memoirs) of Florentine patricians in the fourteenth and early fifteenth centuries.

Rucellai's most distinctive quality was his complacency; he was well satisfied with the world and his place in it. In 1464 and again in 1473, he drew up a balance sheet of his assets: a large mercantile fortune, extensive possessions, a devoted wife and talented children, friendship with the Medici and other prominent families, the benefits he enjoyed as a citizen of Florence, "which is considered the finest and most beautiful city—not only in Christendom—but in the entire world." Rucellai was a devout man. He thanked God for benefits received; he went on a pilgrimage to Rome and made large bequests to churches and monasteries in his neighborhood. But he was not troubled by the fears and anxieties which tormented Guido del Palagio and Francesco Datini; he did not worry about his soul. Other Florentines of his generation, less bountifully endowed with possessions and good fortune, did not enjoy the same measure of happiness and contentment. But most would have agreed with Rucellai that the perils and insecurities of former times had diminished. Under Medici tutelage, Florence had enjoyed some forty years of internal peace, a striking contrast with the political turmoil and social unrest which had disturbed the city in the early decades of the century. Furthermore, Rucellai wrote, "we have had twenty years without war, from 1453 to 1473, with the exception of one year—1467—when we fought with Venice in the Romagna . . . ."

Giovanni Rucellai did not receive a humanistic education and thus could not participate fully in the cult of antiquity whose devotees included his father-in-law Palla Strozzi, and—to a lesser degree—Cosimo de' Medici. Yet the imprint of classical learning upon his thought was clear and unmistakable; it distinguishes him most sharply from Guido del Palagio's generation. His memoirs reveal an acquaintance with a large number of ancient authors (Cicero, Livy, Seneca, Sallust, Aristotle, Epictetus, Lucan), whom he read in translation; he also had intellectual discussions and personal contacts with classical scholars: Giannozzo Manetti, Donato Acciaiuoli, and Marsilio Ficino. His notebooks also reveal that he was primarily concerned with moral values. Thus the main focus of his reading and study was quite similar to that of Guido del Palagio and his friends, Francesco Datini and Lapo Mazzei. Nor was Rucellai satisfied with exclusively Christian solutions to moral problems; like many of his contemporaries, he searched for guidelines to conduct in the writings of classical poets, historians, and philosophers. His intellectual activities reflect that mixture of tradition and innovation which characterized his own life style, and that of the Florentine aristocracy in the Medici period.

FOUR

Politics

THE EVOLUTION OF THE FLORENTINE STATE

The preceding chapters have surveyed Florence's topography, and also some aspects of her economic and social development, from the thirteenth to the fifteenth centuries. They have revealed a pattern of rapid and vigorous growth, of dynamism and vitality, of pluralism and flexibility. By the early Quattrocento, however, there are signs of arrested growth and diminishing vitality, of human activity more systematically and rigidly controlled, of structures more clearly defined. The history of Florentine government in these years displays similar patterns and trends. After an early phase of growth and expansion, institutional and territorial, the political order became more stable, less pliant and adaptable. By 1400, Florentine political life was cast in a well defined mold of institutions and policies which protected the community from radical change, but which also limited the choices and alternatives open to the governing class.

To some degree, the history of the Florentine state paralleled that of other Italian cities which, in the eleventh and twelfth centuries, had established independent communal regimes. Certain aspects of her political experience, however, were quite unique. This chapter will focus upon those atypical qualities and characteristics which set this city-state apart from others in the peninsula. Florence's exceptional size and wealth forced her to play a leading role in Italian affairs, and to become more deeply involved in European diplomacy than smaller cities like

Siena or Perugia or Rimini. Her political concerns extended as far as her merchants traveled; she negotiated with emperors, kings, and princes; with popes, cardinals, and bishops; with cities and monasteries. Reflecting the complexity and diversity of her society and economy were domestic politics which were rarely dull or trivial, often tempestuous and controversial, and concerned with the most fundamental problems of urban life. Conflict between individuals, families, and factions was a basic ingredient of Florentine politics and furnishes much of the grist for this chapter. Dante believed that factionalism and the instability it bred were particularly characteristic of his native city, but every Italian town was plagued by domestic turmoil. Rather, it was Florence's success in controlling these dissensions, in maintaining a viable republican government and in preserving her independence, which distinguishes her most sharply from other city-states.

Similarities between Florence's political experience and that of other Italian cities are most apparent in the early centuries of the communal period. In the heavily urbanized regions of Lombardy and Tuscany, the towns were centers of political ferment, as they struggled to gain autonomy from feudal and ecclesiastical overlords, and ultimately to dominate the surrounding countryside. The story of this development focuses upon the rise of the commune, initially a private association of townsmen who organized to protect their interests. These urban societies assumed responsibilities for certain public functions (administration of justice, military defense, maintenance of a food supply), which the regular authorities were unable to perform effectively. Possessing no status in public law, the communes became the effective governing bodies of the towns, usurping powers previously held by lay and ecclesiastical officials, the counts and the bishops. They recognized the theoretical sovereignty of the German emperor or the Roman pope, while ignoring that authority, whenever possible, in fact and in practice.

The early history of these urban governments was characterized by flexibility and spontaneity, by an ability to confront and solve new problems and unprecedented situations. In response to attack by a neighboring city or feudal baron, the commune mustered a civic militia and created a system for assessing and collecting taxes to subsidize its military operations. If famine threatened the urban populace with starvation, it devised means to commandeer grain from the *contado*, to ration flour, and to impose price controls upon foodstuffs. The communes governed the towns more efficiently than had the bishops and counts and, more important, they created a broader political base. The first secular institutions since Roman times to win the loyalty and devotion of the Italian city-dweller, they provided the political framework for that great surge of creative activity unleashed by Italy's economic revival.

In their embryonic stage, communes possessed two basic institutional features: a legislative assembly representing the urban electorate, and an executive commission responsible for administration. Discernible in the internal histories of these regimes is a trend, reaching its climax in the thirteenth century, toward more popular government as new groups—immigrants from the countryside, parvenu entrepreneurs, affluent artisans— elbowed their way into the ruling class. These political transformations were usually marked by constitutional changes: the establishment of new legislative councils or executive commissions to supplement or replace the older institutions. The administrative structure was also expanded to satisfy the needs of a more complex economic and social order.

The fragmentary nature of the evidence does not permit a detailed account of the early centuries of Florence's communal development. Reforms of the institutional structure suggest, but do not define precisely, important political changes and the more fundamental economic and social transformations which underlay them. But each decade is more fully documented than its predecessor, and by the end of the thirteenth century, there emerges a picture of some depth and detail. With their very different styles and purposes, Dino Compagni (d. 1324) and Giovanni Villani (d. 1348) describe this political community in its various aspects and dimensions. They chart the pattern of Florentine territorial expansion: the subjection of the feudal nobility in the *contado*, the conquest of nearby Fiesole, the wars fought against other Tuscan city-states: Pistoia, Arezzo, Pisa, Siena. Occasionally, their description of a legislative enactment, a famine, or a building project provides clues to some of the critical problems of urban

parvenu
soc-upstart

growth confronting this community. But these prosaic accounts are less successful in depicting the human element, which Dante described so brilliantly. The bitter factional disputes, the personal animosities, the impulses to destroy one's enemies, domestic and foreign, are dramatically portrayed in the *Inferno*, the writing of which must have been a salutary catharsis for the poet, to gain release from the passions that seethed within himself. In the eighth canto, Dante yearns to witness with his own eyes the mangling of his enemy, Filippo Cavicciuli, in the slimy waters of the Styx. "And thereupon my eager eyes beheld such treatment dealt him by his muddy mates for which I still thank God and praise his name."

So writes this Christian poet. But in a calmer, more speculative mood, Dante sought to understand why the Florentines were so quarrelsome and factious, why they hated each other with such intensity. To this question, he formulated a series of responses, each connected with some stage of Florence's transformation from rural village to commercial and industrial metropolis. One source of this discord was racial. The poet believed that every progressive element in Florentine history was Roman in origin, planted and nourished by the colonists of Caesar's time and their descendants. Conversely, the sources of discord and violence in the Florentine character derived from those Germanic tribesmen who had founded Fiesole during the barbarian invasions. Although the incompatibility of these alien races was the primary source of factionalism, Dante found secondary explanations in the pattern of urban growth. The poet idealized Florence's early centuries when the community was small and homogenous, when morals were uncorrupted. But this idyllic age ended with the mass invasion of immigrants from the countryside, and as Dante comments in the sixteenth canto of *Paradiso*, the native populace was overwhelmed by the smelly peasants from Aguglione and Signa, from Figline and Certaldo. These newcomers were attracted by the opportunity for a better livelihood offered by the city, and they contributed to the disintegration of a social order based largely upon landholding. Dante was preoccupied with the moral dimension of this revolution, and he attributed the breakdown of the old values to human greed, which, so he believed, was particularly intense among the parvenus. During their encounter

in the third circle of *Inferno*, Dante asked the glutton Ciacco
to reveal the fate of their native city, "and for what reasons
we are torn by hate." Prophesying the outbreak of violence between the rival factions, the Blacks and the Whites, Ciacco told
the poet that there were only two honest men in that "Babel
of despair," where "pride, avarice and envy are the tongues men
know and heed."

Dante, the aristocratic conservative, perceived and deplored
the trend in Florence toward a regime with a broader social
base, in which "new men" challenged the old ruling class and
obtained a greater share of offices and power. These pressures
were a source of permanent tension and conflict, exacerbated by
features peculiar to this community: an economy characterized
by risk and speculation, sharp fluctuations of wealth and income, a high degree of social mobility. Yet the complex, pluralistic
nature of this economic and social order also contributed to the
strength and vitality of popular government. The great range
and variety of business activity produced an entrepreneurial
class with diverse interests and needs. Although woolen cloth manufacturers formed the most potent interest group in the commune,
they did not enjoy a political monopoly. They shared power with
bankers, traders, and druggists, and also with professional men
(lawyers, notaries, physicians), rentiers, and a few artisans whose
economic interests did not always coincide with those of the textile manufacturers. The size of this electorate was also a deterrent
to the ambitions of potential *signori*. Since wealth, social status,
and political influence was spread among so many, it was difficult
for a single family to emulate the Visconti in Milan or the Gon-
zaga in Mantua, by establishing a despotic regime.

But luck also played a part in the survival of republican government in Florence. On three separate occasions in the fourteenth century, the citizens voluntarily surrendered a part of
their liberty to a foreign prince. In 1313, King Robert of Naples
was chosen *signore* with dictatorial powers for a five-year period, but he was too preoccupied with his own realm to establish
effective control over the distant Tuscan community. Threatened
in the 1320s by the Lucchese despot, Castruccio Castracani,
the commune invited King Robert's son, Charles of Calabria, to
be its military captain and governor for ten years. Charles quickly

asserted his control over the city and was planning to establish himself permanently as Florence's *signore* when he died in November 1328, just two months after the demise of his antagonist, Castruccio. Again in 1342, the commune called upon a military adventurer with political ambitions—the French knight errant Walter of Brienne—to solve its problems. Walter quickly transformed his one-year signorial contract into a life dictatorship and was settling down to enjoy his rich fief when a popular revolution in June 1343 sent him scurrying from the city.

The guild regime established after Walter's departure was more popular, more broadly based, than any of its predecessors, but it was not democratic. Only members of the twenty-one guilds could hold office; excluded were the thousands of laborers in the textile industry, as well as other workers whose economic functions did not qualify them for guild membership. Also barred from the highest executive offices were members of magnate families, which had been disenfranchised by the Ordinances of Justice in 1293.* While the guild community comprised some 5000 or 6000 men in the second half of the fourteenth century, only a minority—perhaps one-third—ever held an administrative post or sat in a legislative council. The instrument for separating this privileged group from the mass of ineligibles was the scrutiny. By this method, a commission of scrutators voted upon the qualifications of guildsmen nominated for a particular office; those with a two-thirds majority were declared eligible, and their names were deposited in the bag from which office-holders were drawn by lot. The scrutinies for the Signoria provide some data for estimating the size of this group. In 1343, only 10 percent of 3000 nominees were certified as eligible for the commune's highest executive office. The number of qualified citizens rose to

*The Ordinances of Justice, enacted between 1293 and 1295, were directed against certain powerful and prominent families (identified by name) with a reputation for violence and lawlessness. In addition to their exclusion from office, the magnates were required to post bond for good behavior. Penalties for certain crimes of violence were doubled for magnates, and they were also held responsible for the delicts of their relatives. Certain provisions of these ordinances were later modified and softened, but they remained on the statute books.

500 in 1361, and twenty years later (1382) some 750 Florentines obtained the approval of the scrutiny, of 5000 nominees.

Following the principle of short tenures which characterized all communal regimes in Italy, the nine members of the Signoria (also called priors) held office for only two months and were then succeeded by another group. Two collegiate bodies, the Twelve *buonuomini* and the Sixteen *gonfalonieri,* advised the Signoria on policy; they also joined the priors in promulgating executive decrees, and in electing officials to minor posts in the communal bureaucracy. Filling the lower rungs of the administrative hierarchy were some fifteen magistracies with diverse responsibilities: supervision of castles and fortifications in the *contado,* administration of the fisc, detection of plots and conspiracies, control of the hiring and disciplining of troops. The Twelve held office for three months, while the Sixteen enjoyed a four-month term. These brief tenures had both positive and negative aspects. Each year, a substantial number of citizens (fifty-four in the Signoria and ninety-six in the colleges) could enjoy the power and prestige of the commune's highest offices, but the system did not provide for administrative continuity, nor did it facilitate the formulation and execution of long-range policies. But these flaws were not as serious as might appear at first glance. The Signoria could rely upon the expertise of a small corps of permanent civil servants, and also upon the knowledge of senior statesmen who were regularly consulted on problems of taxation, foreign policy, and internal security. There developed, too, the practice of appointing special executive commissions *(balìe)* to assume responsibility for waging war, levying forced loans, or reforming the commune's electoral statutes. The increasing reliance upon these commissions, particularly in wartime, was a significant development in Florentine constitutional history after 1350.

In addition to its general responsibility for internal administration and the conduct of foreign affairs, the Signoria also initiated legislation. This aspect of its political function is well documented; these legislative records constitute the basic source for the commune's history in the fourteenth century. Of particular importance are the volumes of the *Consulte e Pratiche,* which contain the minutes of the Signoria's consultative sessions with its colleges, and

...zens assembled to give advice on
...ative problems. Another set of
...*rum,* the "books of beans," record
...council members for and against
...also contain the titles, but not
...hich did not obtain a two-thirds
...thus were not enacted into law.
...councils were inscribed on parch-
...sive tomes of the *Provvisioni,* to
...egislation by which the commune

...lies, the Council of the *Popolo*
...ne, comprised some 500 members
...h terms. Since they could not in-
...played an essentially passive role
...eless, they did constitute a check
...quently rejected legislative pro-
...e Signoria. It is true that a deter-
...usually persuade a recalcitrant
...versial measure. Some provisions,
...legislative mandate; those which
...or forced loans were most likely
to be defeated in the councils.

This cursory survey of Florentine institutions reveals the complex nature of this political and administrative system, with its cumbersome bureaucracy and its tortuous methods of selecting officials. Still, it was the notable achievement of the 1343 regime to preserve the republican institutions inherited from the past when, elsewhere in the peninsula, communes were being replaced by the rule of *signori.* These were tense and anxious times for the city and her government, plagued by the depredations of the military companies, wars with neighboring states, and social unrest arising from famine, pestilence, and economic depression. Compounding the regime's difficulties was the formation of two rival factions in the 1360s. One clique led by the Albizzi family derived its traditions and policies from the Parte Guelfa.* In for-

---

*The Parte Guelfa was founded in the thirteenth century as the political and military organization of the Florentine Guelfs, in their struggle with

eign policy, it advocated the perpetuation of the old Guelf alliances with the Papacy and with Naples; in the domestic sphere, it favored a more aristocratic regime purged of parvenu elements. The rival faction led by the Ricci family advocated a more popular regime with substantial representation by artisans and "new men." Its foreign policy tended to be flexible and pragmatic, less closely tied to Guelf ideology. These internal tensions reached a climax in 1378 and precipitated the Ciompi revolution. Then, after three troubled years of a popular guild regime from which members of ancient families were largely excluded, a new government dominated by conservative patricians was established in 1382.

This regime survived for fifty-two years, until 1434 when the return of Cosimo de' Medici from exile opened a new chapter in Florentine politics. Historians have usually described this government as "oligarchic" but a more accurate term would be "conservative." Its establishment did signify the end of a century-old trend toward popular government and the inauguration of a new era in Florentine politics, characterized by the contraction of the ruling group and the concentration of power into fewer hands. But this change was slow and gradual, not sudden or abrupt, as the patrician leadership moved carefully to establish its control. It did not antagonize the artisans and shopkeepers in the lower guilds by excluding them from office; they continued to receive their traditional allotment of two seats in each Signoria. But the regime did create an elaborate system of electoral controls designed to ensure the selection of loyal officials; it also passed legislation limiting communal office to men of status and substance in the community, those who (or whose fathers) had paid taxes continuously for thirty years. Shaken by the Ciompi experience, this government initially was very defensive and vulnerable, preoccupied with internal security, and fearful of any event or development that might threaten its stability. But these fears, and the measures taken to allay

---

the Ghibellines, the supporters of the German emperors. With the triumph of Guelfism, the Parte became a powerful force in communal politics. The Parte captains formed one of the collegiate groups which advised the Signoria; they also participated in elections and scrutinies for communal offices. The Parte's authority and influence declined in the late Trecento.

them, did not transform this regime into a reactionary, authoritarian state. Within limits, it tolerated disagreement and dissent; it continued to serve as the arena for the articulation and resolution of conflict—economic, social, ideological, personal. During its tenure of power from 1382 to 1434, it was the scene of a dramatic conflict between those forces seeking to preserve the institutions and traditions of republican government and opposing pressures which disrupted the political order and weakened the bonds that held this community together. That contest is the main theme of this chapter.

THE PATRICIAN HEGEMONY (1382–1434): PUBLIC WELFARE AND PRIVATE INTEREST

Most obvious to the modern observer is the coercive and exploitative character of this patrician regime; it governed for the benefit of the rich and the powerful, and often to the disadvantage of the poor and the lowly. Patricians filled most of the communal offices; they enjoyed a monopoly of the most lucrative vicariates and captaincies in the dominion: in Pisa and Arezzo, in Volterra and Cortona. In a less direct manner, the patriciate (or its wealthier members) profited from the tax system. A portion of the republic's revenues came from direct taxes levied upon towns and rural districts in the dominion, and from gabelles assessed on foodstuffs imported into the city. These taxes fell most heavily upon the subject territory, and upon the poor within the city walls. The urban rich escaped the direct levies, and they did not pay an equitable share of the gabelles on wine, meat, and grain, since their households consumed produce on their rural estates during the summer *villeggiatura*. To make up budget deficits, the commune levied forced loans (*prestanze*) upon the urban population, but this system also benefited the wealthy. These loans were commuted into shares of the funded debt (*Monte*), which paid low but regular rates of interest; *Monte* investments were an important source of patrician income in the fifteenth century. In 1427, Palla Strozzi's *Monte* shares totaled nearly 100,000 florins, from which he received an annual income of 1000 florins, sufficient to maintain fifteen households in modest comfort.

Yet it would be a gross distortion to view this patrician government as simply an instrument for the exploitation of the poor and the humble by the rich and the powerful. In a very turbulent age of Italian political history, the durability of this regime was truly remarkable. Its stability and longevity were due to its ability to maintain order and repress dissent and, equally important, to its success in gaining popular support, even among the disenfranchised groups. Although some of these groups accepted the regime because they felt powerless to change it, or because their energies were totally absorbed by their struggle for subsistence, others were fiercely loyal to the republic, the political symbol of their civic identity. This allegiance was stronger and more durable than the personal popularity, often quite fickle, which despots aroused in their subjects and which, later in the fifteenth century, the Medici inspired in many of their fellow-citizens. Most artisans and shopkeepers were apparently content with their token representation in the regime; their influence was minimal but they did belong to the political establishment. The lowliest member of the bakers' guild could hope that, one day, he might qualify for the Signoria, while even among the disenfranchised laborers were many who strongly supported the regime. Least touched by these patriotic sentiments were the residents of outlying areas where local loyalties were still alive and potent and, particularly in the recently annexed communities (Pisa, Cortona, Arezzo), where hostility to Florence was sometimes expressed in overt rebellion.

To a degree rarely achieved in other cities or in earlier regimes, the Florentine government of the late fourteenth and early fifteenth century maintained that delicate and tenuous balance between individual and collective needs, between private interest and public welfare, which is the basis of effective politics. As we shall see, the pursuit of individual and family advantage was a continuous preoccupation; yet most patricians were imbued with a strong sense of their obligations to the commune and willingly accepted the responsibility it imposed upon them. Politically active citizens received both material and psychic rewards for their services, but their labors were heavy and time-consuming, and the benefits did not always repay the effort. Florentines no longer served in the militia, as had their great-grandfathers in Dante's time. But their taxes and forced loans paid for the mercenaries who defended the city. In times of crisis, the council halls reverberated with appeals for fiscal sacrifices. Alessandro Alessandri once announced that he was prepared to sell his children to replenish the communal treasury. Less dramatic was Matteo Tinghi's offer (in 1388) to give his entire fortune to the commune, in installments of 500 florins. Such hyperbolic statements offend modern ears; they seem so blatantly artificial and insincere. But these men were expressing their deeply felt conviction that the requirements of the community took precedence over private concerns, and that they were willing to make any sacrifice to preserve their liberty. "Our city is more important than our children," Messer Rinaldo Gianfigliazzi stated bluntly in 1413, "and for its welfare, everything possible should be done to preserve for posterity what we have received from our ancestors."

The reverence for the past discernible in Gianfigliazzi's statement is a particular characteristic of this regime, a manifestation of its patrician orientation and outlook. Old families naturally demonstrated the most intense fervor for tradition, for their ancestors had literally created the city's history. Their blood had been spilled in the battles enshrined in civic memory: Montaperti, Campaldino, Altopascio.* Descendants of these old houses also believed that they alone possessed the knowledge, discipline, and experience to govern the city properly. The patriciate's conviction that it was born to rule was an important source of its strength, one of the bulwarks of its hegemony. The past was thus a justification for aristocratic government and a source of political stability. Adherence to tradition explains why the constitutional structure changed so little during this regime's lifetime. It also accounts for the continuity of policy, for example, in the generally benevolent attitude toward the local church and the papacy, which derived from the Guelf tradition. Perhaps no other argument counted so heavily in political debate as the contention that a particular measure or policy conformed with traditional

---

*The Florentines were defeated by the Sienese at Montaperti in 1260; they won a battle against Arezzo at Campaldino in 1289. In 1325 a Lucchese army under Castruccio Castracani defeated the Florentines at Altopascio.

practice. While speaking against a proposed change in the method of levying forced loans in 1430, Palla Strozzi argued that innovations were always dangerous, since their consequences were unpredictable; practices might be introduced which, although initially desirable and useful, become detrimental with the passage of time. In the past, he insisted, Florentines did not tamper continually with the tax structure but maintained one system for several years before considering any alterations. "And do we think that they were less expert, less wise, less solicitous of our government than we? Such an opinion is untenable! Our ancestors were more prudent and more dedicated to the public welfare than our own generation. Their record proves this statement for under their guidance, a puny state was transformed into a great power!"

Another patrician trait visible in the public—as well as the private—sphere was an aversion to hasty action and a strong commitment to careful and lengthy discussion of issues. The chronicler Matteo Villani once commented that the Florentines were always slow to arrive at decisions because they debated the issues with such labored thoroughness. In their persistent search for agreement and consensus, the priors would often submit the same problems to the advisory colleges, or to select groups of citizens, in session after session. Much of this discussion, summarized in the *Consulte e Pratiche* records, was repetitious and boring. Yet in periods of trouble and adversity, these deliberations reveal the strengths and virtues of this patriciate: its courage and resolution, its tenacity of purpose. Such times also brought out, in sharp relief, those qualities of shrewdness and astuteness and the firm grasp of reality Florentines typically displayed in their private affairs.

The issues of war and peace, territorial expansion, taxation, and the composition of the electorate were the most significant problems confronting this regime; its decisions on these questions affected the society in fundamental ways. Yet for every hour spent in discussing an alliance with the papacy or the levy of a new gabelle on wine, the Florentine politician devoted an equivalent amount of time to the personal affairs of his relatives, friends, and clients. No analysis of republican politics is complete without some investigation of this poorly documented area of private interest, favor, and corruption. The decisions and compromises formulated in this sphere often influenced the settlement of the important public issues confronting the state.

One episode, described in the correspondence of the Del Bene family, illustrates this intimate connection between the public and the private dimensions of Florentine political life. In a series of letters addressed to his cousin Francesco in the spring of 1381, Giovanni del Bene narrated the vicissitudes of a lawsuit between his nephew Amerigo and an influential politician, Filippo Alamanni. The quarrel began over a claim Amerigo was pressing against the estate of a minor, for whom Alamanni was acting as guardian. While supporting his nephew in this petty suit, Giovanni became involved in an intricate maze of political maneuvers which consumed several days of his time, and which severely tested his patience and reputation.

The Del Bene first petitioned a judge to issue a decree ordering the two parties to negotiate a settlement, or to agree upon arbitrators who would arrange a compromise binding upon both litigants. Apparently, they felt sufficiently confident of their rights to welcome arbitration. In this initial stage of the process, the main concern of the Del Bene was the employment of a competent lawyer with useful connections. They debated the relative merits of Donato Aldighieri (who was called away on an ambassadorial mission), Giovanni Ricci (judged unsuitable on account of his blood ties with the Del Bene), and Baldo da Figline, who was finally hired. But Filippo Alamanni sought to avoid a settlement by arbitration, claiming that it would damage his interests. So he appealed to higher authorities, first the magistracy of the Ten on Liberty (responsible for the settlement of private quarrels), and then the Signoria, to quash the judicial process initiated by the Del Bene. What had been a simple disagreement over money became a complex struggle between two powerful families, each determined to subdue the other.

The most remarkable feature of this controversy was the reluctance of these executive commissions to settle the dispute. No one wished to be responsible for a final solution, which would leave one party aggrieved and bitter. On March 13, the case was brought before an official of the judges' guild, who quickly passed it on to the Ten. Although this commission promised to make a rapid decision, it procrastinated for several days before finally ordering Alamanni to submit the issue to arbitration. But the case was far from settlement. In early April, Giovanni del Bene wrote that Alamanni had petitioned the Signoria to intervene in the dispute, and several times during the month the priors listened to the arguments of the litigants and their lawyers. When Giovanni criticized the Signoria for meddling in an affair which had already been decided by the Ten in the Del Bene's favor, the priors replied that "they did not intend to harm us, but they could not refuse to hear any citizen, and that our adversaries had said many things [against us]." They insisted that they "would do justice to everyone, of whatever class or condition." Despite these brave words, the Signoria refused to settle the quarrel but again shunted it back to the Ten. Meanwhile, owing to personnel changes on this commission, Filippo Alamanni had gained a nucleus of supporters who persuaded their colleagues to abandon their position favorable to the Del Bene. Further delay resulted from Alamanni's departure on an ambassadorial mission to Città di Castello. On May 15, a tired and dispirited Giovanni del Bene wrote a final letter about the case, which was as far away from settlement as ever.

Once this litigation had left the hands of the judges, the nature of the conflict shifted perceptibly, from legal issues to political influence and status. This forced both parties to engage in an exhausting routine of appeals for support to the priors and the members of the other commissions involved in the case. "I spoke with several [citizens] today, and with nearly every member of the Ten; each responded in the customary fashion," wrote Giovanni on March 14. He was able to assess accurately the personnel of each commission, to determine who would support him, and who would favor his antagonist. "Among the new members of the Ten is their close friend, Francesco di Ser Jacopo Cecchi, and I also believe that Baldese [di Torino Baldesi] leans more to them than toward us." Giovanni realized that he was pitted against a potent enemy, whose skein of influential connections was quite as broad as his own. In his efforts to advance his nephew's cause, he had exerted pressure upon his friends, most of whom (he admitted) had loyally supported him. But he also noted that "in this affair I have discovered many more enemies than friends." The most powerful opponent was Giorgio Scali, a very influential politician, who covertly assisted Filippo Alamanni. Scali had arranged for Alamanni's selection to the ambassadorial post, and he also intervened with the Signoria to prevent any settlement during his absence. This potent and tenacious opposition explains the despairing tone which appeared in Giovanni's correspondence, as he realized that his labors had borne no fruit.

Del Bene's ordeal is an illuminating glimpse into the realities of Florentine domestic politics. The case reveals, first, how seriously the civic authorities treated private matters of minor importance, particularly if these involved prominent men. It illustrates, too, how lengthy and time-consuming, for both litigants and officials, these disputes could become. Petitions of private individuals for redress of grievances, or for special privileges, fill thousands of pages of the *Provvisioni*, while the *Libri Fabarum* reveal their fate: those which were consistently rejected in the councils and those which—after several attempts—were finally approved. The range of human problems encompassed by these appeals was broad, but two issues were of paramount importance: taxation and justice. For in these sensitive areas, the power of the state to destroy the lives and property of citizens was directly felt, and the efforts of individuals to escape from the toils of authority were most intense.

Most tax disputes arose from the assessment of forced loans or *prestanze*, which, by the 1370s, had become a major source of communal revenue. These loans brought into the treasury as much revenue as that collected from the gabelles on food and merchandise imported into Florence and the direct taxes imposed on subject territories. The assessment, collection, and repayment of the *prestanze* was an extremely complex procedure, and no modern scholar has had the patience to analyze the system in detail. One major source of controversy was the method of assessment, which, until the introduction of the *catasto* in 1427, involved rough estimates of an individual's wealth by a select committee of his neighbors. While most knowledgeable about a taxpayer's economic status, they were also likely to be either a close friend of a bitter enemy, and thus prejudiced. Giovanni Cavalcanti described a typical scene in his chronicle:

> When the tax lists were posted, everywhere in the city could be heard the laments and bitter cries, and the sounds of hands being struck together. And one man said: "O cursed city, why are you the source of such evil men?" And another identified the man responsible for his assessment, saying: "He knows very well that I cannot pay such an outrageous sum. If he wanted my house, why didn't he ask to buy it? I would have sold it to him for less than its fair price."

Unlike most Italians of this and later ages, Florentines accepted both the necessity of paying taxes and the principle that each citizen should contribute according to his ability. But this sane approach to fiscality did not make taxpaying more palatable, nor did it shake the conviction of many that they were paying more than their share, while others were giving less. The letters and memoirs of prominent and respectable citizens contain information on techniques to avoid taxes and to minimize assessments. Giovanni Morelli instructed his sons to import grain and wine from their country estates in small consignments to avoid the impression of affluence. Any blatant display of wealth could lead to a dramatic increase in *prestanze* assessments, which explains the persistence, in some patrician families, of an austere style of living.

Citizens who sought tax relief used a variety of arguments to win the sympathy of magistracies and legislative councils. Each petitioner claimed that his assessment was excessive, inflated far beyond his ability to pay. Some, like the pawnbroker Barone di Cose, described their penury in the bleakest terms: "This Barone possesses nothing in this world save his own body, his wife and three small children (one other having died in prison), and he [Barone] is dying of hunger in jail, while his family starves outside." Domenico Spinelli reported that in addition to his tax debts, he owed 3000 florins to private creditors, that he had sold all of his furniture, and that "together with his twelve children, he was forced to sleep on straw; in short, he lives in the most abject misery." A father with several nubile daughters would appeal for relief on the grounds that his resources were exhausted by dowries. Normally, descriptions of the petitioners' plight were couched in general terms, but some appellants believed that their case would be improved by citing facts and figures. In 1398, the four sons of Francesco del Bene claimed that their assessment of 48 florins was excessive; their entire estate was worth no more than 7500 florins, and only one of the four, the lawyer Ricciardo, was gainfully employed. The claims of many petitions were certainly exaggerated, but they must all have contained some grain of truth, for it was not possible to disguise completely one's economic condition in Florence. Citizens imprisoned for tax delinquency were probably not lying about their inability to pay their assessments. Several petitioners claimed that their taxes had eaten up most of their assets; Bartolomeo Panciatichi asserted in 1402 that his tax bill for the previous twelve years totaled 93,743 florins. As one of the city's wealthiest merchants, Panciatichi could afford this huge outlay, but the two sons of another rich businessman, Vieri di Cambio de' Medici, claimed that they had been forced to borrow money at usurious rates to pay their assessments, and that their public and private obligations were rapidly depleting their resources. Paolo Davizzi informed the Signoria that he had fled abroad to avoid seizure for tax debts. If relief were not granted to him, he would be forced to choose between perpetual exile or imprisonment.

However eloquent and persuasive, such tales of misery were rarely sufficient to sway the minds of tax officials. The petitioners also appealed to relatives and friends, who in turn directed their oral and written requests to the men in office. To guide a petition for tax relief through the Signoria and the colleges, and then through the legislative councils, was a slow and arduous procedure. It was simpler to exert pressure upon the tax commissions, which were regularly appointed to review assessments and to reduce a limited number. A flurry of correspondence between citizens at home and abroad invariably followed the publication of the membership of these review commissions. Writing from Ferrara in 1395, Lanfredino Lanfredini informed his son Orsino that he had learned that assessments were to be revised, "and I have written to Giovanni and to Nofrio de' Rossi and to Jacopo di Ser Folcho and to Luca del Calvane and to Giovanni Lanfredini . . . appealing to them to make my levy as small as possible. . . ." Donato Acciaiuoli wrote to Ricciardo del Bene in 1409: "I have just learned that you are one of those responsible for reducing the *prestanze*." Acciaiuoli stressed the friendship that had always united their two families, as well as his own poverty, in requesting a reduction of one-half florin in his assessment.

Citizens of high and low estate were aware that personal pressures and influence were valuable weapons in the struggle for tax favors, as this conversation between two obscure citizens reveals. A widow named Margherita Guglielmi greeted an acquaintance: "God help you and you are welcome! What good news do you have of affairs in the city?" Antonio di Piero replied: "It is a good thing for you that I spoke with several of my friends who will aid you . . . so that you will not be too heavily taxed." The grateful widow thanked Antonio profusely for his kindness and remarked that "I have no one else who will help me."

As often as they complained about their individual assessments, Florentines criticized the whole system of tax distribution as inequitable. But revised methods and techniques proposed by the authorities were frequently voted down in the councils, by men who disliked the existing system but apparently feared that others might be worse. In the 1420s, the number and intensity of these complaints reached such proportions that the regime somewhat reluctantly introduced the *catasto*, the most rational and equitable system of tax assessment then existing in Europe. Each taxpayer was required to furnish the authorities with a complete catalogue of his property (real and personal) and his obligations. On the basis of this evidence, his assessment was calculated. The new system did not solve all problems: it did not reduce the total amount of the tax burden, nor did it alter the heavy reliance upon the forced loan. The rate of assessment was fixed at one-half of one percent of capital, less deductions, and this inflexible schedule favored the wealthy. Officials still had wide discretion in calculating the levies of poorer citizens and in negotiating settlements with delinquents, so that personal influence continued to be a factor in the allocation of the tax burden.

In his payments of communal taxes—the *prestanze*, the gate

dues on produce, the salt gabelle, the fees for drawing up contracts —the citizen was reminded daily of his government and its incessant demands upon his resources. The state's authority was also manifest, in a very direct fashion, in the administration of justice. Scarcely a day passed without some public display of the regime's coercive power: the escort of a condemned criminal to the gallows outside the city walls near the Anno, flogging of a prostitute, the hot pursuit of malefactors by police officials, the demolition of a conspirator's palace. Authority was visible and tangible; it was also fragmented. Justice was administered by many agencies, with varying jurisdictions and responsibilities. For physical assault against his neighbor, a Florentine could be prosecuted in one of three criminal courts: the podestà, the captain of the *popolo,* the executor. Apprehended in the act of blasphemy, he might be haled before the bishop's tribunal. If he owed money to a banker, his case would normally be tried in the court of the Cambio guild. Litigation with a foreign merchant was the responsibility of the Merchants' court. In addition to these tribunals, many of the commune's administrative commissions had authority to impose fines on violators of their regulations.

The Florentine was thus surrounded by a truly imposing structure of judicial sanctions to channel his activities along courses approved by society. But this system was very prone to manipulation. Malefactors who possessed money and friends could tamper with the judicial process by quashing a prosecution, mitigating a penalty, or suborning a witness. To be caught up in the toils of this complex structure was rarely as serious as the menacing tone of the statutes and the penal legislation might indicate.

The courts of the podestà, the captain, and the executor were the highest criminal and civil tribunals in Florence. These posts were reserved for foreign knights of high reputation and unimpeachable Guelf sympathies. The importation of outsiders to render justice and to exercise police power was a time-hallowed practice throughout the peninsula. Italians did not place much faith in the principle of judicial impartiality, and they would never permit a neighbor to wield such broad authority over their lives and property. Foreign judges were appointed for short terms (six months), and rarely was their tenure of office extended to a full year. Elaborate precautions were taken to prevent, or to minimize, contacts between judges and the citizenry, which might lead to bribery and collusion. Before a rector was permitted to leave Florence after serving his term, his records were thoroughly examined by a special magistracy seeking evidence of malfeasance.

How honest and impartial was Florentine justice? Very few cases of misconduct in the higher courts are documented in the judicial records, which suggests that the more obvious and blatant forms of corruption were uncommon. The chronicler Marchionne Stefani described the misdeeds in 1382 of one captain, Obizo degli Alidosi, who exiled several innocent citizens, and kidnapped and seduced the daughter of an impoverished nobleman, Riccardo Figlipetri. In 1400, a notary attached to the court of the executor, Giuliano de Rossiano, was convicted of soliciting a bribe (with his superior's consent) of 200 florins from Serpe da Quarata to quash a criminal case which was pending against Serpe's father. The most notorious episode of judicial malfeasance occurred in 1387. The podestà, Rinaldo de Rangoni of Modena, confessed that he had accepted several bribes to quash prosecutions, including one murder case involving a resident of Empoli in the *contado*. Rangoni was forced to resign his office and was fined 2000 florins, which was later cancelled at the request of the disgraced judge's *signore*, the marquis of Ferrara.

In their palaces, the rectors were isolated and shielded from the citizenry, prohibited by statute from establishing social contacts with any Florentine. But such relations did exist, and they could be manipulated for personal advantage, as two extant letters prove. Francesco de Coppoli was Florence's podestà in the spring of 1427, and he corresponded with Forese Sacchetti, then a rector of the subject city of Cortona. Sacchetti had apparently pulled strings to obtain the judgeship for Coppoli, who thanked his friend warmly for his services. "I am grateful to you," the podestà wrote, "for the love which you have for me. . . . God grant me the opportunity to please you in the future." Sacchetti promptly asked Coppoli to intervene in the case of his friend Gherardo Baroncelli, then being tried for some offense in the podestà's court. Nothing so crude as money was mentioned in this correspondence, but Coppoli did acknowledge the receipt of a pair of greyhounds sent by Sacchetti. The judge promised to render every possible favor and assistance to Baroncelli, "and so always in any matter concerning you and your friends, I swear that I will do everything possible and more, as though you were here in person."

Two documents do not prove the existence of a gigantic conspiracy to subvert justice. But together with other fragments of evidence, they do reveal a pattern of close ties of friendship between certain patricians and foreign judges. In his letter to Sacchetti, Coppoli wrote that a prominent statesman, Neri Capponi, was "one of my most intimate friends in Florence." The Count of Macerata appealed to Maso degli Albizzi to help him obtain a rectorship, and announced his willingness "to demonstrate by my actions that I am totally at your will, pleasure and command." Some part of these effusive protestations of loyalty and service was simply rhetorical hyperbole; rectors could not subvert justice openly without incurring recrimination and even criminal penalties. In promising assistance to Gherardo Baroncelli, Francesco de Coppoli inserted the qualifying phrase, "insofar as reason and my honor permit." The administration of justice was watched carefully from the streets, and although only a handful of magistrates and their associates were criminally prosecuted, a larger number incurred public disapproval during their tenures of office. When the legislative councils refused to grant the communal coat of arms to a departing judge, they were informing him that he would not again be invited to hold office in Florence.

Criminal justice was not the exclusive preserve of the foreign rectors; the Signoria could also intervene in this sensitive area. Many petitions approved by the priors and colleges for submission to the councils were requests for the cancellation of criminal sentences. Some of these petitions for leniency were approved by the priors and their collegiate advisers (a two-thirds vote was required), only to founder in the councils, which were too large to be manipulated by the relatives and friends of convicted felons.

A simpler device for executive interference in the judiciary was the *bollettino*, a notice sent by the Signoria to a rector, ordering him to take some specific action in a case before his court. Most *bollettini* granted temporary immunity from prosecution for private debt or tax delinquency. But the Signoria could also issue *bollettini* to a rector, ordering him to quash some prosecution, or to prescribe a specific penalty for a crime. So, in 1415, the priors instructed the captain to desist from prosecuting a group of peasants from Peretola, a village west of Florence, who were accused of seizing a piece of church property. The priors justified this decision by asserting that "from a modest source many noxious things may arise." In the following year, the captain received another notice from the priors, ordering him to sentence one Anastasio di Ser Domenico to life imprisonment for murder, justifying this lenient penalty on the grounds that the culprit was insane. Thus a vigilant Signoria could use its authority to correct judicial mistakes or to mitigate excessively harsh penalties. But these *bollettini* were political tools, by which influential citizens could escape the legal penalties which lesser men could not avoid. The vagaries of criminal justice were noted in 1425, by two lowly transients who had been fined for abducting and seducing a female slave. They argued that they were innocent, and had been convicted only "because they were foreigners and had no friends [in Florence]."

In the administration of justice, as in taxation, there was a perpetual tension between the communal ideals of equity and impartiality, and individual quests for favors and privileges. While the state's authority to enforce justice was greater in 1450 than a century earlier, the demands for special treatment by members of a smaller ruling group were also more intense. The upper classes were not exempt from judicial chastisement. Hundreds of patricians were convicted of crimes ranging from multiple homicide to simple assault, and a dozen of these malefactors were executed between 1382 and 1434. But the documents also show that many aristocrats avoided the penalties for their misdeeds by bribing officials, suborning witnesses, or hiding until their relatives could obtain a cancellation of their sentence. No clear pattern or trend can be detected in this sensitive area; the regime wavered between rigid and lax enforcement of the statutes, between harshness and tolerance. One point is indisputable. While it was possible for anyone to obtain justice in the Florentine courts, the possession of wealth, a distinguished ancestry, and political influence were valuable assets in the search for that elusive commodity.

PATTERNS OF DOMESTIC CONFLICT

The scramble for privileges and immunities, for tax concessions and judicial dispensations, influenced Florentine public life at every level. Politics is the combination of private and public interest. In Renaissance Florence, these two dimensions were joined together in very close and intricate fashion. This was the result, in part, of the small size and intimacy of the ruling group, in which each man was acquainted with his colleague, aware of his economic and social position, his friends and enemies, his strengths and weaknesses. Also contributing to the intensely personal character of politics was the intrusion of individual and familial loyalties into the public arena. Political discord in Florence took various forms: disputes over economic questions, struggles for power between families and social groups, disagreement over such ideological issues as Guelfism and heresy. But every quarrel had its personal dimension. In the background of every controversial public issue were private rancors and animosities, real or imagined grievances, particular interests to be attacked or defended. Behind every effort to reform or overthrow the regime were these same personal factors and motives.

The most direct threat to the patrician republic came from groups that were excluded from office, whose main hope for the recovery of their political fortunes lay in fomenting rebellion. During the regime's early years, the most determined opposition came from the exiled Ciompi. The judicial archives contain the records of several prosecutions against textile workers and artisans who had participated in conspiracies. These lower-class exiles placed their main hope in a mass uprising of the Florentine proletariat. Central to their plans were the flags and slogans of the Ciompi movement, which might arouse the emotions and aspirations of an illiterate mass of laborers. Stirred by the nostalgia for hearth and home felt by exiles of every class, these poverty-stricken workers were also motivated by a vision of a better life for themselves. One Ciompi conspirator, Luca di Guido, announced to a friend that "we will take over the city and kill and rob the rich who have expelled us, and we will be masters of the city and rule it as we wish." Identical sentiments were voiced by another exiled cloth worker, Antonio di Recco, who painted this bright picture of the future: "The time will come when I will no longer wander about begging, for I expect to be rich for the rest of my life . . . and we will live in high estate in Florence."

The genesis of one Ciompi conspiracy in the summer of 1383 occurred within the precincts of Venice's cathedral of S. Marco, where a group of Florentine exiles had assembled. One of their number, Bernardo Velluti, denounced his fellows for their apathy: "You filthy artisans! What is wrong with you, that you sleep . . . and abandon your comrades, because you don't care for anything in the world. You should be organizing a revolution to return to Florence. If you don't act soon, you are all going to swing and the rulers there will starve you." In response to this tonguelashing, these proletarians established contacts with other exile groups in Bologna and Lucca, and laid plans for a revolution in late July. They plotted to organize simultaneous uprisings in three working-class districts (Camaldoli, S. Ambrogio and S. Piero Gattolino); the rebels would seize and open the gates, and then join forces with the exiles lurking outside the walls. The leaders of this conspiracy did enter the city secretly, and at the designated time, they paraded with the flags of the banned laborers' guilds and shouted: "Long live the *popolo* and the guilds, and death to the tyrants! O citizens! O workers! Arise and escape from your yoke of servitude, for your rulers are going to starve you!" But the cloth workers of S. Frediano did not respond to these appeals, and the regime quickly suppressed this rebellion.

These proletarian revolutionaries had scant hope of success, for they had little money and few contacts with their social superiors who might have helped their cause. Potentially more dangerous to the regime were the subversive activities of patrician exiles, who settled in the border cities of Bologna and Faenza, and who maintained regular contacts with relatives and friends in Florence. Included in this group were several members of the Alberti who had been exiled in 1397, and others from the Strozzi, Medici, and Ricci families.

In 1411 and 1412, these exiles organized a major campaign to overthrow the regime during a critical phase of its war with King Ladislaus. The combination of a food shortage and unemployment in the cloth factories had produced widespread unrest in the city. Included in one judicial report was the angry comment of a textile worker, Cola di Maestro Piero: "These traitorous rulers have taken grain from the poultry and fed it to us; by God, we shall eat the good [grain] in their houses shortly; we don't deserve to be treated like poultry." Cola told an acquaintance that he was a partisan of the Alberti, "because they were always good merchants and generous men, and they gave good wages to their employees." One of the exiled Alberti, Bindaccio, made a reconnaissance trip to Florence and reported to his relatives in Bologna that conditions were ripe for revolution: "There are many more malcontents than supporters of the regime; the lower classes complain loudly, and there is dissension between the two leaders, Messer Maso [Albizzi] and Messer Rinaldo [Gianfigliazzi]." Originally Bindaccio planned to seize the palace of the Signoria with a small group of supporters. It would suffice, he believed, to kill only two priors, Rinaldo Gianfigliazzi and Neri Vettori, whereupon their associates would see reason and join the revolution. So great was popular discontent that a parade of communal banners would rally the citizenry behind the new government. But the Alberti considered this plan too risky and advised Bindaccio to establish secret contacts with prominent citizens who might join the conspiracy, and to coordinate the activities of the exiles with a fifth column inside the walls. While engaged in this recruiting campaign, Bindaccio was captured and executed. The Alberti then decided to launch a military attack against the city; in June 1412 they sent an expedition of several hundred exiles and mercenaries across the Apennines toward Florence. But one of the conspirators, Cionettino Bastari, revealed the plot to the authorities. Even before the expedition entered Florentine territory, its leaders learned of this betrayal and returned ignominiously to Bologna.

Potential support for revolution, which seemed quite substantial in the 1380s, slowly ebbed with the passage of time. The last spasm of revolutionary fervor among the lower classes erupted in 1393; after 1412 there were no serious attempts by patrician exiles to overturn the state. There is no simple explanation for this subsidence of political opposition. Did popular unrest diminish as a result of demographic losses from plague, with a consequent rise in the wages and living standards of the poor? More plausible is the theory that effective security measures restrained discontent and silenced potential agitators. A new magistracy responsible for internal security, the *Otto di Guardia,* was established in 1378 after the Ciompi disorders. This powerful agency, one of the first permanent organizations of secret police in Europe, maintained a network of spies and agents which detected many plots before they had matured. No conspiracy could succeed without a large number of adherents, but every recruit was a potential traitor. To reduce further the dangers of revolution fomented outside its territory, the regime granted amnesty and judicial pardons to a number of political exiles. This policy reduced the number of malcontents living abroad, and gave hope to the remainder that, if they behaved with circumspection, they too might be permitted to return to Florence.

This regime withstood the assaults from without, but it finally succumbed to an internal malaise. The process was an old and familiar tale in Italian communal history; it involved the triumph of particular interests and ambitions over civic needs, the spread of fear and suspicion, the gradual weakening of the spirit of cooperation, the sense of community, upon which viable republican government depended. In times of peace and prosperity, the regime functioned quite effectively and smoothly. The allocation of offices, benefits, and perquisites could be arranged, if not always amicably, at least with a minimum of bitterness and resentment. When its borders were secure, its people fed, and its treasury replete, the government could afford to be tolerant—to grant tax exemptions and mitigate judicial penalties, to slacken its control over the private lives of the citizenry. But Florence did not enjoy many years of peace and security in these decades. It was a rare moment when some crisis, domestic or foreign, was not looming on the horizon. The periods of greatest tension occurred during the wars with the Milanese *signori,* Giangaleazzo and Filippo Maria Visconti, and with the ambitious Angevin prince, Ladislaus. During these conflicts, the unity of the ruling group was imperiled. Politicians would accuse others of errors in tactics and strategy, of failing to resist the enemy with sufficient strength, or of neglecting the opportunities to make necessary alliances. Frequently, peace factions would form within the ruling group, demanding that the authorities end the war and reduce the fiscal burdens. In such moments of crisis, too, personal jealousies and antagonisms grew more intense, as ambitious men sought to turn the republic's discomfiture, and that of its leaders, to their own advantage.

In his chronicle, Buonaccorso Pitti narrated an episode in his own career which illustrates this phenomenon. The climax of Pitti's tale occurred in 1412 and 1413, when Florence was at war with King Ladislaus. But the story began several years earlier, when Buonaccorso's brother Luigi first befriended the abbot of Ruota, head of a monastery in the Valdambra district west of Arezzo. The abbot hoped to arrange for a member of the Pitti family to succeed him, but the Ricasoli, a noble clan with large estates and great influence in the region, also had designs upon the convent. Inevitably, this contest between rival houses for a lucrative benefice became enmeshed in communal politics.

The Ricasoli were strong Guelf partisans, belonging to that segment of the Florentine aristocracy which advocated close ties with Rome. Through their friends in the papal curia, they initiated a process against the abbot of Ruota, charging him with maladministration of his convent. The poor monk appealed to the Pitti, who sought to persuade the Signoria to send a letter to Rome defending the abbot. But this maneuver was blocked by Ricasoli partisans in the Signoria. With such powerful opposition ranged against them, the Pitti decided to employ a desperate strategem to save a losing cause. They staged a fake assault against the abbot outside the Ricasoli palace, hoping that their enemies would be blamed for the crime, and that the Signoria would then intervene in the quarrel on their behalf. But the authorities forced Buonaccorso to reveal the details of this amateurish plot, and he himself barely escaped condemnation. Pitti's account of the episode revealed a sharp split in the ruling group. The Peruzzi and Baroncelli families had strongly supported the Ricasoli in the Signoria, and Michele Castellani and Papino Gianfigliazzi had demanded that Buonaccorso be severely punished for his role in the plot. But the Pitti also had powerful defenders in Rinaldo degli Albizzi and Cristoforo Spini, who protected them from the extreme demands of their enemies.

Even with its bizarre overtones, this quarrel does not seem unique, but simply another example of two families with important connections squabbling over a choice ecclesiastical plum. This episode, however, was just one aspect of an internal conflict over foreign policy which then divided the ruling group. It was no accident that the enemies of the Pitti were also leaders of the papal faction. Buonaccorso's brother Luigi had been a member of the Signoria which had negotiated a peace treaty with Ladislaus (December 1410). Opponents of this settlement blamed Luigi for its conclusion; Buonaccorso wrote that they had turned Pope John XXIII against the Pitti "so that ever since we have suffered open and secret persecution at his hands and at those of his clique in this city." Comprising this papal party were the Ricasoli, Peruzzi, and Baroncelli families, and such prominent statesmen as Rinaldo Gianfigliazzi, Gino Capponi, and Niccolò da Uzzano. In his advocacy of peaceful coexistence with the Angevin ruler, Buonaccorso argued that Ladislaus' aggressive policy was simply a defensive response to the machinations of the pope and his Florentine allies, who were continually plotting to embroil the republic in war with Ladislaus. Material gain, not patriotism, motivated the papal faction, for they profited (so Pitti claimed) from the church benefices which the pope lavished upon his supporters. The grant of the monastery of Ruota to Arnoldo Peruzzi was tangible evidence of the pope's benevolence to those Florentines who supported his cause.

This campaign against the Pitti did not end with the Ruota affair. The dispute over foreign policy was not resolved, but became more acute in the spring of 1413 when Ladislaus' army occupied Rome and forced the pope to flee into Tuscany. John XXIII and his supporters sought to persuade a reluctant republic to declare war on the Angevin monarch. Intimidation was a favorite weapon of the papal faction, and the Pitti were its prime targets. Luigi Pitti had imprudently accepted a rectorship in southern Italy from Ladislaus as his reward for promoting Angevin interests. During his absence from Florence, he was accused of transmitting secret information to the king and was condemned to death for treason. Only strenuous efforts by friends saved Buonaccorso and his brother Bartolomeo from a similar fate. After months of rancorous debate, a peace agreement with Ladislaus was finally achieved in June 1414, just two months before the issue became academic with the king's death. By autumn, passions had subsided enough to enable the Pitti and their friends to push through the councils a provision cancelling Luigi's sentence. The "accursed year," Buonaccorso wrote, had finally ended; the family had come within a hair's breadth of political and economic disaster.

The partisan hatreds which flourished during these war years subsided after Ladislaus' death in 1414, and the next decade was an interlude of economic prosperity and peace, both internal and external. But the factional discords had merely gone underground, to emerge again with renewed vigor during the exhausting struggle with Milan which began in 1425. An important source for Florentine politics in these years is the chronicle of Giovanni Cavalcanti. While often inaccurate in historical detail and faulty in analysis, this eyewitness account does portray the animosities and prejudices which motivated the author and his contemporaries. Cavalcanti's description of the political scene in the late 1420s is unrelievedly somber; the city "abounded with men filled with envy and pride, and with other abominable vices." His bitterness was partly inspired by his personal situation; he was a magnate and thus was barred from the priorate and other high offices. Complaining that he was neither "esteemed nor accepted" in the Palace of the Signoria, he claimed that he and his kin were excluded from office by the hostility of "the ungrateful multitude." Cavalcanti described the regime as though it were infiltrated by throngs of artisans and "other mechanical types," for whom his jealousy and contempt were boundless. But he did not direct his barbs solely against the handful of office-holding artisans and shopkeepers from the lesser guilds, who were entitled by law to one-fourth of the seats in the Signoria. Included in his definition of *gente meccaniche* were entrepreneurs whose lineage was less venerable than his own, and who therefore did not merit those political benefits that were denied to him and his fellow magnates.

But Cavalcanti did not believe that the patricians who controlled the regime were more competent than the parvenus and artisans. Himself a man of limited means, he had spent several months in prison for tax delinquency. The fiscal system, he argued, was weighted in favor of the rich, who shift the load "onto the backs of the poor and unfortunate who, without any voice in the government, must sustain these burdens." Even more culpable in Cavalcanti's eyes was the bellicose foreign policy advocated by many aristocratic politicians, particularly Rinaldo degli Albizzi and Neri Capponi. "The greatest citizens," he wrote, "sought to stir up [support for] new enterprises, because they received more wealth and a prolongation of life, in the sense that they gained both fame and reputation. Wealth they received from their administration of the communal fisc; and fame from their involvement in prestigious adventures."

Cavalcanti identified the most divisive issues in Florentine politics: the allocation of the tax burden and the conduct of foreign policy. These problems were at the root of the great wave of discontent which swelled up in Florence, reaching a climax in the early 1430s, during the unsuccessful campaign to conquer Lucca. Taking shape in this confused political situation were two factions, one headed by Rinaldo degli Albizzi, the other by Cosimo de' Medici. Although the emergence of these cliques, and the antagonisms which divided them, were directly connected with the dissatisfactions over fiscal and foreign policy, the factions themselves were not divided by these issues. Indeed, Rinaldo degli Albizzi, the chieftain of the aristocratic group, was instrumental in pushing through the *catasto*, which distributed the tax burden more equitably, whereas Cosimo de' Medici, the leader of the "popular" faction, was very lukewarm in his support for this innovation. The Albizzi group was particularly identified with the disastrous Lucca campaign, but Medici partisans, while criticizing the conduct of this enterprise, did not dare to oppose it openly. Differences between the factions were less political and ideological than personal. Like most political groupings in Florentine history, these parties were tied together by bonds of blood and friendship, which cut across lines of class and economic interest.

The triumph of the Medici faction over its opponents was partly the result of Cosimo's superior financial resources. Controlling the largest banking enterprise in Europe, the Medici were able to buy support in the city and also abroad. Through the judicious dispensation of loans and gifts to impecunious patricians and artisans, Cosimo built up a loyal corps of clients and supporters, which threatened the dominant position of Rinaldo degli Albizzi and his patrician allies. Cosimo also subsidized the military captains in Florentine service and those who were being wooed to fight for the republic. So close were his ties with such *condottieri* as Francesco Sforza and Niccolò da Tolentino that he could influence decisively the conduct of the republic's foreign policy. It was this dimension of his power, combined with his growing political strength at home, which finally persuaded Rinaldo degli Albizzi to force a showdown with his rival. But neither in wealth nor in acumen was Rinaldo a match for the shrewd, resourceful banker. Rinaldo's exile was the penalty which he paid for his misjudgment of the political realities.

Cosimo's most significant contribution to Florentine statecraft was his refinement of the techniques for exercising power covertly, and his masterful handling of opposition and dissent. He was head of a partisan faction recruited largely from the patriciate. Through his manipulation of the electoral system, he filled the important offices with his supporters and excluded those who were hostile or unreliable. The unregenerate and the refractory were sent into exile. Cosimo also used his vast wealth to win political support. He made loans to impecunious fathers with undowried daughters and to men barred from office for tax delinquency. In addition to the impressive sums spent on tournaments and other festivities for the delectation of the populace, Cosimo financed the reconstruction of the collegiate church of S. Lorenzo and the monastery of S. Marco. He further subsidized the building industry by erecting his imposing palace on the Via Larga. Such expenditures advertised his wealth and power, which balanced rather neatly with another facet of his image. This was his posture of disinterest, or rather his pretense that he had no more influence in the republic than any other citizen. When Pope Pius II asked him to commit Florentine resources to the Turkish crusade, Cosimo replied: "You well know how limited is the power of a private citizen under popular government." He never entered the palace of the Signoria except to perform his official duties, or at the invitation of the priors. No one was misled by this pose, but most Florentines were content to live with the deception. So skillfully did the Medici deprive them of their political birthright that two generations passed before they realized fully the value of what they had lost.

WAR AND SOCIETY

This chapter has described facets of the struggle between the cohesive forces in Florentine politics (communal tradition, civic loyalty, mutual cooperation and trust, dedication to the general welfare) and the forces of fragmentation and disintegration (personal ambition and greed, hostility between individuals and groups, the persistence of exploitation and injustice). The burdens and tensions created by war were among the most significant factors in weakening republican institutions and values, and in pushing this community toward a political order dominated first by one family, and then by one man.

In the twelfth and thirteenth centuries, wars fought by civic militias imposed relatively light burdens upon Italian cities, but the advent of mercenary warfare in the fourteenth century sharply increased military expenditures. To meet these spiraling costs, communal governments increased taxes and imposed forced loans. But military budgets continued to rise, as mercenaries demanded higher pay, as the tools of war became more elaborate and expensive. In Florence, moreover, the servicing of the public debt (the consolidated expenditures of past wars) imposed an additional burden upon the populace. Gregorio Dati estimated military costs for the period 1375-1405 at 11,500,000 florins; the conflicts with King Ladislaus and Filippo Maria Visconti in the early fifteenth century were no less expensive. Inevitably, these fiscal burdens were heaviest when the economy was least able to sustain them, when enemy troops had ravaged fields and burned villages in the *contado,* when the blockade of trade routes stifled commerce and industry, and created food shortages and unemployment. During a particularly grave moment in the republic's struggle with Ladislaus in November 1410, Alessio Baldovinetti spoke despairingly: "Our commune has never been in greater danger on account of the war, the pestilence which is imminent, and the shutdown of our factories. . . ." A community of Florence's size and wealth could —and did—support these heavy charges and surmount these difficulties for lengthy periods. But each war piled up new debts and each successive crisis placed a further strain upon the regime. The long and inconclusive struggles of the early fifteenth century were particularly debilitating; by 1430, the city was heartily sick of war and its grim associations.

Still, it is also true that Florentines would not have endured so much travail for so long if the pressures of war had not strengthened the regime in certain ways. These military enterprises aroused patriotic sentiments and encouraged the citizenry to make sacrifices and suffer privation. War also stimulated institutional change. The heavy cost of military operations induced the regime to exploit its resources as fully as possible; this led to a larger bureaucratic apparatus. Administration became more systematic and more professional, as local autonomies and anomalies were suppressed in the interests of effective control and, particularly, of larger revenues to satisfy war needs. Illustrating this trend was a directive sent (November 1418) by the governors of the salt gabelle to the podestà of S. Gimignano in the dominion. This official was ordered to compile a census "of everyone in the district of S. Gimignano . . . under your jurisdiction, large and small, describing the members of each family individually and by age, as well as every foreigner . . . and every priest, friar, monk and nun who inhabits that jurisdiction. . . ." From the perspective of state-building, Florence's wars were positive experiences.

Why did the republic go to war? The answer would appear to be simple and obvious: to defend herself against attack, to protect vital interests. Most historians have stressed economic and strategic factors in their analysis of war and diplomacy in medieval and Renaissance Italy. But in his recent important study, *The Crisis of the Early Italian Renaissance* (1955), Hans Baron has emphasized the ideological dimension of Florentine foreign policy in the early fifteenth century. He has argued that Florence became the main defender of republicanism in a peninsula increasingly dominated by despotic regimes. Often struggling alone against great odds, sometimes assisted by her sister republic Venice, Florence fought to preserve her own liberty, and also that of other city-states seeking to maintain their independence against such tyrants as Giangaleazzo Visconti and King Ladislaus. As a consequence of their involvement in these wars, Florentines became more clearly aware of their republican traditions and developed specific cultural interests inherited from the classical past to justify and to exalt these traditions and values.*

Thus, in Baron's interpretation, an important feature of Italian history in the early Renaissance was the formation of two opposing camps, free republics and despotisms, which were locked in mortal combat. This distinction is almost entirely obliterated by the "materialist" historians, who see no fundamental difference between republican regimes in Florence and Venice and tyrannies in Milan and Ferrara. Both were authoritarian, controlled either by dominant families or by small, oligarchic cliques. Both were governed by similar administrative structures, and both were confronted by similar economic and social problems. In foreign policy, Florence and Milan were guided by a realistic appraisal of their interests. These were, in 1400, essentially what they had been two centuries earlier: the maintenance and extension of control over surrounding territories to protect trade routes, to obtain adequate supplies of food and raw materials, and to prevent enemies from establishing footholds. According to this interpretation, the wars between Florence and Milan were primarily conflicts of material interest. Both states waged propaganda campaigns to justify their activities, which did not always coincide with their professed goals and objectives. But this apologist literature rarely mentions the real issues

---

*The cultural aspects of Baron's interpretation are discussed in Chapter Six, in the section on humanism.

or motives, which must be sought in the minutes of secret council meetings, or inferred from the policies of these governments.

The basic issue in this scholarly disagreement concerns the role of ideals and values in politics. The Florentine experience provides some evidence for both viewpoints, and it also suggests that in this republican context, the formulation of policy was a complex and many-faceted operation. The sources reveal three specific aspects of the process: the ideological, the rational, and the emotional. While the ideological or justificatory dimension was usually emphasized in the writings of Florentine apologists, the arguments based upon material considerations (economic or strategic interest, reasons of state) were rarely mentioned, either because they were universally known and accepted or because they conflicted so sharply with professed motives and objectives. The visceral, emotional reactions of Florentines to foreign policy issues are particularly difficult to identify, for they have left few traces in the sources.

The complexities of this problem are illustrated by the despatches of a Sienese ambassador to Florence, Ser Giacomo Manni, in the spring of 1385. A new regime had just been established in Siena with Florentine assistance, and the ambassador began his mission in an atmosphere of warm cordiality. There had been some suspicion of his government prior to his arrival, but Manni wrote on May 9 that "I cannot walk through the streets without being stopped and greeted by citizens who display such pleasure and show me such honor that it would not be honest for me to describe their sentiments." Two issues were on the diplomatic agenda: the conclusion of a treaty of alliance, and the settlement of border disputes arising from Florence's acquisition of the Aretine *contado* in 1384. Most seriously contested was the possession of Lucignano, a village fifteen miles south of Arezzo, which had long been a bone of contention between that city and Siena.

An unusual feature of this ambassadorial mission was Manni's enthusiastic acceptance of the outlook and viewpoint of the regime to which he was accredited. Perhaps he was overwhelmed by his public reception, but it is more likely that he was influenced by his private meetings with Florentine statesmen who, through secret discussions, endeavored to unravel the knots and dissolve the disagreements which arose in the course of the negotiations. Professing extreme solicitude for Sienese interests, these men promised Manni that they would use their influence to achieve a settlement which his government would accept as just and honorable. They hinted strongly that the Florentine government was prepared to abandon its claim to Lucignano if Siena would become her ally and partner in promoting their mutual interests in Tuscany. So convinced was Manni of their sincerity and good faith that he urged his superiors to place all of the disputed issues in the hands of the Florentine Signoria, and promise to abide by their decisions. It was so obviously in Florence's interest to maintain friendly relations with Siena that she would make large concessions, so Manni believed, to placate her southern neighbor.

Gradually, however, the tone of high optimism in Manni's despatches faded, as weeks passed without any discernible progress in the negotiations. Both the alliance question and the territorial dispute became bogged down in Florence's slow and cumbersome administrative machinery. In every letter, Manni reported yet another meeting with the Signoria and the colleges, or the special committee of seven auditors appointed to examine these issues. Laboriously and redundantly, disputed points were discussed and analyzed. During his frequent meetings with self-styled "friends of Siena," Manni was given tidbits of information about secret council meetings at which Sienese problems were discussed. At one such session, the ambassador's informants told him that the Sienese position was summarized by the Signoria and the auditors, in reply to which "many citizens arose to speak in your [Siena's] favor, warmly commending and praising your regime and your prudence." But these cordial sentiments were never translated into diplomatic act or decision. Tentatively at first, and then more openly, a deluded and chagrined ambassador reported the hardening of Florentine opinion against a compromise over Lucignano. On June 23, Manni informed his government that the Florentines now argued that the border village was legally theirs. Finally, the Signoria refused to make any concessions over Lucignano, while the Sienese would not conclude an alliance without a settlement of the border dispute in its favor. Realizing that his mission had failed completely, Manni asked his government (July 2) for permission to return home.

In his despatch of June 26, the ambassador identified one crucial factor in Florence's *volte-face*. Rumors of a settlement favorable to the Sienese had spread through the city, and these had aroused dormant antagonisms. In his earlier letters, Manni had mentioned the existence of anti-Sienese opinion among the lower classes, but these sentiments did not appear significant, particularly when counterbalanced by the friendly gestures of influential patricians. But while the issue dragged on without settlement, the patriotic fervor of the populace intensified, and the Signoria feared that riots might erupt over the Sienese question. Apparently, the growth of discontent was not spontaneous. Manni reported that propaganda against a settlement was spread by Sienese exiles hoping to discredit their government, and also by certain Florentines who sought to make political capital out of this issue. These groups circulated the story that Lucignano and its surrounding district was a rich source of grain, and thus would provide a valuable supplement to the city's food supply.

This diplomatic episode reveals the complex character of foreign policy issues and their solutions; it also represented a milestone in the relations between these Tuscan republics, with significant implications for the future. Siena's rebuff over Lucignano was the beginning of that regime's alienation from her neighbor, which culminated a decade later in her adherence to Giangaleazzo Visconti's grand alliance against Florence. It is possible that some of Manni's confidants realized the value of making concessions over Lucignano to preserve Siena's friendship and to allay her suspicions of Florentine aggression in Tuscany. In the debate on this issue, several speakers mentioned the desirability of maintaining cordial relations with the Sienese, but no one dared to advocate publicly the sacrifice of Lucignano. There were both imperialist and xenophobic sentiments rampant in the city, probably strongest among the lower classes. And some politicians succumbed to the impulse to push the Sienese to the wall, to concede nothing to that impotent regime which could not retaliate against its powerful neighbor. Reinforcing this aggressive posture was solicitude for the republic's honor, which did not permit any surrender of its legal rights. But opposing such responses was the voice of reason and caution, warning that Florence's true security lay in peaceful relations with her neighbors, and that disastrous consequences might result from Siena's alienation. Yet, the most astute and farsighted statesman would think carefully before advocating a conciliatory policy which bore the earmarks of unpopularity, and which might endanger his political status.

The thorny complexities visible in this minor diplomatic problem were naturally intensified in the more serious questions of war and peace. The stakes were larger, the penalties for failure much greater, in a decision over war with Milan, or an expensive alliance with the King of France. In these critical issues, too, the petty and irrational, the prejudices of the mass and the venality of the few, all undoubtedly played a role. Yet it was a fact that the ruling group was unanimous in its adherence to the main objectives of Florentine foreign policy: independence and the preservation of republican government. Quarrels over foreign policy arose largely, although not exclusively, from honest differences of opinion concerning the achievement of these goals.

The early years of the regime coincided with some fundamental changes in the character of peninsular politics, which presented the leadership with new problems and dilemmas. Prior to 1375, Florentine foreign policy had been built on two foundations: alliances with other Italian Guelf states (the papacy, Naples), and with neighboring communes (Siena, Pisa, Perugia, Bologna, Città di Castello). These supports were crumbling in the 1380s. Florence's war with Pope Gregory XI had severed the city's traditional bond with the Holy See, and this breach was not fully repaired after the peace settlement in 1378. Throughout the duration of the Great Schism (1378-1417), the Roman papacy was too weak to defend herself and her territory effectively. Her value as an ally to the Arno republic was very limited. Meanwhile, republican regimes in central Italian cities were weakened by a combination of economic crisis and political disorders. In their debilitated state, they were dubious allies and they attracted foreign predators. Thus the imperialist policy which Florence fitfully and sporadically pursued in these years had some justification on defensive grounds. As the communal regimes in Tuscany and Umbria collapsed one by one, falling prey to a native despot or a foreign invader, the Florentine republic had to consider the risks, costs, and potential benefits of acquisition. Fear was probably a stronger motive than greed in the regime's expansionist course, which led to the incorporation of Arezzo (1384), Montepulciano (1390), Pisa (1406), Cortona (1411), and Livorno (1421) into the Florentine dominion.

But while Florence was establishing her hegemony in Tuscany, two northern powers were similarly expanding and consolidating their territory. Giangaleazzo Visconti had achieved marked success in his efforts to build a compact and unified state in Lombardy, and farther east, Venice was laying the foundations for her *terrafirma* empire. Florence was transforming herself into a regional power; so were Milan and Venice, and some decades later, Naples and the Papal States. The most direct threat to Florence was Giangaleazzo Visconti, the intelligent and astute lord of Milan who displayed an unusual talent for deploying military and economic resources to achieve his political goals. Florence was weaker and more vulnerable than her Lombard foe, a fact that her citizens understood fully. The fears which this confrontation aroused in the city were not chimerical fantasies, but the reactions of rational, intelligent men to a menace of grave proportions.

The Florentine response to this crisis, and to later ones, assumed two different forms. These positions were never rigid but shifted and vacillated according to situation and circumstances. One response tended to be aggressive and bellicose, the other more cautious and pacifist. One posture harked back to the glorious days of the international Guelf alliances of the late thirteenth and early fourteenth centuries; the other was the direct heir of the more flexible, pragmatic policy which had characterized Florentine diplomacy in the middle decades of the Trecento.

Neither position was so clearly defined and articulated as to constitute a program, but each had certain characteristics and each rested upon specific, and quite different, assumptions. Proponents of a dynamic, aggressive foreign policy were naturally expansionist; they supported most projects of acquisition which

the regime considered. Not only did these men favor the enlargement of Florentine territory, but they also pressed for more
effective control of the communities within the dominion. They
frequently argued that timidity and caution in foreign policy
inevitably led to disaster, and that the prize went to those
states which acted with vigor and speed. Ever suspicious of
the plans and motives of potential enemies, they were the apos-
tles of preparedness, the opponents of truces, the advocates of
wars fought to definite conclusions. Their outlook and viewpoint
were well articulated by Rinaldo degli Albizzi in 1424: "I wish
we were real men and would beat the Duke [of Milan] to the
draw; it would be greater glory than the Romans ever achieved!"
Those Florentines who opposed this bellicose posture often used
arguments derived from the city's business experience. War is
expensive and involves enormous risks; therefore it should never
be declared until the last moment, when the issue is clear-cut,
and when all doubts of the enemy's motives have disappeared.
Although they could not be described as appeasers, the spokesmen for this viewpoint often favored truces to end a military
stalemate, or to gain a breathing space for an overtaxed citizenry.
They criticized the imperialist designs of their opponents, warning that such acquisitions were expensive and troublesome, since
they inevitably antagonized those who were incorporated into
the dominion, as well as their neighbors on the frontier. The
Signoria expressed this viewpoint in a letter (1407) to the
Florentine captain in Arezzo concerning the possible acquisition
of a small border village. We would like to acquire this territory, the priors wrote, if it can be done without incurring the
antagonism of local notables. "For you know how easy enterprises are begun, and how frequently, for smaller affairs than
this, great inconveniences and dangers ensue."

These opposing positions were represented in most major
debates on foreign policy in these decades. Usually the discord
was muted, but occasionally it flared up into open conflict. The
wrangling over the republic's relations with King Ladislaus, so
graphically described by Buonaccorso Pitti, was one occasion
when the rivalry between the two factions was particularly acute.
Debate on the renewal of hostilities with Milan in 1423-1424
likewise revealed a sharp cleavage in the political community.

But the most controversial foreign policy issue in the regime's history was the campaign to conquer Lucca.

The Lucca enterprise began in November 1429, when Florence had not yet recovered from her exhausting four-year war with Milan, and just weeks after she had suppressed a serious rebellion in the subject city of Volterra. Florence was patently unprepared for a long struggle, and the spokesmen for the war party, Rinaldo degli Albizzi and Neri Capponi, claimed that the campaign to subdue Lucca would be brief and decisive. To justify the aggression on legal grounds, the war party claimed that the Lucchese *signore*, Paolo Guinigi, had secretly supported Milan during the recent conflict. Florence and her Tuscan possessions could not be secure, so this argument ran, until such independent nuclei were eliminated, for they were open invitations for enemy powers to gain a foothold in Tuscany. In response to these arguments, the opposition, led by Niccolò da Uzzano, could only assert that Lucca was not guilty of any overtly hostile act against Florence, and that the war faction could not guarantee the rapid, easy victory it confidently predicted. On this question, the peace faction did not have the popular support it had enjoyed in its efforts to conclude a diplomatic settlement with Milan. The Lucchese were roundly hated by the Florentine lower classes, and Rinaldo degli Albizzi was able to manipulate this xenophobic sentiment to his advantage.

The campaign was an unmitigated disaster. The Lucchese energetically resisted the Florentine assault, which was hampered by inept leadership and poor coordination between political and military authorities. Unwilling to abandon Lucca to his enemy, Filippo Maria Visconti furnished assistance to the beleaguered city. To counter Milan's entry into the war, Florence persuaded Venice to join her in an alliance between free republics against the forces of tyranny and oppression. But Venice did not move the scales decisively in Florence's favor. To terminate a war which she could not win, the frustrated republic signed a peace treaty with her antagonists on April 26, 1433 and withdrew her army from Lucchese territory. The domestic animosities engendered by this conflict contributed directly to the political crisis of 1433-1434 and the establishment of a new regime controlled by the Medici and their supporters.

This analysis of Florentine politics has placed heavy emphasis upon dissension and conflict within the city, and upon the weakening of communal values as a result of internal tensions. Perhaps these themes have been overdrawn, and too little attention has been paid to the regime's positive accomplishments: the successful defense of the city and her territory against foreign domination; the preservation of the republican constitution, of open debate, and the right to vote against candidates and laws; the strengthening of the executive authority and the utilization of that authority to maintain order, to develop new public services, and to harness civic energies for useful purposes. This political legacy, which was inherited and maintained (with modifications) by the Medici, was no small achievement in Quattrocento Italy, where authoritarian regimes predominated and where force and violence played an increasingly large role in political life. In Florence the rule of law, and not the arbitrary will of the executive, was the norm throughout the 1400s.

While it is true that Florence was governed more efficiently, and that life and property were more secure, in the fifteenth century than before, this was achieved at a certain cost. Some measure of freedom had been sacrificed for order; some sources of political vitality had been stifled to achieve greater stability. The medieval commune had never been a democracy, but it had accommodated a broad range of diverse interests. By excluding many of these groups from power, by limiting the size of the electorate, the patrician regimes of the Quattrocento did "tranquilize" politics. The ruling class was more homogeneous, less divided by social and economic issues. But the regime grew weaker and more vulnerable as its social base contracted, as citizens were transformed into subjects, as more Florentines became passive onlookers instead of active participants in the political life of the republic. In foreign affairs, the regime was trapped in a vicious circle similar to that which operated in the domestic sphere. In its quest for security from external aggression, it pursued a course of territorial expansion which aggravated its internal problems and sapped its strength. Incorporated into the dominion were thousands of Tuscans who never accepted Florentine rule willingly and who constituted a permanent threat to state security. To govern this alienated population, and to defend it from foreign invasion, the republic spent large sums on garrison troops and fortifications and, in wartime, on mercenary forces. Both citizen and subject had to bear this heavy fiscal burden, which increased resentment and discontent in the city and throughout the dominion, and weakened still further those associative impulses—the feelings of loyalty, of mutual interest, and cooperation—which held this polity together.

FIVE

The Church and the Faith

UBIQUITY AND PROPINQUITY

Religion is the least explored aspect of Florentine Renaissance history. Much of the writing devoted to the subject is superficial in content and polemical in tone, even though the source materials exist for a comprehensive analysis of the church and the faith. Studies of Florentine religion tend to fall into two categories. One interpretation, particularly favored by clerical authors, emphasizes the continuity of religious institutions and traditions, and the vitality of Florentine spirituality, from the Middle Ages through the Renaissance and beyond. Evidence to support this viewpoint is abundant if not conclusive: the popularity of cult ceremonies; the uninterrupted flow of bequests to monasteries and charitable foundations; the wave of religious fervor inspired by the Dominican friar Girolamo Savonarola at the end of the fifteenth century. At the other extreme are those historians like Jacob Burckhardt, who minimize the importance of Christianity in Renaissance Italy. For Burckhardt, the most significant feature of Italian religious history in the Renaissance was the secularization of institutions and beliefs. Clerics and laymen alike pursued their worldly interests in a society no longer influenced or guided by spiritual ideals. For the masses, superstition replaced faith; while the upper classes, although psychologically dependent upon the traditional rituals of the cult, were attracted intellectually to the philosophies of pagan antiquity.

172

Both of these perspectives are flawed, the one because it denies change, the other because it posits a revolutionary break with the past. So venerable and so deeply enmeshed in the city's history and traditions, the church was one of the most conservative forces in Florentine life. The ecclesiastical institution and the spiritual values which it represented were bastions of security and stability in this volatile urban milieu. Yet, throughout the medieval period, the church had altered its customs and policies, adjusted to new conditions, responded to new demands and pressures. The forces and circumstances which instigated and stimulated ecclesiastical change did not abate, but rather intensified, during the fourteenth and fifteenth centuries. The degree and direction of change—of institutions, practices, and beliefs—are the central issues in the study of the Florentine Renaissance church, and the particular focus of this chapter.

Certain aspects of Florentine religious history are more susceptible than others to description and analysis, either because the material is more abundant or the problems themselves are more concrete. From ecclesiastical and secular sources, we have detailed information on the church's institutional structure, and the changes wrought by the crisis of authority during the Great Schism (1378–1417)*. Communal archives, more complete and accessible than ecclesiastical records, throw light upon the church's relations with the secular world. The materials for a detailed study of the church's economic resources are extant, although one valuable source—the *Conventi Soppressi* in the *Archivio di Stato*—was badly damaged by the 1966 flood. But the most obscure and elusive problem is the nature of Florentine piety. A century ago, Burckhardt warned of the hazards involved in defining the religious and moral values of a society. "The more distinctly our evidence in these matters seems to

---

*After the election of Pope Urban VI in 1378, a group of dissident cardinals left Rome, elected a rival pope, Clement VII, who established his court in Avignon. For nearly forty years, Latin Europe had two popes. Some European states (like Florence and England) gave their allegiance to Urban VI and his successors in Rome, and others (like France and Aragon) accepted the legitimacy of their rivals in Avignon. The schism was finally ended in 1417, when the Council of Constance elected an Italian pope, Martin V.

speak," the Swiss historian wrote, "the more we must be on our guard against unqualified assumptions and rash generalizations."

Outwardly, the Florentine church of the fifteenth century resembled closely the institution which St. Francis had known two centuries earlier. It was still overwhelmingly a medieval church architecturally; the classicism of the Renaissance had scarcely made an impact. Florence's medieval church was active, busy, noisy and colorful; the Renaissance church retained all of these qualities. It was a church of large and frequent processions through the streets, sweeping up clergy and laity in their wake. It was a church of begging friars making their rounds, and also of distinguished scholars like the Augustinian Luigi Marsili and the Dominican friar and saint, Antonino. Its symbols and monuments were visible everywhere: the street corner crucifix and the Virgin's illuminated portrait; the small, cramped parish church and the grandiose monastic foundation. The church touched the life of every Florentine at frequent intervals and on several levels. Its most notable characteristics were its ubiquity and its pervasiveness.

Owing to the active participation of the laity in cult ceremonies, the secular and ecclesiastical worlds were in regular and intimate communication. Attendance at morning mass and evening vesper service was a standard part of the daily routine of many Florentines. The clergy officiated at baptisms, marriages, and burials; they were often witnesses to the last testaments dictated by the moribund. Many wills contained elaborate and detailed provisions for masses to be recited for the souls of the testator and his family. The implementation of these bequests forced their heirs to maintain close contact with the clergy, who were charged with this responsibility. How demanding this burden might become for a conscientious executor is revealed in a 1377 testament—by no means unique—made by Francesco Niccoli. This merchant bequeathed some real estate to the Augustinian convent of S. Spirito in Florence, "with the proviso that the friars of the chapter are required to celebrate mass every morning in perpetuity, in which they shall pray to God for the soul of the testator and his relatives; and also that every year in perpetuity on the feast day of the Virgin Mary, they shall celebrate a mass, in which they must light twelve candles . . . and in this chapel in perpetuity there shall be lighted a lamp both day and night." Niccoli further stipulated that if these provisions were not fulfilled, the bequest was to be withdrawn from S. Spirito and the property given to the society of Orsanmichele "to be expended by that society on the paupers of Christ for the soul of the testator."

Contacts between the religious and lay communities resulted, too, from the church's traditional claim to exercise jurisdiction and control over a broad range of secular activities. In Florence, with its complex economic structure, the problem of usury was particularly acute. Episcopal courts normally did not prosecute suspected usurers during their lifetime, but waited to bring suit against the estate of the deceased. Since these court records have not survived, it is impossible to estimate the incidence of usury prosecutions. Other sources provide fragments of evidence about a handful of cases, all involving businessmen of considerable wealth. In a letter written in 1385 to a relative living abroad, Domenico Lanfredini described his quarrel with the bishop over this issue: "After the death of my parents and my brother, the bishop initiated a process against Sandro's [his father's] estate, accusing him of usury. This has been a source of great embarrassment, and I am still not absolved, nor will I be absolved without loss. . . . There are others at the bishop's court who are claiming the usury which they had paid to Sandro in the past." While these cases were not common, they did remind Florentines that the church possessed the instruments to regulate and penalize their economic activities, even though its surveillance was not as thorough as that of the secular authority.

In the absence of court records, one can only speculate about the number and variety of offenses against canon law which were prosecuted in ecclesiastical tribunals. Heresy cases were the exclusive preserve of the Inquisitor's court; heretics condemned to death were turned over to the secular authorities for punishment. Blasphemy was perhaps the most common misdemeanor for which men were haled before the inquisitor or the bishop's vicar-general; Giovanni Villani once complained about an inquisitor who levied a fine "for every little word which someone wrongly uttered against God." Moral offenses and attacks upon the clergy were violations of both civil and canon law; information on such crimes is abundant in the records of the secular courts. For example, the scion of a prominent mercantile family, Adoardo Peruzzi, was sentenced to death by the podestà in 1400 for conspiring to murder a priest, and for complicity in the assassination of an abbot. One case tried in the court of the vicar of Valdelsa (1413) describes a remarkable variety of sacrilegious acts committed by Antonio di Tome of Castro Tremoleti, "in violation of divine, as well as civil and canon, law." Antonio had incestuous relations with his cousin, by whom he had a child, and also with his niece. In a fit of anger occasioned by his gambling losses, he slashed a painting of the Virgin, and later used his knife to deface a coin upon which her image was engraved. For these crimes, Antonio was sentenced to be burned to death in a wooden cage, but this punishment was later changed to decapitation.

Some of the bonds connecting the church and lay society involved all groups in the community. Rich and poor alike crowded into parish churches to observe the Host and to receive the spiritual ministrations of the clergy; aristocrats and lowly vagabonds appeared together as defendants in ecclesiastical tribunals. But only the upper stratum of Florentine society was involved in two spheres of contact between the secular and religious worlds, where relations were unusually close and sensitive. These were property and personnel.

Like ecclesiastical structures elsewhere in Catholic Europe, the Florentine church—or more accurately, the various foundations which comprised that church—owned a substantial amount of property in Tuscany. A record of rents and land transactions of the Carthusian monastery near Galluzzo, five miles south of Florence, reveals that the convent's investments were about equally divided between city and countryside. The Certosa's property in the city included a cloth factory in the Via Maggio, a tailor's shop in the Via del Garbo, a barber shop in the parish of S. Piero Gattolino, a dwelling in the Borgo Ogni Santi. Farms and vineyards owned by the Carthusians were scattered throughout Tuscany, and furnished not only such staples as wheat, wine, and oil for the monastic kitchen, but also surpluses for sale in local markets. Elio Conti's recent study of land ownership in twelve *contado* zones reveals two significant facts. First, ecclesiastical foundations owned 13½ percent of the land in these zones in 1427; the figures for individual zones varied from 2 to 45 percent. Second, church ownership increased dramatically in these districts during the century, to 23.2 percent in 1498, with zonal variations from 7 to 60 percent. These figures suggest that the claim made by the republic's ambassador to Rome in 1452, that the church possessed one-third of the real property in Florentine territory, was not a wild exaggeration.

Much of the revenue from ecclesiastical property was expended on quite legitimate objectives: the stipends of parish priests; the subsidy of monasteries, hospitals, and educational institutions; the payment of papal taxes. Some of this income, however, found its way into secular hands, with little or no benefit accruing to the church. For centuries, the Visdomini family had enjoyed certain lucrative rights to the bishop's revenues; the Arrigucci had a similar (but smaller) claim on Fiesole's episcopal *mensa*, an annual subsidy of 120 bushels of grain. Many patrician families had the right of presentation to parish churches in the city, or to baptismal churches *(pievi)* in the *contado*. Sometime in the thirteenth century the Medici acquired patronage rights to the church of S. Tommaso adjacent to the Old Market. The revenues accruing to the family from such livings were usually not large, although they did provide opportunities for granting a modest income to a poor relation or client. Not economic interest but pride induced families to engage in lengthy and expensive litigation to vindicate their patronage rights over a church. It was doubtless for similar reasons that Pandolfo Ricasoli, member of that powerful noble family residing in the Chianti region southeast of Florence, assaulted a priest, Ser Giunta Casini, asserting that "we have done this to you because you have celebrated [mass] in the church of S. Piero de Montegonzi at the request of the parishioners and against the wishes of Albertaccio and Pandolfo [Ricasoli], and if you dare to celebrate mass again, we will kill you."

By 1400, however, these traditional patronage rights had lost much of their value and importance for the Florentine patriciate. More significant were the lucrative benefices and the prominent careers in the ecclesiastical hierarchy which were open to aristocratic clerics with good connections in the Roman curia. In 1342, Giovanni Villani noted that very few of his fellow-citizens had ever entered the College of Cardinals, "since the Florentines make little effort to induce their sons to become clerics." After the Black Death, however, the number of Florentines in holy orders increased substantially. Was this influx the result of the psychological effects of the plague, of a more intense piety, or rather a desire for economic and professional security? For many of these priests and monks, the church must have seemed an attractive alternative, more stable and more respectable, to a business career with its risks and vicissitudes.

The traffic in Florentine benefices was no more crassly materialistic than elsewhere; the exploitation of ecclesiastical office by local aristocracies had been a fact of European life since the fourth century. But in a society so permeated with mercantile values, the economic dimension assumed particular significance. The issue is discussed with unusual candor by Lanfredino Lanfredini in a letter to his son in September 1406:

> I write to inform you that your close relative—the Augustinian friar, Maestro Bernardo Angioleri—has been made bishop of Thebes, which is in Romania near Negroponte, with a yearly income of 2500 ducats. We are his only kin, and he asked me to send him one of my sons, whom he will treat as his own; he will leave him his estate and procure good benefices for him. So I wrote him about all of you: where you were and what you were doing. He replied that he would particularly like to have you, that he would cherish you and bequeathe you his entire estate. You should know that he is an old man of eighty, distinguished, and very well liked by the Pope and [the members of] the Roman curia. If I may be permitted to advise you, I would urge you to visit him as soon as possible, and see how he treats you.

Normally, benefices did not fall so easily into Florentine hands, but were obtained after long and arduous effort. The correspondence of a papal secretary, Francesco Bruni, describes the efforts by Francesco del Bene in 1364 to obtain a local church, S. Maria sopra Porta, for his son Bene, a law student at the University of Bologna. This church was in the papal gift, and competing for the office with Florentine aspirants were curial cardinals who sought the post for their favorites. Besieged by this throng of petitioners, Pope Urban V endeavored to sift out the unworthy and the unqualified. A commission of cardinals appointed to review candidates scrutinized educational requirements, which Bene fulfilled only partially, for he had not yet obtained the doctorate at Bologna. Letters of recommendation were important and Bruni urged Francesco del Bene to obtain testimonials from several sources: papal legates, the governors of the University of Florence, the captains of the Parte Guelfa, and the directors of the Alberti company, who were the leading papal bankers in Avignon in the 1360s. In this competition with five cardinals and several Florentine candidates, Bene del Bene finally obtained the prize. Contributing to his success was the factor of residence, which gave him an advantage over the necessarily absent curialists, but his greatest asset was undoubtedly the influence of Francesco Bruni, who could sway papal judgment in favor of his clients.

This scramble for ecclesiastical office had certain unfortunate consequences; it tended to exacerbate relations between families, particularly if they belonged to rival political factions. Since the middle of the fourteenth century, a group of patrician conservatives identified with the Parte Guelfa had advocated close ties with the papacy and support for papal policy in Italy. Their opponents suspected these men of advocating this course to obtain benefices for their relatives, as Buonaccorso Pitti charged in his quarrel with the Ricasoli over the abbey of Ruota. Two years before the Ruota incident, Pitti had lost another contest for a benefice. While seeking a papal grant of a hospital in Altopascio (near Lucca) for a nephew, he encountered the opposition of Niccolò da Uzzano, an influential member of the papal faction. Although Buonaccorso had been encouraged to apply for this benefice by Cardinal Baldassare Cossa (later Pope John XXIII), the prelate later reneged on his promise to support the Pitti candidacy, since he did not wish to offend Niccolò da Uzzano. The Altopascio and Ruota incidents prompted Buonaccorso to admonish his sons: "Take example from this case wherein we suffered from trying to vie with the powerful, meddling in squabbles over church benefices and getting involved with priests. Have no dealings with them and you will be wise."

For most patrician families, however, the church was too ubiquitous—and too wealthy—to be ignored. No systematic study has been made of the contribution of ecclesiastical resources to the fortunes of particular Florentine families, but scattered evidence suggest that it could be very important. Gregorio Dati admitted that his brother Leonardo, while general of the Dominican order, saved him from bankruptcy with a timely loan which was never repaid. A recently published account book of the Corsini family reveals that during the tenure of Andrea and Neri Corsini as bishops of Fiesole (1348–1377), their relatives took over the management of the episcopal patrimony and exploited it for their economic advantage.

This pattern of intimate and frequent contact between clergy and laity fostered the anticlericalism which was so pervasive in Florence. The hostility which the clergy aroused in the secular mind was probably due less to the occasional scoundrel or blackguard in clerical robes than to the fact that priests and monks were so ubiquitous, so visible. Some of the roots of Florentine (and Italian) anticlericalism can be traced directly to the ambivalent position which the priest occupied in a society still imbued with the primitive values of Europe's feudal age, the values of a warrior nobility. The priest was a figure of contempt because his vows prohibited him from filling the masculine role. But given his peculiarly close relationship with women, he was also in a strategic position to break his vow of chastity, and to deprive the male of two cherished possessions: a virtuous wife and virginal daughters. In yet another sense, the priest was a menace to the lay community. As a man of God, he was a neutral and uncommitted figure in secular affairs; his clerical garb was his badge of innocence and noninvolvement. But whenever he abandoned his neutral posture to join a faction or a cause, he was particularly dangerous, since his movements did not normally arouse suspicion. Priests and monks were often recruited as agents and messengers in conspiracies and assassinations; their complicity in these enterprises intensified the anticlerical feelings among the laity. In appearance so weak and defenseless, the men of God were powerful, privileged, and dangerous.

THE INSTITUTIONAL CONFRONTATION

Relations between ecclesiastical and lay society were thus defined and conditioned by the thousands of daily contacts between members of these communities. From these associations, there developed the circumstances of institutional confrontation between the church and its secular counterpart, the commune. The long and complex history of this confrontation in Tuscany had created the traditions and the rules which regulated the communication between these two worlds. Over the centuries, the church had won a privileged position for itself, a broad but not total immunity from secular control for its personnel and its possessions. It devoted much energy to maintaining these privileges against direct attack, or the slow erosion of its rights by individuals or corporate groups in lay society.

It is possible to define certain basic elements, some of which are unique to Florence, which influenced the pattern of church-state relations after the outbreak of the Great Schism in 1378. Particularly important was the commune's fundamental advantage over an ecclesiastical institution which was not the monolithic, hierarchical structure often described in textbooks, but rather a congeries of particular entities, frequently in bitter conflict with each other, and very imperfectly and ineffectively controlled by the papacy and the episcopate. During the fourteenth century, the commune had pursued a policy of limiting ecclesiastical privileges, and of intervening in areas which had been the church's exclusive preserve. The climax of this trend occurred during the commune's war with Pope Gregory XI (1375–1378). Not only was the Florentine clergy taxed heavily to subsidize this war, but ecclesiastical property was confiscated and sold to the laity. The commune also sought to control appointments to the episcopal sees of Florence and Fiesole, and exercised a broader supervision over the clergy than at any time in its history. Some of these secular curbs and burdens on the ecclesiastical community were removed or relaxed when peace was made with Rome in 1378, but the Great Schism created additional problems for the vulnerable and beleaguered Florentine church. During the Schism, conditions were certainly ripe for the establishment of a church largely independent of papal control and dominated by the state, similar to those in Milan and Venice. But this did not occur. One important deterrent was the survival of some fragments of a Guelf ideology. Ever since Guelfism had become the official Florentine creed at the end of the thirteenth century, the republic had tied its political fortunes to the papacy, and had based its foreign policy upon a community of interest with Rome (and later Avignon). With some reservations, it had also accepted the principle of papal control over the local church. This tradition had fostered certain habits and attitudes of respect for Rome's authority which were never erased, even at the height of the war with Gregory XI, and which reasserted themselves strongly after 1378.

The strength of this commitment to the Roman papacy was demonstrated most clearly after the outbreak of the Great Schism. Immediately after the election of a rival pope, Clement VII, by a group of dissident cardinals, Florence gave her allegiance to the Roman pope, Urban VI, and never wavered in her devotion until the Council of Pisa in 1409. She remained loyal to Urban and his successors even though other Guelf states —Naples, Hungary, France—supported Clement VII in Avignon. The commune's allegiance to Rome was severely tried by the irascible Urban VI (1378–1389), whose activities once prompted an exasperated citizen, Maffeo di Ser Francesco, to call the pope "a quarrelsome enemy of our commune" and to urge that all ecclesiastical revenues accruing to the papacy be confiscated. Hostility to the Roman pope was also widespread within the inner circle of the ruling group after Cardinal Piero Corsini's defection to Avignon in 1380. The Albizzi-Corsini faction sought to promote a rapprochement with Avignon in 1387, when Pope Clement VII sent an embassy to persuade the commune to break with Urban VI. Clement's ambassadors conveyed his promise to install the republic as vicar over large parts of the Papal States. But none of these inducements could persuade the citizens to switch their allegiance, and the leaders sympathetic to Avignon wisely refrained from pursuing a policy that had little popular support.

The republic's posture with respect to the Schism was symptomatic of its ecclesiastical polity. Relations between commune and *ecclesia* were characterized by a cautious, hesitant groping toward a *modus vivendi,* in which the parties sought to avoid any serious quarrels or any direct conflict that might disturb the equilibrium. Although definitely the stronger partner, the state treated the ecclesiastical community with surprising gentleness and restraint, demonstrating an unwillingness to push its advantage against a debilitated and vulnerable adversary. For its part, the church willingly accepted its protected status and rarely roused itself over an issue, or threatened to invoke ecclesiastical penalties to protect its interests.

The issue of personnel caused the greatest friction between the commune and the Roman curia in these decades. The Florentine government had not resisted the growth of papal provisions in the fourteenth century, which saw the papacy everywhere replace the local patron as the bestower of church office. Owing to the city's traditionally cordial relationship with the curia, many Florentine clerics had profited from the provision system. But like secular governments everywhere in late medieval Europe, the Florentine commune complained about the abuses which the system fostered, particularly absenteeism and pluralism. The stream of recriminatory letters sent by the Signoria to Rome reflects the commune's policy on this issue. Its goal was a church staffed by Florentine citizens or subjects who were qualified, not only in terms of education and vocation but also in a political sense, as loyal supporters of the regime. In 1396, a communal magistracy wrote to Rome about the Franciscan provincial in Tuscany, Fra Arrigo of Massa, "who is politically suspect to our regime and who governs the province in an evil and scandalous manner." Letters addressed to the pope frequently complained about the number of benefices granted to absentee clerics who enjoyed the revenues of office and either neglected the cure of souls entirely, or appointed unqualified men to fulfill this responsibility. But the one specific action taken by the commune to remedy this abuse was to pass legislation in 1406 which stipulated that after five years, the revenues of a benefice held by an absentee incumbent would accrue to the commune.

Selection of Florentine bishops had long been a papal perquisite, and the commune was notably unsuccessful in its efforts to influence appointments to that important office. The most distinguished Florentine cleric in the late Trecento was the Augustinian friar and scholar, Luigi Marsili, highly respected by the regime. Although strongly recommended to Urban VI by the Signoria, Marsili never obtained the Florentine episcopate, which was thrice vacant in the 1380s, nor did he receive any other high position in the hierarchy. The most serious dispute over the bishopric occurred in 1400, when Pope Boniface IX removed the incumbent, Nofri Visdomini, and the Signoria sent embassies to remonstrate with the pope, to no avail. Not all papal appointments which ignored the commune's recommendations were unfortunate or unwise. In 1446, Eugenius IV disregarded the Signoria's candidates to select an obscure Dominican friar, Antonino Pieruzzi, as archbishop of Florence; his great distinction in that office was recognized by his canonization in 1523.

As long as the commune received its share (and perhaps more) of the offices in the papal gift for its citizens and clients, it did not challenge Rome's authority to dispose of local benefices at its discretion. In similar fashion, the curia and the republic compromised their differences over the issue of clerical taxation. The commune regularly imposed forced loans upon its clergy in these decades, usually obtaining a papal license for such exactions in advance. To justify this practice, Florentine envoys in Rome pointed out that the laity were heavily taxed to support military expenditures, and that the clergy benefited from the monies spent on defense. Popes were generally disposed to accept these arguments, particularly since they levied their own taxes upon the Tuscan clergy and needed the commune's cooperation to collect these assessments. In this mutual exploitation of the Tuscan church, neither party challenged the other's right to tax the clergy, but they occasionally protested against the method and extent of the fleecing. In 1432, for example, an indignant Eugenius IV placed the city under interdict when the republic failed to request his approval for a forced loan of 100,000 florins, to be levied on the church during a four-year period. The penalty was removed and the license granted after a communal embassy hurried to Rome to explain the government's need. Voicing their concern for the well-being of the Tuscan clergy, popes occasionally reduced the amount of the assessment. For its part, the republic made some desultory attempts to limit papal taxation of the Florentine church, but its protests were half-hearted and quite ineffectual.

The profile of Florentine-papal relations outlined here has emphasized the dominant position of the republic and the relative impotence of Rome. This situation changed during the fifteenth century, as the papacy recovered from the effects of the Schism and reasserted its temporal and spiritual authority. Beginning with the pontificate of Nicholas V (1447–1455), Roman popes resisted more tenaciously Florentine requests to tax the clergy (although invariably approving some levy), and they acted more vigorously to protect ecclesiastical rights and jurisdictions. By the end of the century, the balance had shifted decisively in favor of Rome; Florence was on the defensive in her negotiations with the curia. The most significant evidence for this trend is the increasing number of judicial cases transferred to papal tribunals, the Rota and the Cameral court, from Florentine secular courts. Prior to 1450, decisions of the republic's courts were rarely appealed to Rome; the commune strongly resented this practice which challenged its sovereignty. But the number of these appeals (many on the grounds of justice denied) increased so rapidly that, by 1500, Florentine ambassadors were devoting much of their time and effort to these cases.

Inevitably, the republic paid more attention to the diplomatic niceties in its relations with the Roman curia than with the local clergy. The Florentine church was a privileged corporation, its special status and its immunities sanctioned by law and custom. But not infrequently, the commune had violated ecclesiastical privileges without compunction and without too much regard for the consequences. The weapons in the local church's arsenal were not very potent or menacing, particularly since the bishop did not have complete and effective control over his diocese. Although the clergy could appeal to Rome for protection, bitter experience had taught them that the curia was not a staunch defender of their rights. The threat of episcopal interdict did not cause great apprehension in the palace of the Signoria. Imbued with the values and traditions of this political community, and connected by blood ties with the ruling class, the

Florentine clergy accepted a considerable degree of secular interference in its affairs without serious complaint.

In the occasional dispute between clergy and commune over rights and jurisdictions, the latter usually triumphed, if only because it possessed superior coercive power. When, in 1431, Jacopo degli Agli arranged for the imprisonment by secular authorities of Andrea and Tommaso Lamberteschi, his opponents in a usury case then being tried in the archbishop's court, he was fined by the vicar-general for violating the court's jurisdiction. But this penalty was unenforceable, since the commune had imprisoned the Lamberteschi and had ordered the transfer of this litigation to a secular court. In another usury case tried before the court of the archbishop of Pisa, the Florentine Giuliano de' Ricci, the Signoria levied a fine of 1000 florins against the prelate's brother Ugucciozzo, unless within a month he had somehow arranged to quash the case.

The commune reacted most sharply to any sign of clerical interference in political affairs. In October 1382, the bishop's vicar-general initiated a judicial process against the Duke of Anjou, then the regime's favored candidate for the Neapolitan throne. In a heated debate over this action, some speakers demanded that the vicar-general be expelled from Florence, while others favored his imprisonment and the immediate suspension of the process. Five years later (April 1387), certain friars who had criticized the policies of Pope Urban VI in sermons were sharply reprimanded and warned "not to involve themselves in public affairs." When two clerics in the diocese of Pistoia voiced their disapproval of the republic's diplomatic relations with the Council of Constance in 1417, they were exiled for one year. An official of the papal curia, Messer Francesco Bartolini, was sentenced to death in 1399 for allegedly posting subversive writings in Florentine churches, but his condemnation was cancelled when he swore that he was innocent of the charges. Any priest or monk so rash as to involve himself in conspiracy against the state could not hope to obtain protection from his clerical robes or his tonsure. Implicated in a plot against the commune in 1375, a Prato friar was hanged by the secular authorities. A canon from Arezzo named Matteo di Angelo was tortured in 1395 to obtain evidence of his complicity in a conspiracy and was then condemned to death. In a letter to the bishop of Arezzo describing this affair, the Signoria requested his approval of the death sentence.

But these incidents tend to distort reality, for they were the critical moments of extreme friction between church and state. A more balanced picture of this relationship would take into account the crises and ruptures (and their subsequent readjustments), but would also incorporate the everyday experiences and confrontations. This story would be less dramatic, more placid; it would reveal these two communities working together in relative harmony to reconcile diverse and often conflicting interests. Such a view is presented in the diary of a Florentine patrician, Paolo Sassetti, as he described the selection of a priest for his parish of S. Piero Buonconsiglio.

The incumbent priest, Ser Antonio, had died on June 3, 1388; Sassetti reported that he had led a dissolute and scandalous life. Perhaps to insure that his successor would be more qualified for the office, twenty-six parishioners assembled in the church to select Messer Niccolò of Urbino, then vicar-general of the diocese, as their spiritual leader. Elections of priests were quite rare in fourteenth century Italy, and this selection was noteworthy for its popular character. In addition to representatives from the prominent families of the parish (Sassetti, Malegonelli, Anselmi, Pigli), there were present and voting two blacksmiths, a baker, two ironmongers, and a linen manufacturer. The parishioners had taken the precaution of obtaining an episcopal license for the election, and the bishop promptly certified the validity of Messer Niccolò's appointment. Unfortunately for the parish, however, the incumbent died in Rome two years later, and S. Piero Buonconsiglio was again without a priest.

When news of Messer Niccolò's death reached Florence in June 1390, the parishioners assembled for another election. Their choice fell on Ser Zanobi Francesci, a chaplain in the Florentine cathedral and a brother of the barber Nuto, who operated a shop on the Piazza della Signoria. Procurators appointed by the parish members informed the priest-designate of his election and also requested episcopal confirmation. But legal problems snarled this appointment. Two lawyers appointed by the bishop stated that the election was valid only if it took place a month after

Messer Niccolò's death. Conforming to this legal decision, the parishioners again assembled to elect Ser Zanobi. But on July 3, the bishop received a letter from Cardinal Bartolomeo Uliari, forbidding him to ratify the election of any priest by the parishioners. Uliari had his own candidate for the benefice, a monk whom he sent to take possession of the church. But the parishioners refused to accept this challenge to their electoral rights and appealed to the Signoria for help.

The issues were legal and delicate. They involved the question of the traditional electoral privileges of this urban parish, the authority of the bishop, the juridical basis for the cardinal's efforts to gain control of the benefice, and, finally, the commune's legal and political position in this complicated dispute. The parishioners were aware of the power and influence of their antagonist, but they fought tenaciously to defend their rights. They hired lawyers and instituted legal action in the bishop's court, and also before the Signoria, to challenge the cardinal's high-handed occupation of their church. Sassetti wrote that he and his neighbors addressed strong letters of protest to the cardinal, and they also complained to the prelate's friends among the Florentine clergy. The strength and unanimity of parish opinion on this issue undoubtedly made an impact upon the authorities, both lay and ecclesiastical. Although unwilling to intervene directly in this legal tangle, the Signoria did expel the cardinal's candidate from the benefice, and a communal official took possession of the church until the dispute was settled. It was Oleari himself who, sensing the hostility which his interference had aroused, broke the impasse. "After we had spent some 50 florins or more," Sassetti wrote, "[the cardinal] gave orders to Messer Bartolomeo [dell 'Antella] and Giovanni [di Salvino] to the effect that our election should stand, and that Ser Zanobi should have possession of the benefice, in reverence to God and St. Peter."

THE MONASTIC WORLD

A constant preoccupation of the Florentine church was the preservation of its identity in a society whose secular interests were alien to its professed goals and purposes. Historically, the

Italian church had enjoyed only marginal success in its efforts to free itself from mundane entanglements. After centuries of trying to impose its values upon the turbulent rural society of medieval Italy, it was then confronted by the different needs and concerns of urban communities. The priests in the rural *pievi* and the canons and administrators of diocesan centers were particularly vulnerable to the secularizing tendencies of the age. Their livelihood was often dependent upon the benevolence of lay patrons; their daily routines varied little from that of the laity. Those clerics with no strong sense of vocation simply absorbed the values of the secular world. Among the volumes of the *Conventi Soppressi* in Florence's state archives is an account book of a parish priest, Giuliano Benini, rector of the suburban church of S. Jacopo di Campo Corbellino in the early fifteenth century. Benini was an ecclesiastical capitalist; his concept of his office was indistinguishable from the merchant's view of a business investment. He hired chaplains to perform the spiritual functions of the benefice, paid them low salaries (8 to 12 florins annually) and discharged them without provocation. Only a small portion of the church's income was spent on its fabric and maintenance; the remainder lined Benini's pockets.

Monastic communities were less susceptible to mundane influences and temptations. In the thirteenth century, the friars had broken down some of the traditional barriers separating convents and lay society. They begged in the streets; they preached to crowds in churches and squares. Yet, although they were more intimately involved with the urban community than the inhabitants of older foundations, their vows and regulations limited their contacts with the outside world. And within cloistered walls, they pursued their corporate activities of prayer, study, and labor. As organized and disciplined communities, they could withstand more effectively the lures of the secular world; they could also make a greater impact upon that world than the isolated and vulnerable priest or even—save in rare instances—the bishop.

One important monastic service to the community was to provide a haven for the spiritually intense: to permit the members of this small, devout minority to work out their religious problems in a regulated, disciplined milieu. Another function was intercessory. Florentines bequeathed their property to the monasteries in order that their souls might benefit from the regular prayer services for the dead. The burial vaults which today line the cloisters of S. Maria Novella and SS. Annunziata are mute evidence of the intimate ties between these foundations and Florentine society.

When the Dominicans, Franciscans, and Carmelites established themselves in the city in the thirteenth century, they added new and important dimensions to the monastic role. They stimulated, and succeeded partially in controlling, the waves of religious enthusiasm which developed in this expanding urban community, its members so recently recruited from the farms and villages of rural Tuscany. Franciscan and Dominican friars, each with their particular techniques and their particular messages, furnished spiritual sustenance to an immigrant mass which was poorly serviced by the secular clergy. As visible symbols of poverty, charity, and humility, the friars were also the church's most effective propagandists for Christian virtues. This function they continued to fill even after they had built those large and expensive churches of S. Croce and S. Maria Novella, which muted the impact of their commitment to poverty. Not least among the mendicant contributions was their teaching function. In S. Croce, S. Maria Novella and S. Spirito (the home of the Augustinian hermits), *studia generale* provided higher education not only for the members of their respective orders, but also for laymen. Dante's intellectual debt to the Dominican *studium* in S. Maria Novella is well known. At the end of the Trecento, the liveliest cultural center was the Augustinian convent of S. Spirito, where Luigi Marsili headed an informal colloquium of scholars interested in philosophical problems. In the 1430s, Ambrogio Traversari, prior of S. Maria degli Angeli, promoted Greek studies in his Camaldolese monastery.

Not every part of the monastic establishment contributed to the spiritual and intellectual welfare of the community; some orders and foundations were in serious difficulty in the fourteenth and fifteenth centuries. Several had lost the zeal and enthusiasm of their founders, and instead of responding imaginatively and creatively to new conditions and responsibilities, they had adopted a posture of sterile and reactionary conservatism. Still other monastic problems were wholly beyond human control. The plagues which swept through Tuscany at regular intervals after 1340 took a particularly heavy toll of conventual lives. Statistics drawn from the mortuary roll of S. Maria Novella reveal this grim pattern: seventeen deaths in 1340, eighty in 1348, twenty-one in 1363, twelve in 1383, twenty-one in 1400, eight in 1417. From a complement of more than 100 friars in 1348, the number had fallen to forty-four in 1419. But S. Maria Novella's losses were surpassed by those of other foundations, for example, by the Dominican convent of S. Jacopo de Ripoli where in 1348 only the prioress and two tertiaries survived from a community of 100 nuns.

Paralleling this decline in the human resources of Florentine monasticism was the reduction or, more accurately, the maldistribution of material wealth. Many Florentines preferred to establish their own tiny hospital or nunnery instead of bequeathing their property to a larger institution. The Via S. Gallo, a main thoroughfare leading north to Bologna, was lined with these miniscule houses, many of which were as transitory and as economically insecure as the fly-by-night businesses which border the main traffic arteries leading into a modern metropolis. Their inhabitants decimated by the plague and their revenues unreplenished by new bequests, these small convents often foundered after a brief existence. A papal bull of 1455 described one of these institutions, S. Maria in Verzaria in the Borgo S. Frediano, which was inhabited by two aged nuns who could not subsist on the convent's paltry revenue. The serious nature of this monastic crisis is clearly revealed by the visitation record (1463–1464) of Francesco Altoviti, general of the Vallombrosan Order. The major Vallombrosan convents in and near Florence were relatively strong: S. Salvi had a total complement of thirty-five (including professed monks, novices, and *conversi*); S. Trinita had eleven monks and S. Pancrazio nine. But in the rural areas surrounding the city, the situation was critical. The walls of S. Bartolomeo de Ripoli enclosed four monks; S. Mauro de Grignano three; S. Mauro de Tagliafumi, only two. Several of the priories in the *contado* were inhabited by a single religious, and none of the Tuscan foundations outside of Florence contained more than ten professed monks. Such was the personnel situation in one of the most renowned monastic orders in central Italy.

In these small and undernourished foundations, breaches of the rule and relaxation of monastic discipline were most likely to occur. They were the scenes of those spectacular cases of immorality which have always exercised a morbid fascination on the secular mind. In convents with so few inmates, one errant regular could break his vows with relative impunity, particularly if he—or she—occupied a position of authority. Nunneries were particularly vulnerable to charges of sexual misconduct, the sin most deplored by secular critics, and for which the evidence was most visible. The Augustinian convent of S. Caterina de Cafaggiolo was the subject of one letter from Pope Nicholas V to Archbishop Antonino in 1452; two of the nuns had borne children during the previous year, which was sufficient reason for instituting a reform. In the 1430s, a lurid scandal involving certain Franciscans and Clares from the convent of Monticelli attracted the attention of Eugenius IV, who ordered the transfer of the inmates to other foundations. For some of Florence's high-spirited youth, the challenge presented by convent walls was too attractive to be ignored, as the criminal court records reveal in abundant detail. One nocturnal incident in 1421 involved three young patricians who used ladders to scale the walls of the convent of S. Silvestro. For two hours, they searched in rooms and under beds for a young nun named Dorotea, terrorizing the other women and threatening the abbess with death if she did not reveal the girl's whereabouts. Unsuccessful in their hunt, they finally escaped through the convent gates and fled the city to avoid paying 1600 *lire* in fines.

Such incidents prompted the government (June 1421) to create a commission of nine men, all married and over fifty, with authority to inspect nunneries and insure their proper governance. This magistracy was authorized to correct and punish conventuals, and also any outsiders found guilty of molesting the nuns. But Eugenius IV considered the establishment of this commission a violation of ecclesiastical privilege, and in 1436 he ordered its dissolution. However, he later abandoned his opposition to this magistracy, which became a permanent fixture in the republic's administrative structure. Its few surviving acts pertain to laymen accused of breaking into convents; there is no evidence that it intervened directly in the internal affairs of these foundations. Eugenius IV's response to the problem of conventual discipline was more constructive, for he attacked a main source of the malaise. He closed down several small nunneries, particularly those with bad reputations, and transferred their inhabitants and their assets to other foundations. This certainly improved the economic health of the surviving convents but, as the Signoria informed the curia in 1436, it also led to quarrels among the nuns, whose established routine had been disrupted.

Many nuns were not strongly committed to the religious life. They were victims of a social system which used the convent as a dumping ground for undowried daughters. Throughout the fifteenth century, Florentine dowries rose steadily while incomes and prices remained relatively stable. Fathers with several nubile daughters often had no choice but to send one or two girls to convents for an expenditure of 100 florins, instead of arranging a respectable marriage at a cost of 1000 florins. The problem is illustrated by the tax declaration of Ser Lodovico della Casa in 1433. This notary informed the tax authorities that "he had a daughter, Piera, in a convent in Faenza, and the convent was demanding that she take her vows; he would have done this some time ago but for his taxes; but now he cannot delay any longer and it will cost 50 florins."

Nuns from aristocratic families who were forced into convents might gain some comfort from living among social equals. The Vallombrosan nunnery of S. Verdiana was one of the most exclusive convents in Florence. In 1464, the abbess was a Medici, and her companions all came from prominent families: Cavalcanti, Gherardi, Cerchi, Guasconi, Altoviti, Rondinelli. The convents of S. Felicita near the Arno and S. Appolinaria on the Via S. Gallo also catered to an exclusive social caste. A diary entry (1490) of the latter foundation reported that Ippolita Baroncelli was accepted as a novice with a small dowry of only 54 florins, as a special favor to Lorenzo de' Medici.

Given the sparse and fragmentary evidence, and the lack of systematic study devoted to this subject, it would be dangerous to generalize about the state of Florentine monasticism in the

fifteenth century. Each convent possessed its unique characteristics: its economic resources, its traditions, its connections with
particular families. Each house had its own historical experience,
its phases of decline and its moments of revival, perhaps stimulated by a large property bequest, an administrative reorganiza-
tion, or the tenure of a vigorous and talented abbot. The following
paragraphs describe conditions in some Florentine monasteries
which, though perhaps not typical, throw some light upon this
cloistered world.

Among the surviving monastic account books in the *Conventi
Soppressi* is one register from the Vallombrosan foundation of S.
Trinita, whose Gothic church adorned by Ghirlandaio frescoes
still stands on the Via Tornabuoni. S. Trinita was a convent
of middling size and status in the city's monastic hierarchy. This
register was kept by a monk, Lorenzo Martini, who recorded
"all of the money which I have spent for the material sustenance
of the monastery, and also for any other necessary items." The
ledger's most striking feature is its meticulous accounting for
every penny spent: the 4 *d.* for salad and the 3 *s.* 6 *d.* for a
dozen eggs disbursed for the evening meal of September 25,
1360, or the 5 *s.* expended three days later for mushrooms
"which the lord abbot bought outside the city gates when he
went to Ema." Such careful attention to fiscal matters was not
unusual; monasteries had long recognized the importance of
keeping accurate records of income and expenditure. But not all
convents were as careful and precise as S. Trinita. The majority
may have been as slovenly in their accounting procedures as
those employed by one monastery whose spokesman reported
(1427) his inability to describe the precise location of the foundation's property, "because it would be too tedious to record
these boundaries, and they could not be determined anyway,
and it's simply not worth the effort."

There is probably a direct connection between S. Trinita's
careful scrutiny of minor household disbursements and the
general impression of prosperity which this account book con-
veys. The convent dispensed hospitality lavishly to visiting
Vallombrosan monks and also to other clerics. On July 8, 1360,
Dom Lorenzo wrote: "Today the lord abbot entertained at din-
ner the abbots of Rezzuolo, Alfiano and Spugna [all Vallombrosan

S. Trinita, interior. (Alinari-Art Reference Bureau)

convents in Tuscany], and Ser Gherardello and another priest who was with the abbot of Alfiano, and there was also Dom Francesco who has left Forcole." A more significant index of prosperity was the construction of a new dormitory in these years, with Neri di Fioravante as master builder. The convent was also sufficiently affluent to subsidize, in this three-year period, two journeys by its abbot to Rome and Avignon.

The Vallombrosan order stressed austerity and the contemplative life; perpetual silence and rigid enclosure were cardinal features of its rule. But the evidence from Dom Lorenzo's account book suggests that the walls of S. Trinita were not effective barriers for those religious who were striving for spiritual perfection through isolation and silence. The views of monastic life furnished by this record suggests neither asceticism nor withdrawal; S. Trinita had learned to live comfortably and even intimately with its neighbors. Laymen were frequent visitors at the abbot's table: the lawyers Andrea Peruzzi, Piero Corsini, and Lapo da Castiglionchio, the physician Maestro Biagio, the architect Neri di Fioravante. In June 1360, the count of Poppi, a prominent lord in the Casentino east of Florence and a benefactor of the order, stayed in S. Trinita while he was being treated for an eye disease. On the feast day of John the Baptist (June 24), Dom Lorenzo recorded the expenditures for purchasing and roasting meat and for carrying the victuals to a house where the count and the abbot were watching the horse races and dining with companions. On each feast of the Trinity (May 31), the convent provided an outdoor banquet for the neighborhood at a cost of some 30 florins. Nearly 200 pounds of beef were roasted on a spit; this fare was supplemented with eggs, wine, bread, salad, and fruit. The convent hired musicians and singers to entertain the crowd, and the account book noted the payment of 1 *lire*, 10 *s.* "to a Catalan named Bartalotto who performed many fine tumbling acts and feats of strength and other marvelous things." Even when, in 1363, plague was raging in the city, the residents of the quarter gathered to celebrate the feast of S. Trinita, and incidentally to spread the contagion which, before summer's end, had taken the lives of three monks. That one of these victims, Dom Simone Gianfigliazzi, did not die in the convent but in his mother's house is another illustration of S.

Trinita's involvement in the world outside its walls. The account book contains this entry: "I gave Monna Isabetta, mother of Dom Simone di Bertoldo Gianfigliazzi, 2 florins and 22 *lire*, which she had spent on the illness of Dom Simone, our monk, who stayed in her house during his malady and died there."

This diary affords a limited glimpse of one segment of Florentine monastic life at a specific moment in time. A broader view emerges from the travel record (1431–1434) of Ambrogio Traversari, who was elected general of the Camaldoli in 1431. Traversari was a distinguished Greek scholar, prior of his monastery of S. Maria degli Angeli, when he was chosen to the generalship. The convents of his order were concentrated in the central Apennines, from Perugia north to Bologna, and along the Adriatic coastal plain from Cesena to Venice. In many respects, Traversari's account of his travels is typical of visitation literature. His inspection of Camaldolese establishments invariably included a presentation of credentials, a formal greeting, a service celebrated by the general in the monastic church, followed by interrogation of the inmates and the final criticisms, admonitions, and judgments of the visitor. Still, the *Hodoeporicon* (Traversari's title for his story) is a more interesting narrative than most visitation accounts. The Latin is clear and expressive, and by stressing dramatic incidents and significant themes, the author avoids the mechanical, repetitive quality which characterizes much of this genre. Traversari may have touched up his narrative for effect, but the record of his inspection trips attests to his energy (he was constantly on the move), his genuine concern for the welfare of his order, and his reforming zeal.

No clear, sharply defined image of Camaldolese monasticism emerges from Traversari's account. The picture is mottled and blurred, with some black and some white and a predominant shade of gray. A few houses, like the isolated Apennine nunnery at Pratovecchio, were distinguished for their discipline and spirituality; a few—for example, Querceto and Silva—Traversari described as brothels. Although the urban foundations were usually in better physical and moral condition than the rural establishments, this was partly due to the latter's vulnerability to despoliation by military forces. Traversari discovered that the monastery of S. Ippolito in the Apennines near Faenza had been ravaged by troops, had fallen into total disrepair, and was inhabited by an infirm abbot and two novices. But large foundations in an urban environment were not immune to corruption. In the monastery of S. Salvi outside Florence's walls, the abbot was accused (correctly, in Traversari's opinion) of maintaining a mistress whom he smuggled into his cell at night. Few convents received a clean bill of health from the general; even the well disciplined establishments had their flaws and their breaches of the rule. If only one or two monks were guilty of minor infractions, like the two from S. Salvatore with a penchant for wandering about Florence, the defects could be repaired by admonitions to the errant, and a warning to the abbot. The cases of delinquent priors and abbots were more serious, for their lapses directly affected monastic discipline. Mariano, the abbot of Silva, had taken a peasant's wife as his mistress and then tried to murder the cuckolded husband. He was deprived of his office, as was the abbot of Anghiari near Arezzo, whose immoral life had contributed to the disorderly state of his monastery. To the nuns in a convent in southern Tuscany who had confessed to sexual relations with male visitors, Traversari delivered a dire warning, that he would order the physical destruction of the convent if he heard any further rumors of their evil conduct.

Insofar as the Camaldoli general's program for reforming his order is revealed in the *Hodoeporicon,* it was traditional. Camaldoli had been founded in the eleventh century as a hermitic order, but some houses later organized themselves on a communal basis. While approving both systems for monks, Traversari believed that only communal living was suitable for nuns, and he emphasized this point in his exhortations to the women under his charge. With only limited success, he urged the convents of Regulars to adopt an Observant discipline. Perhaps the most serious obstacle to his reform plans was the spirit of autonomy within each convent. These parochial instincts were particularly obdurate when supported by local political influences, in the person of a feudal baron or a commune. Some of these local authorities—for example, the count of Poppi—were warmly disposed toward the order and cooperated with Traversari; but others engaged in jurisdictional disputes, or challenged his right to depose an abbot who came from a prominent local family. Such interference naturally complicated the problem of discipline within the order, for an errant or disobedient monk could usually find some secular authority, or even a convent, which would offer sanctuary. While on a visit to Rome in 1432, Traversari met several Camaldolese who had left their houses to enjoy the attractions, presumably more temporal than spiritual, of the Eternal City.

Although he never commented directly on this problem, Traversari was hampered by a shortage of competent personnel to assist him in administering and reforming the Order. The human resources at his disposal were limited; apparently, only a handful of Camaldolese monks possessed the necessary qualifications of education and character to assume positions of responsibility. After deposing a corrupt or incompetent abbot, the general was often forced to appoint a member of his own staff to govern the convent. An improved system of monastic education was one solution to this problem, and Traversari was pleased to meet, in the convent of S. Maria de Carceri near Este, an industrious abbot who was teaching ten young novices. But this was the only specific reference to monastic education in Traversari's journal. Learning was evidently not one of Camaldoli's strongest features. This may explain the order's modest contribution to Italian religious life in the fifteenth century, and it bolsters an impression—which Traversari's own talents and zeal do not efface—of a monastic organization which was not pulsating with vitality and religious fervor.

Of the religious orders in Florence, the Dominicans were the most active and distinguished in the late Trecento and early Quattrocento. In an age that produced relatively few candidates for sainthood, the friars of S. Maria Novella and S. Marco counted one saint (Antonino) and three *beati* (Alessio Strozzi, Giovanni Dominici, and Fra Angelico) among their number. A more significant index of distinction is the number of Florentine Dominicans who became bishops. Twelve held sees between 1360 and 1430, and another (Leonardo Dati) was elected general of the order. If a defective system of education contributed to Camaldolese mediocrity, then the traditional Dominican commitment to learning may explain the order's prominence in the fifteenth-century Italian church. The biographical researches of

Stefano Orlandi reveal that a high proportion of friars attached to S. Maria Novella received degrees in the various Italian *studia* of the order, while several had studied theology in Paris. Perhaps the most remarkable feature of the Florentine Dominican tradition, so oriented toward the training of administrators and professors, was its strong reformist bent, its impulse to create and maintain a higher quality of monastic life.

Fra Antonino Pieruzzi (1389–1459)—Observant friar and vicar-general, archbishop of Florence, and saint—was the most distinguished member of this Dominican community prior to Savonarola. When this son of a Florentine notary entered the order in 1405, he became a disciple of Giovanni Dominici, whose strong reformist views had been nourished by his contact with followers of St. Catherine of Siena. Within the Dominican hierarchy, Antonino rapidly established a reputation as an efficient administrator and reformer. In convents in Fiesole and Cortona, in Rome and Naples, he held positions of responsibility, and in 1436 he was named prior of the new Dominican foundation at S. Marco, which was given to the Observants by Eugenius IV. His reputation for piety and learning, as well as his demonstrated talent for administration, were factors in Eugenius IV's happy decision to appoint him to the Florentine archdiocese.

Distinctive features of Antonino's episcopal career were his gift for combining traditional attitudes with progressive ideas, and his clear understanding of the realities of urban life. Antonino took his pastoral responsibilities very seriously; he sought to improve the morale of a listless clergy which had become lax and indifferent to its responsibilities. When appeals and admonitions failed, the archbishop did not hesitate to use force. Delinquent priests were deprived of their benefices, imprisoned, sometimes tortured. Antonino's theology was as traditional as his conception of the pastoral office; his ideas, which he developed in a ponderous *Summa Moralia*, were largely derivative. Yet this massive work contains interesting passages which reveal the author as a knowledgeable and perceptive analyst of the contemporary scene, who had confronted the problem of the two cities and who—like Aquinas and unlike Augustine— believed that a constructive and harmonious relationship between the heavenly and earthly realms was possible. Two centuries before, Aquinas had conceded that merchants (like knights and peasants) were also children of God, and that their activities, which satisfied important social needs, did not automatically condemn them to perdition. Antonino accepted this premise without question. His specific contribution was to define, as precisely as possible, those business activities which were licit, and those which were forbidden. For example, he approved the traffic in *Monte* shares, while condemning the practice of dry exchange, the employment of money-changing transactions to conceal loan operations. He defined "just price" very flexibly, taking into account the variables and imponderables of the market.

The archbishop's political views were also influenced by his Florentine origins. Although he stoutly defended the privileges of the ecclesiastical corporation which he headed, Antonino admitted the state's right to tax the clergy in case of need. He threatened to excommunicate some recalcitrant Pistoia clerics who had refused to contribute to a forced loan levied by the Florentine republic and approved by the pope. The most notable aspect of Antonino's political philosophy was his strong commitment to republicanism. His relations with Cosimo de' Medici were friendly; the banker had subsidized the rebuilding of S. Marco and had his own private cell in the convent. But Antonino did not approve of the methods by which Cosimo subverted the constitution to establish more effective control over the state. In his famous protest of July 1458 against the breach of voting secrecy in the councils, he opposed Medicean efforts to consolidate their power. His protest had no practical effect, and he was reprimanded by the Signoria for interfering in politics. But he had raised his voice in defense of traditional republican values, and a half century later Savonarola would reaffirm this position, with very dramatic consequences.

PIETY

Not innovation, but rather the persistence of traditional forms and attitudes, is the dominant impression gained from an examination of the institutional structure of the Florentine church,

its internal problems, and its relations with the secular world
in the early fifteenth century. Tradition is also the most distinctive feature of Florentine piety in the Renaissance. Some
changes did occur in the modes of religious expression, and in
the influence of spiritual values upon behavior, but these were
not as striking as some historians—following Burckhardt—have
suggested, in stressing the worldly, secular orientation of this
society. Yet so little is known about the history of Florentine
piety that generalizations must be formulated with great caution.

The city's religious life continued to focus upon the cult, the
elaborate structure of service and ritual by which Florentines
gave expression to their faith and performed the propitiatory
acts considered essential for salvation. Although the basic features of the cult were both ancient and universal in the Latin
West, there had developed over the centuries an accretion of
custom and tradition peculiar to Florence. These unique features of the religious scene included the celebrations on the
feast day of the patron saint, John the Baptist (June 24), the
veneration accorded to the paintings of the Madonna in S.
Maria Impruneta and in SS. Annunziata, and the custom of
Sunday pilgrimages in search of indulgences along "monastic
row," the Via S. Gallo. Florentines were a churchgoing people;
they participated frequently and fervently in the religious services of the cult, as well as in many special forms of worship
and devotion. Today, the vast, cavernous interior of the cathedral is filled only on rare, ceremonial occasions or by an exceptional confluence of tourists. But in the fifteenth century, the
church was always crowded on the major feast days, and particularly during the cycle of Lenten sermons preached by renowned friars, whose appearances were solicited and arranged
by the commune.

Not all of this involvement in cult activity was motivated by
deep and sincere piety. Rote habit, the pressures of social
conformity, and even less worthy personal motives contributed
to these visible and formal manifestations of devotion. One may
question the piety of a merchant who begins his business correspondence with the invocation: "In the name of God and of
profit." The renowned Franciscan preacher Bernardino of Siena
criticized the female members of his audience who came to his

sermons to gossip. As did their contemporaries in the *Canterbury Tales,* some Florentines went on pilgrimages for the sake of their souls, others to enjoy a holiday promenade. When Francesco Datini followed the bishop of Fiesole, Jacopo Altoviti, on a penitential pilgrimage to Arezzo, he was certainly concerned about his salvation. But he did not accept the premise that his soul could be purified by asceticism.

On this 18th day of August 1399, I, Francesco di Marco, through the inspiration of God and his Mother our Lady, resolved to go on a pilgrimage, clothed entirely in white linen and barefoot, as was the custom then from many people in the city. . . . For at that time all men, or at least the greater number of Christians, were moved to go on a pilgrimage throughout the world, for the love of God, clothed from head to foot in white linen. . . . And that we might have what was necessary, I took with us two of my horses and the mule: and on these we placed two small saddle chests, containing boxes of all kinds of comfits . . . and candles, and fresh bread and biscuits and round cakes, sweet and unsweetened, and other things besides that appertain to a man's life. . . . The two horses were fully laden with our victuals; and besides these, I took a great sack of warm raiment, to have at hand by day and night. And the mule I took in case one of us, through sickness or any other cause, could not walk. . . .

Confronted by grave crisis, this society naturally sought aid and comfort in its faith. Indeed, its reaction to crisis provides clues to those aspects of its spiritual life which it cherished most deeply. When plague or famine struck, Florentines sent for Impruneta's portrait of the Madonna, which was then paraded through the city streets at the head of a great procession of clergy and laity. During the earthquake of 1453, one observer reported that "the entire populace rushed to their devotions and during a period of four days, there were great processions of men and women. People of the lower classes assembled under the leadership of their parish priests and at night marched to S. Trinita singing hymns and praying for their safety." Particularly revealing was the community's response to the interdict imposed by Pope Gregory XI in 1376, which disrupted normal religious life for two years. This interdict did not suspend all cult activity, but it drastically limited the laity's participation.

Behind the closed doors of churches, priests performed the sacrifice of the mass, to which they were the sole witnesses. Florentines were not unduly disturbed by the prohibition against confession and communion, but they exhibited a particular urge to observe the Host, and this deprivation certainly aroused some feelings of anxiety. The populace took part in outdoor religious processions throughout the war's duration. The most intense anxieties and fears were doubtless felt by the dying, who were not permitted to receive extreme unction and were also refused burial in holy ground. While the citizenry gained some solace from the widespread belief that the interdict was unjust and therefore illegal, the authorities were unwilling to violate its provisions.

Certain forms of religious enthusiasm, which characterized this crisis of the 1370s, declined in popularity during the fifteenth century. For example, the throngs of flagellants traveling along Italian roads in the fourteenth century are rarely mentioned in chronicles and public documents after 1400. The flagellation mania reached a climax during the papal war, and became the subject of several debates among worried priors and counselors in the palace of the Signoria. A decade later (December 1388), the government placed a ban upon flagellant processions, and this official disapproval may have played some part in their decline.

One of the greatest manifestations of religious fervor in Florence before Savonarola's time occurred in the summer of 1399. This was the phenomenon of the Bianchi, so called because its adherents wore white linen cloth as a sign of repentance and regeneration. From Lombardy, where the movement originated, throngs of white-clad penitents moved southward toward Rome, attracting thousands of followers from the cities and villages along the way. The specific catalysts of this movement are obscure, although plague had struck many parts of the peninsula, and war between Milan and Florence had contributed its measure of misery and destruction. The impact of the Bianchi upon Florence was profound. For nine days, the city's shops remained closed while the inhabitants went on pilgrimages to Arezzo, to Vernia and Camaldoli in the Apennines. Not only did Florentines of all classes join the movement, but they were unusually lavish in their provision of alms for the pilgrims who, in the words of one astonished witness, "committed no damage to fruit trees nor to anything else during this pilgrimage, but paid for everything." So intense was the spirit of brotherhood generated by the Bianchi that some enthusiasts tried to open the gates of the communal prison and release the inmates. Responding to this impulse which threatened public security, the commune enacted a law which conceded that these humanitarian impulses were divinely inspired, and then simplified the legal procedure whereby individual prisoners might be freed. Dozens of feuding families signed peace agreements. For this brief moment, Florentines treated each other with the charity and compassion which, according to the hagiographic sources, St. Francis of Assisi aroused 200 years earlier in his flying visits to Tuscan towns. But as in the thirteenth century, this enthusiasm quickly waned, and its effect upon social behavior was soon obliterated by the resurgence of the old problems, the old passions and enmities.

If the flourishing of heresy is an indication of a society's spirituality, Trecento Florence was a devout city. The Fraticelli movement, led by radical Franciscans who preached strict compliance with the vow of poverty, had attracted many adherents in the city and elsewhere in central Italy. Little is known about the size and social composition of this heretical community, although it has been suggested that its membership was recruited primarily from the cloth workers and the inhabitants of the city's slums. By the 1370s, the heretics were so numerous and so well organized that there was talk of a formal debate, to be arranged by the Signoria, between the bishop and a spokesman for the Fraticelli. Some voices were raised against the heretics; particularly hostile were those patricians sympathetic to the papacy and the Parte Guelfa. Others, with no strong commitment to orthodoxy, nevertheless denounced the Fraticelli as potential subverters of the political and social order. But Florentines were characteristically tolerant of religious and intellectual aberrations; even the orthodox felt some sympathy for Fraticelli views, particularly their exaltation of poverty, and their criticism of the ecclesiastical hierarchy. In November 1383, one year after the passage of a harsh law against the Fraticelli by the new conservative regime, six artisans (including two cutlers, a harness-maker, a carpenter, and a belt-maker) were convicted of harassing officials of the Inquisition and the podestà who were attempting to arrest a suspected heretic, Lorenzo Puccini. When Lorenzo's son Angelo pleaded with bystanders to prevent his father's seizure, the artisans shouted, "Let us stone those buggering friars and the police!" The crowd responded enthusiastically to this appeal, and the officials had to flee for their lives.

These ambiguities were all present in the trial and execution (April 1389) of Fra Michele da Calci, a native of the Pisan *contado* who had been captured while ministering to the Fraticelli community in Florence. The judicial act which sentenced Michele to the stake accused him of "persuading many men and women of the city of Florence . . . to join the sect of the Fraticelli, describing to them the above mentioned sect, and with false words and erroneous arguments, insisting that this sect was the true religion and the true observance of the rule and life of the blessed Francis, and that all those who observe this doctrine and life are in a state of grace and that all other friars and priests are heretics and schismatics and are damned." There has survived a vivid description of the condemned friar's last hours, written by an anonymous member of the group who asserted that "everything which I now describe, I who write both saw or heard." Like other hagiographic writing, this account may have been colored to serve the purposes of the author and his cause, but it is a credible description. As Michele was paraded through the streets on his way to execution, the crowds urged him to recant and save himself. Rejecting these appeals, the friar invited his listeners to "repent of your sins, your usury, your gambling, your fornication." If this anonymous source can be believed, members of the heretical community publicly identified themselves by urging Michele to remain steadfast throughout his ordeal. The authorities, religious and secular, obviously hoped that Michele's execution would be an object lesson to the faithful, but this account suggests that some Florentines were very disturbed by the friar's execution:

Many of the witnesses [to the execution] said: "He seems to be a saint!" Even his adversaries whispered it, and they slowly began to return to their homes. They discussed Michele, and the majority said that he was wrong, and that no one should speak such evil of the priests. And some said, "He is a martyr," while others claimed that he was a saint, and still others denied it. And there was a greater tumult and disturbance in Florence than there had ever been.

This was the last execution of a member of the Fraticelli sect in Florence, a fact which emphasizes the decline of the movement, and indeed of unorthodoxy generally, in Tuscany during the fifteenth century. Although the evidence is fragmentary, the infrequency of prosecutions suggests that heresy had lost much of its popular appeal, and was confined to a few intellectuals. I have discovered only three heresy cases for the first half of the fifteenth century, none of which involved a large group or mass movement. In 1410, Pope John XXIII absolved the Florentine bishop Jacopo Palladini of a heresy charge arising from his treatise on the book of Daniel. Eight years later, a rural priest in the Fiesole *contado* was reprimanded for preaching that the Dominican saint Peter Martyr was in hell and that he died "not for the love of God but as a result of a vendetta." This priest allegedly told the women of his parish that they were not breaking any divine law by sewing or weaving on Sundays or other feast days. The most sensational heresy case occurred in mid-century; it terminated in the execution of a well-known physician, Giovanni Cani of Montecatini, in 1450. Cani was accused of harboring Fraticelli opinions, and also of dabbling in sorcery. His execution was a rare blemish on the city's record for intellectual and religious toleration. The physician was the only man to die in Florence for his beliefs in the 110 years between the executions of Fra Michele da Calci (1389) and Savonarola (1498).

After 1400, Florence witnessed fewer displays of mass religious enthusiasm and a dwindling interest in heretical ideas. There was a similar decline in the number of individuals judged worthy of sainthood. Compared to the galaxy of Florentine saints and *beati* in the fourteenth century (a dozen by the author's rough count), the fifteenth century produced only S.

Antonino who, unlike the ascetic friars and nuns of the Trecento, won renown as a distinguished scholar and prelate. These trends did not signify a decline in Florentine spirituality, but rather the channeling of religious impulses along different routes.

In 1244, the Dominican friar and saint Peter Martyr organized a confraternity in Florence for the specific purpose of combating the Patarine heresy. Following this example, other groups of clergy and pious laymen assembled regularly in chapels and monastic cloisters, some to sing hymns at vespers, others to indulge in flagellation, and still others to perform acts of charity. This last activity was particularly favored by those societies that were allowed to function after 1419, when a law was passed which dissolved all confraternities and permitted a few to reorganize with the consent of the Signoria. Two of the most prominent (which still survive today) were the *arcifraternità della Misericordia,* which specialized in tending the sick and burying the indigent, and the *compagnia di S. Maria del Bigallo,* which in the fifteenth century concentrated its efforts and resources upon caring for orphans and foundlings.

The constitution of one society, S. Maria della Pieta, describes the functions of a popular and active confraternity which had been founded in 1410. Its members came from every social class except the lowest; they included the patrician Bindo Guasconi, the lawyer Bernardo Muscini, the silk manufacturer Parente di Michele Parenti, and a cloth shearer named Bindo. The constitution defined the rules of behavior prescribed for the brethren: "to observe the laws of God," to abstain from frivolous company, to avoid taverns and gambling halls, to confess at least once a month, and to take communion twice a year. The society met each month for business, every second Saturday for prayer sessions, and it also assembled on major feast days. On Holy Thursday, for example, the regulations stipulated that "the governors will wash the feet of the brethren, and will offer a simple meal, to commemorate this day on which Christ washed the feet of his disciples and then shared a meal with them."

This confraternity's primary mission, however, was charitable. Each weekend the members distributed bread and wine to those indigents whom the society undertook to succor.

We hereby decree [reads the constitution] that the orderlies shall identify the poor who live in the city and *contado,* and shall assign them to a pair of the brethren. To each pauper shall be given three loaves of bread and a flask of wine once a week. The orderlies will be penalized 4 *d.* if they fail to have the alms ready for distribution to the poor by the brethren, at the latest on Saturday at noon. . . . And from nones on Sunday to the hour of vespers on Sunday, at least one of the orderlies must be on duty at all times, to give alms to each pair of the brethren who come for their quota. . . . And each [brother] who takes these alms must indicate the name of the pauper to whom he is distributing them before he leaves . . . so that each one knows who has been visited and who has not, to avoid a double distribution to one, and nothing to another.

Any surplus of funds could also be applied to purchasing the release of prisoners from the communal prison, "only those who are imprisoned through misfortune and not through vice," to clothing the poor, and providing temporary shelter for pilgrims.

For those Florentines who could not participate actively in pious works, there remained an alternate means of expressing their religious zeal: the bequest. The *catasto* records of the 1420s and 1430s are liberally sprinkled with references to these benefactions, some as outright gifts of property or income to religious foundations, others as life annuities for members of the regular clergy. Many of these obligations were perpetual charges established by ancestors. In his tax declaration, Piero Girolami noted that his family did not receive a penny of the annual rent (44 florins) from a tower on the Por S. Maria. Through the testamentary stipulations of deceased Girolami, this money was used to distribute alms on the feast day of S. Zanobi, to maintain a chapel and provide a commemorative meal annually in the parish church of S. Stefano a Ponte.

Although there was no discernible slackening in the size and number of religious bequests in the fifteenth century, a significant change did occur in the pattern of giving. Florentines were channeling more of their resources into institutions which were specifically concerned with social problems. In the twelfth century, the Benedictines and Vallombrosans, and in the thirteenth, the Dominicans and Franciscans, had been the main beneficiaries of Florentine philanthropy. But these orders attracted less attention from Florentine testators in the Quattrocento. A wealthy partner in the Medici bank, Ilarione de' Bardi, devoted most of his charitable expenditure to providing dowries for poor girls. Prato's richest citizen, Francesco Datini, left no legitimate heirs; with his fortune of 80,000 florins, he established a foundation to succor the indigent of his native city. In 1362, a knight from Parma named Bonifazio Lupi donated 300 florins to purchase land for building a hospital to care for "the infirm poor."

From this modest beginning, the "hospital of Messer Bonifazio" became one of Florence's largest charitable institutions, receiving numerous testamentary bequests. In the 1430s, the hospital's buildings were valued at 24,000 florins, and it received an annual income of 700 florins from its property. Elio Conti's researches into the patterns of land ownership in the Florentine *contado* reveal that Bonifazio's foundation, the hospital of S. Maria Nuova, and the Foundling Home of the Innocenti significantly increased their real estate holdings in the fifteenth century. In the twelve zones which Conti analyzed in detail, he discovered that S. Maria Nuova had acquired property valued at 5300 florins between 1427 and 1498. Bonifazio's hospital also shared in this largesse, increasing the value of its holdings in these zones by an estimated 2100 florins, while the foundlings of the Innocenti benefited from a single bequest worth 1000 florins. One of Florence's richest men, Niccolò da Uzzano, stipulated in his will that the bulk of his fortune be spent on constructing a hospice for poor students attending the university.

How can one measure the intensity and sincerity of these manifestations of piety in Quattrocento Florence? The evidence does suggest that this society (contrary to Burckhardt's judgment) was still devout, profoundly concerned about spiritual values, and troubled by the conflicting demands of this world and the hereafter. It is true that the more extreme and manic forms of religiosity—heresy, flagellation, mass peregrinations—are less common after 1400 than before. Church and state joined forces to channel these impulses into more disciplined patterns, for example, into confraternities whose members concentrated less upon whipping themselves and more upon performing char-

itable acts. There were, however, occasional outbursts of popular religious enthusiasm in the fifteenth century. In 1423, a
Dominican preacher, Manfredo of Vercelli, attracted a large
following in Tuscany and led some 400 pilgrims to Rome. One
of his disciples was a Florentine matron named Ginevra Mannelli who followed the friar with her three children and some
700 florins in cash. In 1450, thousands of Florentines journeyed
to Rome to obtain the jubilee indulgences proclaimed by Pope
Nicholas V. Three years later, the terrors aroused by an earthquake provoked a surge of religious emotion comparable to the
Bianchi phenomenon of 1399. Nor did Florentines cease to respond to the appeals of crusade preachers. In October 1455 a
Dominican friar from Naples attracted widespread sympathy
and support for his fiery sermons on behalf of Pius II's crusade
against the Turks. A crowd estimated at 20,000 participated in
one procession organized by this preacher, and Florentines contributed several thousand florins to the crusade fund.

There is no evidence of any movement in Quattrocento Florence comparable to the *Devotio moderna* of the Netherlands,
which focused upon the inner spiritual life of the individual
and his private relationship with God. This intensely personal
form of religious experience was foreign to the Florentine mentality, with its emphasis upon corporate, public religiosity. Only
rarely do the sources contain any sign or hint of an attitude
characteristic of northern piety. In the trial record of a servant
girl accused of stealing a Bible is the curious statement that its
owner, Tedaldo Tedaldi, "was accustomed to read it frequently,
and at night left it on his table." Denouncing the Florentine
practice of making vows for every conceivable purpose, Franco
Sacchetti wrote that such practices were idolatrous, and not
acts of Christian faith. "And I, the writer, have actually witnessed someone whose cat has strayed making a vow that if he
recovered it, he would send a wax image [of the cat] to the
Virgin at Orsanmichele. And he actually did this! Now while
this may not be a violation of the faith, surely it is a mockery
of God, the Virgin and all the Saints. For [God] desires our heart
and our mind; he is not interested in our wax images, nor in
such conceits and vanities." Sacchetti's view was a minority
opinion; the majority of his fellow-citizens accepted the tradi-

tional beliefs and practices of the cult. Florentines prayed
to the local saints; they were eager to witness miracles; they believed in the efficacy of relics. In 1454, the hard-headed industrialists of the Lana guild spent 800 florins for relics brought
from Constantinople: a piece of the true cross, a fragment of
Christ's clothing, and part of a cane with which he had been
whipped. These were displayed above the high altar in the
cathedral. The citizenry applauded their acquisition quite as
fervently as had their ancestors a century earlier, on the occasion of the purchase of another relic, the right arm (later found
to be counterfeit) of S. Reparata.

SIX

Culture

FOUNDATIONS AND PREMISES

For two centuries, from the age of Dante and Giotto to that of Machiavelli and Michelangelo, Florence was one of Latin Europe's most dynamic and creative centers of intellectual and artistic activity. This chapter will attempt to define the nature of that cultural achievement, and to relate it to the city's institutions and values, and to her experience. Perhaps no problem of historical analysis is so challenging and provocative, and so beset with pitfalls, as the attempt to explain the relationship between social and cultural phenomena. Every student of Florentine history is confronted by these questions: Why was this society so creative, and so receptive to change and innovation? Of all the major Italian cities, why did Florence—and not Milan or Genoa or Venice—achieve the greatest distinction in art and learning during these centuries?

The Florentine contribution to Renaissance culture was not limited to a few specialized areas; it encompassed many fields and disciplines. In painting, sculpture, and architecture, the city's achievement was spectacular. Florentine artisans excelled in a variety of craft activities, from terracotta and metal casting to the weaving of silk brocades. A long tradition of technological skill and innovation lay behind the work of the architect Brunelleschi and the inventor Leonardo da Vinci. In classical studies and in those disciplines—history, poetry, moral philosophy —stimulated by the renewed interest in antiquity, Florentines were preeminent. The city's jurists, physicians, and theologians made significant contributions to their disciplines. The catalogues of the *Biblioteca Nazionale* describe thousands of manuscripts that indicate the broad range of Florentine cultural interests. These include copies of the Villani chronicles and Boccaccio's *Decameron;* French chivalric romances translated into the Italian vernacular; saints' lives and moral tracts; books on medicine and cuisine; Latin classics in the original and in translation. The list of works composed or copied by Florentine hands would be even longer and more diverse if certain categories—for example, heretical literature and occult writings —had not been systematically destroyed.

The ingredients which were fused together into Florence's cultural matrix derived from two distinct sources: the Graeco-Roman-Christian tradition, universal in scope, hierarchical and authoritarian in structure; and the vernacular tradition, which gave expression to the particular attitudes and values of this Tuscan community. The classic-Christian tradition was based upon the Latin language, upon the principles of Roman law, and upon certain philosophical concepts derived from Greek antiquity and reformulated in European monasteries, cathedral schools, and universities during the medieval centuries. This tradition was professional in its orientation; it trained—and imposed its values upon—theologians, lawyers, notaries, rhetoricians. Its educational organs were the grammar schools, the *studia* in the Florentine monasteries, and the universities. The vernacular tradition, on the other hand, was quite flexible and unstructured. Its modes of communication were largely oral and visual; its written form was not yet bound by rules of grammer and orthography. Both of these major traditions were divided into segments or disciplines, each with its educational method, its subject matter, and its professional concerns. From antiquity and the Christian tradition came the legal culture of Florence's lawyers and notaries, the classical culture of her humanists and certain of her artists, and the scholastic culture of her learned priests and monks. The vernacular tradition embraced the mercantile culture of the city's business community, the chivalric culture of her nobility and pseudo-nobility, and a cluster of more

obscure subcultures: those of the streets and slums, of the popular heresies (most notably the Fraticelli), and of the occult.

The most distinctive feature of Florentine intellectual life
was not its variety and complexity—which was matched, to
some degree, by Milan, Venice, and Naples—but rather the unusually close rapport between these cultural traditions. Contributing to this atmosphere of free communication was the
social structure, perhaps the most flexible of any major Italian
city. But another important factor was the towering figure of
Dante Alighieri. The poet represented a crucial stage in the
fusion of the universalist, hierarchical ideals of the classic-
Christian tradition with the parochial values and interests of the
local milieu. In the Florentine schools and *studia* (and perhaps
also at the University of Bologna), Dante had absorbed those
universal ideals which had been summarized so brilliantly by
Thomas Aquinas. The poet wrote scholastic treatises, and he
also composed essays praising the Christian virtues. His political ideas, his veneration for the Empire and the values of
ancient Rome, were likewise universal and hierarchical. Yet
his *Divine Comedy* was written in the local Tuscan dialect, not
in Latin. And although this work contains the universal concepts
of the classical and Christian traditions, it is also a Florentine
poem, replete with the particular values, emotions, and concerns of that community. The poet did not succeed in reconcil-
ing all of the contradictions between the two traditions, but his
genius enabled him to surmount these discordant elements, and
to create a magnificent synthesis combining ideal and reality,
the universal and the particular. He also established a lofty
standard of excellence, to serve as challenge and inspiration for
later generations of Florentine intellectuals.

In the realm of the visual arts, Giotto di Bondone (d. 1337)
filled a role similar to Dante's in literature. Giotto's subject matter was traditionally Christian; he learned to paint in the Byzantine style of the thirteenth century. His great contribution
to fresco painting was to humanize the wooden, stylized figures
of Byzantine art, to create scenes that were naturalistic and life-
like but also grandiose and monumental. His fresco cycle in
Padua of Christ's life and the scenes in S. Croce from the life

of St. Francis are supreme statements of these qualities in Giotto's art, worthy of comparison with the *Divine Comedy*. Certain attempts have been made to identify the sources of Giotto's inspiration and genius, for example, in the Franciscan emphasis upon Christ's humanity, and the striving for a more intense religious experience. Rather less persuasive is that interpretation which depicts him as a representative of the Florentine bourgeoisie, whose monumental human figures reflect the self-confidence of a rising social class, emancipating itself from subjection to the church and the feudal nobility. Giotto's fame during his lifetime was enormous, although his reputation declined during the second half of the fourteenth century. But his frescoes made a profound impact upon the revolutionary generation of Florentine artists in the early Quattocento, who recovered Giotto's sense of the monumental, which had disappeared from the Florentine art of the preceding age.

Complexity of social structure, variety of intellectual interests, a history of fruitful intercourse between different traditions—these are some factors which fostered cultural vitality and innovation in Florence. The aristocracy did not merely patronize art and learning; it was actively involved in the city's cultural life. Nearly every prominent family counted a lawyer and a cleric among its number; and by the middle of the fifteenth century, many houses—Strozzi, Corbinelli, Rossi, Medici, Davanzati, Alessandri—could also boast of a humanist scholar. The intellectual interests of many Florentines cut across cultural and disciplinary barriers. Cosimo de' Medici is a good example: banker, statesman, scholar, a friend and patron of humanists (Bruni, Niccoli, Marsuppini, Poggio), artists (Donatello, Brunelleschi, Michelozzo), and learned clerics (Ambrogio Traversari, Pope Nicholas V). The library of a wealthy merchant, Piero di Duccio Alberti, was inventoried in 1400; it contained a large number of business papers and ledgers, a book of hours, several Latin grammars and works by the classical authors Aesop, Cicero, Seneca, Eutropius, and Vigentius. A notary, Ser Matteo Gherardi, died in 1390, leaving a collection of legal treatises (decretals, commentaries, works on canon law), but also a nucleus of religious works (a book of homilies, a psalter, a prayer collection, and a Bible), and the writings of Aesop and Boethius. Lapo Mazzei's letters to Francesco Datini contain references to the Bible and to Christian authors (St. Augustine, St. Bernard, St. Francis, St. Thomas Aquinas), to ancient writers (Cicero, Seneca, Sallust, Horace, Livy, Vergil, Valerius Maximus, Boethius), and to the vernacular works of Dante, Jacopone da Todi, and the Vallombrosan hermit Giovanni dalle Celle. In a treatise on the subject of fortune written about 1460, Giovanni Rucellai incorporated citations from an unusually wide range of classical, Christian, and Italian authors. Aristotle, Epictetus, Sallust, Cicero, Seneca, St. Bernard, Dante, Petrarch, and a Florentine theologian, Leonardo Dati.

Communication between merchants, politicians, artists, and scholars was also facilitated by certain attitudes and conventions, to some degree institutionalized, of this society. Wealthy bankers and poor artisans sat together as equals in the Signoria, a political tradition which must have facilitated intellectual discourse between aristocratic patrons and the sculptors, painters and other craftsmen they employed to build their palaces and decorate their chapels. The open and candid discussions about the problems of cathedral construction (in which bankers, lawyers, friars, and craftsmen participated) also cut across social and professional barriers. Among the citizens invited to counsel the Signoria were men representing all of the major professions and occupations (with the sole exception of theology). These included the lawyers Filippo Corsini, Lorenzo Ridolfi, and Giuliano Davanzati; the physician Cristofano di Giorgio; the humanists Leonardo Bruni, Palla Strozzi, and Agnolo Pandolfini, who were thus provided with an arena for voicing their political opinions and for publicizing ideas and perspectives derived from their disciplines. This forum may have stimulated interest in classical antiquity, and thus contributed to Florence's precocious adoption of humanism as a moral and educational system.

Another device for promoting communication between men of diverse disciplines and cultural interests was the Florentine version of the salon. One of these meetings was described in the *Paradiso degli Alberti* by Giovanni da Prato; other groups gathered around the Augustinian friar Luigi Marsili, the humanist chancellor Coluccio Salutati, and the Camaldolese prior of S.

Maria degli Angeli, Ambrogio Traversari. Scholars have also discovered references to an informal gathering which met in the early 1400s under the Tettoio dei Pisani, a pavilion adjacent to the Piazza della Signoria, and another two decades later organized by the Augustinian scholars, Fra Evangelista of Pisa and Fra Girolamo of Naples.

Participants in these *convegni* came from every social class except the lowest, although the majority were either professional scholars and writers, or patricians with strong intellectual interests. Giovanni da Prato's assembly at the Villa Paradiso included himself, the son of a used-clothes dealer who had obtained a law degree at the University of Padua; Marsilio da S. Sophia, a distinguished professor of medicine; Guido, count of Poppi, scion of a noble family in the Casentino; several Florentine patricians—Alessandro Buondelmonti, Giovanni de' Ricci, and Guido del Palagio; and Luigi Marsili as the sole representative of the clergy. Only a few of the "most excellent and highly reputed men of this city" who frequented Marsili's discussions have been identified by name: Coluccio Salutati, Poggio Bracciolini, and three young Florentine patricians interested in classical studies: Niccolò Niccoli, Roberto de' Rossi, and Giovanni di Lorenzo. More patrician and secular in composition was the group of Greek enthusiasts who met with Ambrogio Traversari in the 1420s: Cosimo and Lorenzo de' Medici, Giannozzo Manetti, Leonardo Dati, Ugolino and Filippo Peruzzi, Franco Sacchetti, Bartolomeo Valori, and two friars, Fra Michele and Fra Jacopo Tornaquinci.

One important consequence of this intellectual cross-fertilization was the relatively open and tolerant cultural climate in Florence, in which no single tradition or professional caste became so powerful that it could dominate others. In some parts of Latin Europe (but not in Italy), the church had long maintained a cultural hegemony through its monopoly of education. In Florence and generally throughout the Italian peninsula, secular learning had flourished since the thirteenth century, thus providing an alternative to the schools and intellectual interests of the clergy. Theology was a respected discipline in Florence; it was taught both in the conventual *studia* and in the university. But its appeal was never strong, and it occupied a relatively low place in the hierarchy of Florentine intellectual concerns. Moreover, the church's role as cultural censor was quite firmly restricted by the state. The small number of heresy trials was due less to the orthodoxy of the populace than to the commune's restrictions upon the Inquisition. Supporters of the Fraticelli in the fourteenth century were rarely molested by the authorities, and the execution of a sorcerer condemned by the Inquisition in 1383 aroused widespread opposition. An anonymous chronicler remarked that "there was much discussion in the city, because no inquisitor in Florence had done anything similar for many years, and the bishop and the clergy and many doctors of canon law were opposed to this execution." A century later (1493), when a Franciscan preacher, Bernardino da Feltre, denounced the Florentine government for permitting the Jews to live in the city and engage in usury, he was expelled by the authorities.

In Italy, the most serious threat to cultural pluralism did not come from the church, but rather from the eminence which certain disciplines enjoyed in the universities, most notably in Bologna and Padua. Civil and canon lawyers dominated Bologna's intellectual life, while Padua was the preserve of the natural scientists, students of Aristotelean philosophy. Florence was saved from a similar fate by the chronic weakness of her university. The instruction in Greek offered by Manuel Chrysoloras in the 1390s did stimulate interest in classical studies and contributed to that wave of enthusiasm for the *studia humanitatis* in the Quattrocento. Yet, while humanism became the most potent intellectual force in Florence by the mid-fifteenth century, it did not oust the other disciplines. Nourished by their strong and viable traditions, and by their useful contributions to the community, they continued to thrive.

This analysis of the foundations of Florence's Renaissance culture has emphasized those social and institutional elements which promoted creativity and innovation. Another dimension of the problem is the identification of those particular qualities of mind and personality fostered by the Florentine historical experience. Throughout its history, this community had always existed precariously, and had engaged in perilous enterprises which made heavy demands upon its resources. Much of its wealth derived from participation in an international economy encompassing many markets and regions, and involving great risks. To protect itself, the city extended its control over much of Tuscany and thus aroused the enmity of its neighbors. Survival in this hostile and dangerous milieu required intelligence, astuteness, and fortitude. Within Florence itself, the competitive atmosphere and the high degree of social and economic mobility also made heavy demands upon the inhabitants. In balance, these pressures were constructive; they induced Florentines to sharpen their wits and to expand their intellectual horizons. These stimuli may also have played a part in the development of particular mental attributes: a sense of quality, and particularly of esthetic quality; and sensitivity to the distinctive, the particular, the unique.

The Florentine sense of quality was a product of the city's craft tradition and the exceptional skills of her artisans. The industrial and craft guilds had developed a system of quality control to protect their trades; every Florentine realized that the maintenance of high standards benefited the city's economy. This appreciation of quality, and a corresponding disdain for the shoddy and the inferior, became a characteristic feature of the Florentine mentality and mode of perception. It is revealed in this letter written by a lawyer, Rosso Orlandi, to a friend in Venice, Piero Davanzati, about a very small problem, the purchase of a piece of cloth:

I received your letter in which you instruct me to buy and send you twelve yards of good blue cloth. One of my neighbors is a good friend and a cloth expert. First we looked around in the cloth factories, where occasionally one may find some nice remnants at a discount, but we didn't see anything we liked. Then we visited all of the retail shops which sell for cash. It is not their custom to allow buyers to examine and compare the cloth of one shop with that of another. However, we did find a way to examine the finest and most beautiful cloth in each shop, and we also seized the opportunity to compare these pieces side by side. From them all, we chose a cloth from the shop of Zanobi di Ser Gino. There were none that were better woven or more beautifully dyed. Furthermore, the cloth was nearly a foot wider than the others, even after it had been washed and trimmed. Since the Florentine shearers do better work than those in Venice, I have had the cloth washed and trimmed here. When you see it, I believe that

you will be pleased with it. You will like it even better after you have
worn it for several months; for it is a cloth which will wear extremely
well.

The Florentine esthetic sense was derived from this appreciation for quality; it is stamped upon the physical city and upon
the rural landscape, fashioned by generations of men who
prized beauty. It is revealed too in contemporary writing, for
example, in a letter from a banker, Jacopo Pazzi, to his friend
Filippo Strozzi in Naples (1464), thanking him for a consignment of gold coins: "They are so beautiful that they give me
great pleasure, because I love coins which are well designed; and
you know that the more beautiful things are, the more they are
cherished." Writing in his diary in the 1460s, Giovanni Rucellai
described "the most attractive and pleasing aspects" of his villa
at Quarachi, a few miles west of Florence near the Arno. He
mentioned the house, the garden planted with fruit trees, the
fish pond surrounded by fir trees, and another wooded grove at
the edge of the garden adjacent to the road. "This park is a
source of great consolation," Rucellai wrote, "not only to ourselves and our neighbors, but also to strangers and travelers
who pass by during the heat of summer . . . who can refresh
themselves with the clear and tasty water. . . . And no traveler
passes who does not stop for a quarter of an hour to view the
garden filled with beautiful plants. So I feel that the creation of
this park . . . was a very worthy enterprise." Also illustrating the
Florentine concern for esthetic values is a document in the files
of the republic's diplomatic correspondence. During a crucial
period of the Milanese war (December 1400), the Signoria
wrote to the general of the Camaldolese order concerning the
sale of a grove of fir trees which were to be cut down, near the
ancient monastery of Camaldoli in the Apennines. Expressing
their shock and dismay at this vandalism, the priors reminded
the general that the trees had been planted and nourished by his
predecessors "for the consolation of the hermits and the admiration of the visitors." Four years later (September 1404) the commune again raised this issue, urging the general to cease the
despoliation of the monastic patrimony, whose beauty was as
pleasing to God as to man.

Florentines were unusually sensitive to physical environment, and they possessed a rare talent for communicating their perceptions. They were also intensely aware of other men: their features and habits, their character, their virtues and vices. This curiosity led them ultimately to develop an introspective interest in themselves. Professor Kristeller has noted that humanist writing is characterized by "the tendency to express, and to consider worth expressing, the concrete uniqueness of one's feelings, opinions, experiences and surroundings. . . ." These qualities are displayed in Latin treatises and letters, and also in the diaries and private correspondence of ordinary Florentines. Even such prosaic documents as tax declarations are frequently couched in very expressive language, as they describe the topography of a hill farm or the antipathetic character of a surly peasant. This appreciation of the concrete, the specific, and the unique was fostered not only by the literature of antiquity, but also by the social and intellectual climate of Renaissance Florence.

CULTURAL PATRONAGE IN RENAISSANCE FLORENCE: STRUCTURES, MOTIVATIONS, TRENDS

Renaissance culture, so the textbooks assert, was subsidized by a new social class, the urban bourgeoisie. Replacing the nobility and the clergy as the dominant group in society, the bourgeoisie also supplanted them in their traditional role as patrons of culture. With the wealth gained from their mercantile, banking, and industrial enterprises, they were able to hire the poets, scholars, and artists whose brilliant achievements brought fame and glory to them and their city. Through these intellectuals and artists, their employees and agents, the bourgeoisie were able to express their own ideals and values. Stated so simply and crudely, this analysis is valid, but it does require elaboration, qualification, and refinement. One must examine the methods and techniques by which this society encouraged and nourished—materially and psychologically—its intellectuals. How was talent recognized and merit rewarded? What were the peculiar and unique opportunities Florence offered for creative achievement? How effectively were the city's intellectual resources exploited, and how much talent was attracted from abroad? Finally, how were changes in the structure and values of the society reflected in different forms of patronage?

Intellectual activity in medieval and Renaissance Florence was predominantly—almost exclusively—functional; it was related to specific vocational and professional purposes, and directed toward the satisfaction of social needs. The educational system was organized to train some boys for mercantile careers and others for professional careers in law, the notarial discipline, medicine, and theology. In his statistical survey of Florence prior to the Black Death, Giovanni Villani cites some interesting figures on school enrollment. In a population of approximately 100,000, between 8000 and 10,000 youths were enrolled in the city's private schools. While the majority attended elementary schools, which taught the rudiments of the vernacular, 1000 advanced students went to special schools to learn the mathematics necessary for a business career, and another 500 enrolled in preprofessional academies which taught Latin grammar, rhetoric, and logic. Although these figures may be inflated, they do indicate the great value attached to education in Florence, and also the unusually high literacy rate, perhaps one-fourth or one-third of the male population. A basic knowledge of reading, writing, and arithmetic was an essential prerequisite for a business career, even in one of the artisan trades. An incident described in the protocols of the Merchants' Court illustrates this recognition of the value of education among the city's underprivileged. A young emigrant from the Perugian *contado*, Antonio di Manno, instituted a lawsuit for the recovery of a gold florin which he had paid in advance for some elementary instruction. Antonio worked as an apprentice in a shoemaker's shop where a fellow employee, Miniato, agreed to teach him reading and writing for a year, but then broke his promise when he left the shop.

The size and quality of Florence's educational system (which included conventual *studia* and a university as well as primary and secondary schools) was one factor in the city's ability to attract talent from abroad. Alongside the institutions which provided formal schooling were the guilds with their system of instruction for apprentices. Young artists like Giotto from the

Mugello and Masaccio from S. Giovanni Valdarno came to Florence to study in the workshops of the great masters, to live and work in a stimulating intellectual environment, and to gain wealth and fame in a community which subsidized the arts. The city's attraction for men with professional training is documented by the unending flow of petitions from foreign lawyers, notaries, and physicians who sought Florentine citizenship. In 1381 a young physician, Ugolino of Montecatini, had just begun his professional career in Pisa, where he had a small practice and a lectureship in the university. He was then invited to become the town physician of Pescia in the Valdinievole. The most compelling reason for abandoning his teaching post at Pisa to accept this offer was the opportunity to pursue his medical studies in Florence, to take part in disputations, and to enlarge his experience. Ugolino admitted that the move to Pescia would not redound to his honor, but he believed that it would benefit his career. Apparently, his ultimate goal was to practice medicine in Florence and lecture in the university, but he was realistic about the difficulties confronting him. It required years to build a medical reputation, and then the physician had to endure the jealousy of his colleagues. But Ugolino was willing to accept the challenge of the metropolis, aware that "our profession is one of those influenced by fortune." In 1429, a young Lucchese lawyer, Filippo Balducci, was contemplating a move to Florence from Siena, where he taught and practiced law. To a Florentine acquaintance, he wrote: "Since I have always had a great affection for that magnificent and glorious city, which I consider one of the three [greatest] in the world, I would rather be there than here, even though I will earn less."

Public recognition of distinguished achievement in Florence took various forms. The most tangible mark of distinction was the bestowal of a public office, a university professorship, or an artistic commission upon the meritorious, and these were distributed quite generously to prominent scholars and artists. In 1375, Coluccio Salutati became the first humanist chancellor of the republic; his successors in that office were men of great learning and reputation: Leonardo Bruni, Poggio Bracciolini, Carlo Marsuppini. In 1300, the commune granted a tax exemption to the architect Arnolfo di Cambio, "since this master is the most renowned and the most expert in church construction of any other in these parts; and that through his industry, experience and genius, the Florentine commune . . . from the magnificent beginning of this church . . . hopes to have the most beautiful and the most honorable cathedral in Tuscany." A century and a half later, Leonardo Bruni and Poggio Bracciolini obtained similar exemptions; Poggio had claimed that "he cannot pay the assessments levied against citizens who have profited from trade and the emoluments of public service, since he plans to devote all of his energies to study. . . ." Although Filippo Brunelleschi obtained no tax exemption from the state, he did receive a rare public acknowledgement of his talent. Described in a provision of June 1421 as a "man of the most perspicacious intelligence and admirable industry," he was granted a three-year patent on a boat he had invented, which apparently reduced the costs of transporting goods on the Arno. In reserving all benefits for this invention to Brunelleschi, the law stated that its objective was to prevent "the fruits of his talents and virtue from accruing to another," and also "to stimulate him to greater activity and even more subtle investigations. . . ."

During his lifetime, Dante Alighieri received no accolades from his native city, but after the poet's death, the Florentines made some belated gestures of apology. Giovanni Villani wrote that "because of the virtues and knowledge and worthiness of this citizen, it seems proper to grant him perpetual memory in our chronicle, even though his own noble works, which he has left to us in writing, bear witness to him and bring renown to our city." Giovanni Boccaccio's appointment (1373) as the commune's official lecturer on the *Divine Comedy* was an unprecedented sign of Dante's exalted reputation. Twenty-three years later, the councils passed a law authorizing the officials in charge of the cathedral to arrange for the return of the bodies of five illustrious Florentines who had died and been buried abroad. Munificent tombs were planned for these men in the cathedral, where no other interments were to be permitted. Four of the charter members of this Pantheon—Dante, Petrarch, Boccaccio, and Zanobi da Strada—were literary men, and the fifth was a distinguished lawyer named Accursius (d. 1260?) who taught for many years in the University of Bologna. This project failed completely, for the guardians of these bodies refused to surrender them. In 1430, the Signoria again appealed to the lord of Ravenna for Dante's remains. "Our people," so the official letter read, "harbor a singular and particular affection for the glorious and undying memory of that most excellent and renowned poet, Dante Alighieri; the fame of this man is such that it redounds to the praise and splendor of our city. . . ."

Not every distinguished citizen remained home to adorn his native city with his talents. Petrarch was never attracted to Florence, nor was Boccaccio an enthusiastic admirer of the city. After 1400, however, the pendulum swung quite decisively in Florence's favor, and during the first half of the Quattrocento, her cultural magnetism was particularly intense. Native artists and writers—Masaccio, Brunelleschi, Ghiberti, Manetti—stayed home and made only brief excursions abroad, while their ranks were supplemented by foreigners: Bruni, Poggio Bracciolini, Gentile da Fabriano. S. Croce, not the cathedral, became Florence's Pantheon, and the tombs in that Franciscan basilica are visual evidence of the magnitude of Florentine genius, and also of the city's inability to retain and exploit that genius fully. Dante, Petrarch, and Boccaccio are still missing, although Dante is commemorated by an ugly modern cenotaph. From an esthetic viewpoint, the two most noteworthy tombs are those of the humanists Bruni and Marsuppini, both of whom received imposing state funerals. Lorenzo Ghiberti, Niccolò Machiavelli, and Michelangelo are all buried in S. Croce, although Michelangelo died where he had lived and worked, in Rome. His body was spirited away to Florence by agents of Duke Cosimo I. Some distinguished Florentines of the Quattrocento are not interred in S. Croce. These include Palla Strozzi, who died in Padua while living in involuntary exile, Leon Battista Alberti, who died in Rome in 1472, and Leonardo da Vinci, who abandoned both Florence and Italy to spend his last years at the French court of Francis I.

The official recognition of intellectual and artistic distinction was one aspect of the collective, public nature of artistic and scholarly patronage in early Renaissance Florence. The great architectural monuments of the fourteenth and fifteenth centuries were supervised by commissions of *operai* selected by the guilds. In 1402, Lorenzo Ghiberti won a commission for the Baptistery doors in a public competition organized by the consuls of the Calimala guild, and judged by a special committee of thirty-four painters, sculptors, and goldsmiths. In the realm of letters and scholarship, official patronage was also important and useful, generally assuming the form of a communal office or a university professorship. The bestowal of the chancellor's office upon distinguished humanists like Salutati and Bruni was a reward for their fame and reputation, as well as payment for services rendered to the republic. By the middle of the fifteenth century, however, public subsidy of culture was declining, and the role of the private patron, and of culture created exclusively for private needs, now assumed greater importance than before. This trend can be charted in two quite different contexts: in the history of the Florentine Studio, and in Medicean patronage of the arts.

The fortunes of the city's major institution of higher learning provide a valuable corrective to the idealized picture of this society as totally committed to intellectual distinction, and willing to make heavy sacrifices to achieve and maintain excellence. From the beginning, Florence's efforts to create a university of the first rank met with very limited success. In 1321, a *studium generale* was established by the commune; it never flourished and ceased to function in the 1330s. But even before the Black Death had run its course, a courageous and imaginative Signoria enacted a decree (August 26, 1348) which authorized the reopening of the Studio, and bravely proclaimed that "from the study of the sciences, the city of Florence will receive an increase in honors and a full measure of wealth. . . ." Although the circumstances of its foundation could not have been less promising, the university did survive and gradually developed a modest reputation. But its existence was never secure, and it limped along on the rather meager resources which the commune grudgingly provided. Records of the deliberations on the university's budget in the 1360s reveal that some citizens doubted whether the school was worth its cost. During its most flourishing period, in the 1380s, the university operated with a substantial budget of 3000 florins, which paid for a staff of twenty-four professors. But one consequence of the debilitating wars with

Giangaleazzo Visconti was the closing of the university in 1406; it did not reopen again until 1413. Thereafter, its budget was repeatedly cut during the Milanese wars of the 1420s; it was finally reduced to 200 florins in 1426. Four years later, the Studio governors candidly admitted that the university was in a parlous state. "It grieves us sorely," they announced, "that this glorious republic, which has surpassed the rest of Italy and all previous centuries in beauty and splendor, should be surpassed in this one respect by some of our neighboring cities, which in every other way are inferior to us."

This failure of the university to achieve the distinction which its founders and supporters envisaged is perhaps the crucial factor in the reluctance of Florence's ruling class to provide adequate and sustained support. The solid reputations of Bologna and Padua were never really challenged by the Studio, and shrewd politicians may have realized that no amount of money would change that fact. Patrician interests were not affected adversely by the mediocre quality of Studio instruction; wealthy citizens could send their sons to other Italian universities, and particularly to Bologna, to acquire the skills and the degrees needed to further their professional careers. Also contributing to the declining importance of the university was the tendency, in Florence and elsewhere, for humanistic studies—rhetoric, moral philosophy, poetry—to flourish outside of the university. Although these subjects were offered regularly in the Studio, occasionally by such distinguished scholars as Chrysoloras, Filelfo and Marsuppini, most teaching in the humanities occurred in a private context: tutors instructing students in their homes, scholars assembling in monasteries or in private palaces to discuss classical texts. Like other facets of patrician life in Quattrocento Florence, learning and education were becoming more private, aristocratic, and exclusive.

The most renowned institution of higher learning in Florence in the second half of the fifteenth century was not the Studio, but the Platonic Academy, an informal coterie of scholars and students united by an interest in Platonic philosophy. Its leader was Marsilio Ficino, whose translations of Platonic writings were subsidized by the Medici. The Academy had a geographical focus in Ficino's villa at Careggi outside of Florence, but it possessed no formal organization, nor did it provide any regular instruction. Its only scheduled events were irregular lectures by Ficino and occasional banquets and symposia held infrequently at the Careggi villa. Ficino did provide loose and informal guidance to his disciples and to visiting scholars like Pico della Mirandola and Jacques Lefèvre d'Étaples. But the essential qualities of this community were privacy, intimacy, and learning pursued for its own sake, without any concern for vocational or practical benefits.

This shift in the form and object of patronage from the public-corporate to the private sphere also occurred in the plastic arts. Communal and guild patronage was at its height between 1375 and 1425, when the Loggia dei Lanzi and the cathedral dome were built, when guilds were commissioning Baptistery doors and statues for Orsanmichele and erecting new headquarters for themselves. In these decades, too, private subsidy of the arts was largely (although not exclusively) directed toward public enterprises. The first architectural projects financed by Cosimo de' Medici were reconstructions of churches and monasteries: S. Lorenzo, S. Marco, the Badia of Fiesole, and the church of S. Francesco in Bosco in the Mugello. This pattern was sanctioned by tradition, and so too was its collective form, since other families were involved in several of these projects. If only because of his superior resources, Cosimo's voice in these collective enterprises tended to predominate; S. Lorenzo, for example, was finally completed with Medici money twenty years after the project had been initiated. Cosimo's reluctance to finish this work earlier was apparently due to his unwillingness to appear too bold and ambitious as a patron. His plan to rebuild S. Marco was thwarted when other families with burial rights in the convent refused to surrender them.

Despite these limitations imposed upon Cosimo's patronage by community sentiment and tradition, and by his own sense of propriety, his total contribution was impressive. His greatest achievement was, of course, the palace on the Via Larga, and it was within the confines of that structure that later Medici generations satisfied their esthetic needs. Lorenzo was recognized as the premier connoisseur of the arts in Italy, and his advice on painters and architects was sought by princes throughout the peninsula. As one dimension of his foreign policy, he sent Florentine artists to work for those rulers whose favor he desired. But Lorenzo's material subsidy of the arts in Florence was niggardly. Most of his money for this purpose was spent not on ecclesiastical or civic projects, but on his private collection of precious gems and antique art. This had been assembled for his enjoyment, and for that of close friends and visiting dignitaries, whose appreciation of the gesture might be politically advantageous as well as personally gratifying. Lorenzo's collection of *objets d'art* was the esthetic counterpart of the Platonic Academy.

FLORENTINE HUMANISM: ITS EVOLUTION AND SIGNIFICANCE

From 1380 to 1450, the central theme in Florentine cultural history is the emergence of classical antiquity as the major source, focus, and inspiration of intellectual life. These years witnessed the development of an educational curriculum founded upon the *studia humanitatis,* the subjects of grammar, rhetoric, poetry, history, and moral philosophy which had formed the basis of classical education, but which had been changed and modified—although never entirely rejected—by the different needs and interests of the medieval world. This phenomenon, usually described as the "rise of humanism," occurred in an atmosphere of great enthusiasm for classical literature, both Latin and Greek, similar in its intensity to the excitement created in twelfth-century France by the discovery of Aristotelean logic and its application to theological problems. Some manifestations of the rise of humanism are the striking increase in the number of students pursuing classical studies, the formation of groups linked by their common interest in the writings of antiquity, and the intensive search for unknown manuscripts of ancient authors. Progress in humanistic studies can also be measured by the perfection of techniques for the study of classical texts, and greater knowledge of the character of Greek and Roman civilization. Another dimension of Florentine humanism was the broadening of classical interests from purely literary sources to other disciplines: to architecture and sculpture, to music, to mathematics and the physical sciences. Its most controversial aspect, which has been much discussed and debated, concerns its influence upon contemporary values, and its role in stimulating the changes in the ways that Florentines viewed their world and themselves.

This interest in classical antiquity, and acquaintance with its literary heritage, was not a wholly new phenomenon; it had a long and continuous history extending back to classical times. Medieval Europe had never lost its fascination for ancient Rome, nor had it ever abandoned its study of Roman literature. Generations of students destined for ecclesiastical careers learned to read Latin by studying passages from Livy and Horace in medieval grammars. This sympathetic interest in the classical past was strongest in Italy, whose natives took pride in their descent from the ancient Romans. In their studies of Roman law, the beginnings of which can be traced back to Bologna in the eleventh century, Italian legal scholars became acquainted not only with the codes and digests, but also with the political and institutional history of republican and imperial Rome. And while the Bologna lawyers were immersing themselves in the intricacies of Justinian's Code, other young men were preparing for notarial careers, the basic discipline for which was rhetoric. These students read Cicero and Livy, and while their future professional activity was devoted to such prosaic tasks as the composition of wills, deeds of sale, and mercantile contracts, some continued their study of the classics as an avocation.

The foundations for a strong interest in the ancient world and its literature were thus well established in the fourteenth century, and it was upon these foundations that Petrarch fashioned his crusade for the "new learning." He was born in Arezzo in 1304, the son of an exiled Florentine notary who later found a position in the papal court at Avignon. Sent to Bologna to study law, Petrarch abandoned that discipline in favor of poetry; it was as a writer of verse in the Tuscan vernacular that he first gained an Italian reputation. His lyrics were enormously popular, and they exercised a profound and lasting influence upon the writing of poetry, not only in Italy, but also in France and England. Early in his student career, Petrarch had developed a strong enthusiasm for the works of Latin authors, Cicero in particular, and he became the most influential spokesman for the new learning and its staunchest defender against critics. During his lifetime and largely as a result of his efforts, the study of the classics became a controversial issue in the Italian scholarly world. It also exhibited the characteristics of a cult, with disciples, a program, and a strong proselytizing impulse.

A crucial figure in Florence's development as a center of the new learning was Coluccio Salutati, a notary from the village of Stignano (in the Valdinievole between Lucca and Pistoia), who càme to Florence in 1375 to accept the post of chancellor of the republic. He held that important office until his death in 1406, becoming a powerful and influential statesman and a respected member of the patriciate. Salutati's entrenched position in Florentine society was an important factor in his successful promotion of humanism. Although Petrarch achieved much greater fame as a writer, he never lived and worked in Florence, and so his influence there was limited. Less brilliant intellectually, and less renowned in the Italian literary world, Salutati was nevertheless able to achieve more for classical studies in Florence.

Salutati was a member of that group of scholars and citizen savants who met in the Augustinian convent of S. Spirito under the aegis of Luigi Marsili to discuss moral and philosophical issues. After Marsili's death in 1394, Salutati became the titular leader of this group, and the leading champion of the classics in Florence. His disciples includes some of the leading humanistic scholars of the next generation—Leonardo Bruni, Pietro Paul Vergerio, Poggio Bracciolini—and also a group of young Florentine patricians whom he encouraged to pursue classical studies and who regarded him as their patron and mentor: Niccolò Niccoli, Angelo Corbinelli, Roberto de' Rossi, Cino Rinuccini. For these men, Salutati was an example and a secure foundation upon which to build their scholarly and literary interests. Under his guidance and patronage, they met regularly to discuss their problems. They borrowed books from the chancellor's library, probably the best private collection of classical works in Florence, and widened their acquaintance with the literature of antiquity. The chancellor was the bridge between the world of learning and scholarship and the world of commerce and politics.

Aspiring humanists could point to Salutati's fame and reputation, his political influence and social standing, in arguments with their elders who might question the value of classical studies. Vespasiano da Bisticci described one such skeptic, the merchant Andrea de' Pazzi who "knew little of learning, thought it to be of little value, and had no desire that his son [Piero] should spend time over it."

Through his professional career and his writings, Salutati endeavored to make classical studies relevant to the world in which he lived. His state letters, written in a style considered elegant and Ciceronian for the time, and replete with classical allusions, served as models for Italian chancery correspondence. According to a widely circulated story, Giangaleazzo Visconti once said that a Salutati letter was worth an army of 1000 lances. This hyperbolic statement does indicate the inflated importance which was attached to humanist talents employed for political purposes. In 1394, the Florentine Signoria requested the lord of Padua, Francesco da Carrara, to refrain from sending diplomatic notes in the vernacular, "for either through some stylistic flaw or a secretary's error, your letters might be misinterpreted. . . ." The value of rhetorical training for members of an ambassadorial mission had long been recognized, and the commune paid increasing attention to this qualification in making ambassadorial appointments. The *Consulte e Pratiche* records provide further evidence of the impact of rhetoric upon political thinking and practice. The early volumes of this source, compiled in the middle decades of the Trecento, contain very short and pithy summaries of speeches, which suggests both oratorial brevity and the notary's reluctance or inability to write long and detailed summaries. Coinciding with Salutati's tenure as Florentine chancellor, the accounts of these speeches were greatly expanded, written in a more elegant style, and occasionally embellished by classical references and quotations. By the beginning of the fifteenth century, if not earlier, oral eloquence was a significant political asset, although it occasionally prompted some criticism, illustrated by Gino Capponi's caustic remark that a speech of Piero Baroncelli "was very pretty but lacking in substance."

Salutati's social and cultural values have been subjects of

scholarly controversy. The difficulties arise primarily from certain contradictions in his writings, and other discrepancies between his words and his actions. In his defense of classical studies, he was quite consistent, repeating arguments which had been formulated earlier to justify the reading of pagan literature. He insisted that the concern of many classical authors with moral problems legitimized their study by Christian scholars. But on other issues, Salutati was ambiguous and contradictory. His chancery correspondence contained some very eloquent statements eulogizing political freedom and liberty, praising republican government in Florence and condemning the despotism of Milan. However, in his treatise *De tyranno*, he argued that monarchy is the best form of government, and he condoned the destruction of the Roman republic by Caesar. His essay, *De seculo et religione*, was a restatement of an old medieval theme, the superiority of the monastic life of solitude and prayer. Yet in private letters to friends, Salutati developed a coherent and persuasive justification for the "active life" which he led. In another letter, Salutati was severely critical of a man who had abandoned his literary studies to pursue a notarial career to improve his economic circumstances. This letter idealized the figure of the indigent scholar intent only upon learning, and it contrasts sharply with Salutati's own professional career, which brought him wealth and high social rank.

The inconsistencies and contradictions in Salutati's writings appear to reflect the doubts and confusions of his generation, searching for meaningful values. The most comprehensive analysis of this problem is Hans Baron's book, *The Crisis of the Early Italian Renaissance*. Baron argues that a new cultural phenomenon, civic humanism, came into being in Florence after 1400. Although its classical orientation was inherited from Trecento scholars, its outlook and values differed significantly from those espoused by Petrarch and Salutati. The origins of civic humanism are to be found in the Florentine political scene around 1400 and, more specifically, in the threat to the city's independence posed by Giangaleazzo Visconti. This crisis had a profound impact upon the Florentine mentality. It strengthened the citizenry's commitment to its republican government and to the ideals of liberty and freedom traditionally associated with that government. The humanists became the leading exponents of those political values, the most articulate propagandists for Florentine republicanism. They developed a new interpretation of Florentine history based upon the city's founding by Sulla when the Roman republic still flourished (and not by Caesar, who destroyed the republic). And in their writings and speeches, the humanists also formulated an ideology for the Florentine citizenry which, while derived from classical sources, was also firmly rooted in the realities of the city's experience. This ideology exalted the civic virtues of participation in public affairs, the concept of the "active life" pursued by merchants and statesmen, as opposed to the contemplative life of ascetics and scholars. Furthermore, it viewed the acquisition of wealth not as an impediment to knowledge and salvation, but instead as a resource to be used in the promotion of learning and morality.

This rough summary of the Baron thesis does not do justice to the richness and complexity of the author's analysis, nor to his vast erudition, which can only be appreciated by a careful reading of his works. The thesis rests upon certain premises and assumptions which are not clearly articulated in his writing or in much of the criticism which his arguments have stimulated. Perhaps the most striking feature of his interpretation is the sharpness of the distinction between the two stages of humanism. Separating Salutati, the spokesman for the older humanism dominated by medieval preoccupations and values, and Leonardo Bruni, the voice of the new civic humanism, is a generational gulf which forms the dividing line between medieval and Renaissance Florence. Baron is committed to a sociological view of culture, and he views intellectual innovation as a direct response to change in the material world. By dating, as precisely and accurately as possible, the writings of Florentine humanists around 1400, he has sought to demonstrate that the political crisis of 1402 had an immediate and profound impact upon their ideas. Also underlying Baron's interpretation of Florentine culture is the concept, which is clearly formulated in Von Martin's *Sociology of the Renaissance*, of a dominant social class which expresses the values and ideals of the whole society.

Criticism of Baron's interpretation has focused upon his concept of civic humanism, and his theory of intellectual change as a response to political crisis. A recent article by Jerrold Seigel (*Past and Present*, No. 34, July 1966) illustrates the direction and tone of this criticism and develops a very different theory about the historical development of Florentine humanism. Much of Seigel's argument is concerned with the chronology of Bruni's early writings; he believes that two important treatises, the *Laudatio Florentinae Urbis* and the *Dialogi ad Petrum Istrum,* were written prior to 1402 and thus were not influenced by the crisis of that year. Seigel concludes that Bruni's motives for composing these treatises were neither political nor ideological, but professional and practical. Bruni was exhibiting his rhetorical skills; he was demonstrating that he could develop eloquent and persuasive arguments on both sides of an issue, as he does in the *Dialogi.* By writing these laudatory treatises, Seigel further suggests, Bruni may have hoped to obtain a position in the Florentine chancery under Salutati. Seigel then surveys the development of Florentine humanism around 1400 and concludes that humanism was not affected significantly by social and political conditions. Changes which occurred in humanist thinking were internal, inspired by new attitudes and viewpoints arising from the rhetorical tradition, and not as a response to outside stimuli. Instead of viewing ideas as the product of specific historical events or circumstances, Seigel prefers to treat them as developing within a particular intellectual tradition or discipline. He emphasizes the occupational differences, the professional castes —lawyers, humanists, theologians—and suggests that men in these fields pursued their interests quite independently, as untouched by developments in other disciplines or professions as by social upheaval or political crisis.

The central issue in this debate is the nature of the relationship between ideas and experience. Although quite sympathetic to Baron's conception of this relationship, the author is not persuaded by every part of his analysis. One can accept his thesis that a fundamental change in humanist values and perception occurred in the early Quattrocento, and still be skeptical of his explanation for this intellectual revolution. Although the Milanese threat to Florentine independence was certainly a factor in this mental and psychological readjustment, it was not the sole—or perhaps even the most important—stimulus. The

Consulte e Pratiche protocols, those records of deliberations by the Florentine political class, furnish some clues to the state of the civic mind in the early Quattrocento. While not conclusive, the evidence from these protocols suggests that the most critical moments in these "crisis" years did not occur during the Milanese wars, but a decade later, during Florence's struggles with Genoa and King Ladislaus of Naples (1409–1414). A significant aspect of political discussion in these years is its critical and introspective quality, its harsh and bitter judgment of Florentine institutions, practices, and attitudes which—so the blunt and candid critics assert—were responsible for the city's perilous condition. In these deliberations, the traditional appeals to defend Florentine liberty and republican institutions were supplemented by a tough and realistic appraisal of the flaws in those institutions, and a demand for reform.

These protocols support the hypothesis that Florence's cultural revolution of the early Quattrocento was not simply a response to a particular moment of crisis, a specific catalytic event; it was a gradual process stimulated by several factors and circumstances, both internal and external, which impelled Florentines to examine themselves more objectively and realistically. The origins of this cultural revolution should not be sought in Florence's status as a beleaguered republican city, but in the particular character of this society and its political traditions, which facilitated communication between intellectuals, merchants, and statesmen, and which provided a unique forum for the spread of new ideas and opinions. From these institutions and circumstances, there developed that symbiotic bond, so peculiarly Florentine, between the worlds of thought and action. Unusually sensitive to their society and its needs, the humanists of Bruni's generation exploited the literary resources of their discipline to provide Florentines with the techniques and the materials for reexamining themselves, their values and goals.

One of the most important humanist tools was a new historical perspective which—as Hans Baron has shown—was developed by Leonardo Bruni. Whereas medieval historical thinking was universal in scope and teleological in character, concerned with tracing the implementation of the divine plan, Bruni's historical outlook was temporal, secular, and particular. In his judgment, the historical experience of Florence and republican Rome merited the highest praise, for these communities had created the optimum conditions for human existence, the pursuit of an active civic life. The temporal existence of these cities was justified not by any reference to a divine plan, but in terms of their secular achievements. Moreover, the historical record of that experience provided a model for emulation and a framework by which human actions could be comprehended and judged. The first documented utilization of this perspective in political deliberations occurred in the spring of 1413, during the war with Ladislaus. Messer Piero Beccanugi made this statement, the first of its kind recorded in the extant protocols: "To administer public affairs intelligently, it is essential to look to the past [for guidance] to provide for the present and the future." Thereafter, the appeal to historical example, as justification for a particular policy or viewpoint, became a standard feature of political discussion. Most commonly cited were events from the Florentine past, embracing not only recent occurrences familiar to every citizen, but others going back nearly a century: the dictatorship of the Duke of Athens in 1342–1343, the war with Pisa in the 1360s, Emperor Charles IV's invasion of Tuscany in 1368. It is perhaps significant that the protocols contain several references to Florence's wars with Giangaleazzo, but none that points specifically to the crisis of 1402. Speakers also utilized the sources of classical antiquity. Messer Filippo Corsini cited events from the Punic wars—the massacre of the Roman army at Cannae and the siege of Saguntum—to bolster his arguments concerning Florentine policy toward Ladislaus. Messer Rinaldo Gianfigliazzi quoted Seneca: "Only that which is honest is good," and the example of the Spartan king Lycurgus who "in promulgating laws stated that public affairs are properly directed by the few with the authority of the many."

Another example of humanist influence upon Florentine political thinking, and upon policy, was the radical transformation of the city's self-image in the early fifteenth century. Although Trecento Florence had many cosmopolitan features, its inhabitants were quite insular and parochial in their outlook: fearful of the outside world, suspicious of all foreigners, and of distinguished visitors in particular. From 1273 to 1419, no pope or emperor came to Florence; princes and prelates were frequently rebuffed wren they sought permission to visit the city. The first signs of a change in this defensive attitude are visible in the deliberations of 1407, in which a few speakers proposed Florence as the site for an ecumenical council designed to end the Schism which had divided Latin Christendom for thirty years. This idea disturbed many citizens, who did not enjoy the prospect of their city overrun by foreigners, and sheltering a large group of ecclesiastical and secular dignitaries. Advocates of the council argued that God would reward those devout Christians who had contributed to the healing of the Schism; they asserted, too, that Florence's reputation would be enhanced throughout Christendom. One speaker, Antonio Alessandri, claimed that nothing would gain greater merit in the eyes of God, and greater fame among men, than to assemble a council in Florence to restore church unity. This argument added a new dimension to the idea that civic fame could be achieved not only by the construction of magnificent cathedrals and palaces or through the exploits of famous sons, but also by creating a setting for a major historical event. Here in embryonic form is the vision of Florence described by many Quattrocento humanists: a city known and admired throughout the civilized world, an international city. Pisa, not Florence, was finally chosen as the site for the ill-fated council of 1409. But those Florentines who had developed this new and enlarged vision of their city were rewarded in 1438, when Pope Eugenius IV transferred the council, assembled to reunite the Greek and Latin churches, from Ferrara to Florence.

The records of the republic's deliberations thus provide some clues to the movement of new attitudes and values, new modes of perception, from the realm of ideas to the world of action, from the *vita contemplativa* to the *vita attiva*. As a result of fundamental changes in educational method and philosophy, these values became more firmly established in the city. Since Dante's time, classical studies had attracted a minority of Florentine students, but after 1400 the *studia humanitatis* became the core and foundation of the aristocracy's academic curriculum. In his biography of Filippo Brunelleschi, Antonio Manetti noted that when Filippo was a boy (he was born in 1377), "few persons among those who did not expect to become doctors, lawyers or priests were given literary training [i.e., instruction in Latin]." But in his memoirs written about 1420, the merchant Giovanni Morelli prescribed an academic program for his sons which contained such traditional features as reading, writing, mathematics, and the Bible, but also a surprising emphasis upon the classics:

> Every day for at least an hour, read Vergil, Boethius, Seneca and other authors. . . . Begin your study with Vergil. . . . Then spend some time with Boethius, with Dante and the other poets, with Tully [Cicero] who will teach you to speak perfectly, with Aristotle who will instruct you in philosophy. . . . Read and study the Bible; learn about the great and holy acts which our Lord God accomplished through the prophets; you will be fully instructed in the faith and in the coming of God's son. Your spirit will gain consolation and joy. You will be contemptuous of the world and you will have no concern for what may happen to you.

It is instructive to compare this passage with Leon Battista Alberti's views on education contained in his treatise on the family (1435). Alberti based his curriculum exclusively upon classical authors (Cicero, Livy, Sallust); he did not mention the Bible or any work by a Christian author. These Latin writers were the foundations of his own education, and during his lifetime (he died in 1466), they formed the essential academic diet for the children of the Florentine aristocracy.

THE ARTISTIC REVOLUTION

Coinciding with, and closely linked to the emergence of humanism as the premier intellectual concern in early Quattrocento Florence were developments in the plastic arts which marked the beginnings of a new style. A distinctive feature of this artistic revolution was the revived interest in ancient art, and the intensive study of those physical remnants of classical antiquity which had survived the ravages of time. From this investigation, Florentine artists rediscovered the formulas and principles that had guided the buildings and sculptors of the ancient world. And in painting, the medium for which no ancient examples had survived, the Florentines developed particular techniques to create a more realistic image of the physical world. As the humanists had discovered and exploited the dimension of time as an essential element in their mode of perception, so the artists used perspective and proportion to organize space in a manner which expressed their particular view of reality.

In contrast to the humanistic movement, which is amply documented, very little evidence concerning the artistic revolution has survived, either in written or plastic form. Art historians have been very diligent in combing archives and libraries for contemporary documents—letters, commissions, tax records —that throw light upon this development, and in analyzing the extant paintings, sculptures, and architectural monuments, many of which have been damaged by the elements and inept restorers. They have plotted the course of this revolution, identifying and dating the works which marked the significant advances in style and technique.

Quite as much controversy has developed over the origins of this artistic revolution, as has been generated by the concept of civic humanism. The central problem, the focus of much of the discussion, is the degree to which changes in the plastic arts have been influenced by a transformation of the intellectual milieu, or by a significant recasting of the political and social order. Many art historians, perhaps the majority, deny that this question is a legitimate concern of their discipline, which they define as the patient accumulation of data about artistic works and their creators and the close analysis of style. Their approach to their subject is similar to that of the intellectual historian who focuses his attention exclusively upon his texts, treating ideas as an independent and autonomous dimension of history. At the opposite pole of the spectrum is the Marxist scholar who views all cultural phenomena as mirroring the structure and values of the society that creates them. Significant changes in the arts are thus indices of alterations and readjustments of the social order and indeed can be utilized to show the direction and tempo of that transformation. When presented in its most dogmatic form—as, for example, in Frederick Antal's *Florentine Painting and its Social Background*—the Marxist viewpoint has won few adherents or sympathizers. Between these poles, however, much significant work is being done by scholars who are examining the connections between Florentine society and its artistic achievement. They have studied the incomes of painters, sculptors, and goldsmiths; their relations with corporate and individual patrons; the social and political function of artistic works, as devices for advertising family power, prestige, and wealth; and their ideological function, as expressions of the values and ideals of the community and, particularly, its ruling elite.

Why did the new Renaissance style originate in Florence? The city was a likely site for this development, with its exceptional size and wealth, and its tradition of excellence in the crafts and plastic arts. The community of artists was large, active, and well patronized by clients, public and private, secular and ecclesiatical. Giotto's frescoes in S. Croce and Andrea Pisano's Baptistery doors lay conveniently at hand, to be admired, studied, and copied by young artists. These material factors may help to explain why the revolution occurred in Florence and not in Arezzo or Genoa; but they do not reveal why it occurred at a specific time—in the second decade of the fifteenth century—or why it assumed a particular form. Perhaps the most puzzling fact about the new style was the suddenness of its appearance, after three decades of artistic stagnation. No painter or sculptor of the first rank was active in Florence between 1370 and 1400. The recurring plagues of the late fourteenth century may have killed off many young and promising artists or disrupted the workshops that trained them. Perhaps the political and social disturbances of these years strengthened the conservative tendencies among artists and patrons. The distinctive features of "late Gothic," the dominant style of the period, were its linear and decorative qualities, its concern with detail and color. It was an attractive, charming, graceful style which made only a muted appeal to the emotions and none to the intellect.

Perhaps the limitations of this style and the mediocrity of its practitioners contributed to the artistic revolution, by inducing the leaders of the new generation—Brunelleschi, Donatello, Ghiberti, Masaccio—to search elsewhere for guidance and inspiration. With the exception of the painter Masaccio, these men all received their initial training in goldsmiths' shops, even though Brunelleschi specialized later in architecture, Ghiberti and Donatello in sculpture. In their chosen fields, therefore, they were largely autodidacts, free to develop their interests and techniques without the inhibiting hand of a master. These men were strong and independent personalities, endowed with a sense of their unique talents and capacities, an enormous curiosity, and a willingness to experiment. In his *Commentaries,* Lorenzo Ghiberti praised the great artists of the early fourteenth century—Giotto, Niccolò and Andrea Pisano—who influenced him, but he did not mention any of his own teachers. Nor does Brunelleschi's biographer, Antonio Manetti (who knew his subject personally), identify the masters who instructed the young sculptor and architect. Brunelleschi and Donatello journeyed to Rome to study classical ruins; this was not the only excursion into unfamiliar areas which these artists undertook to increase their knowledge and experience. Manetti is our source for the information that Brunelleschi learned some mathematics—so crucial for his discovery of perspective—from Paolo Toscanelli. He also noted that Filippo was very interested in theology and often frequented the disputations held by masters in that discipline.

The creators of the Renaissance style rejected their contemporaries and went back a century to the work of Giotto. The quality they most admired in this master was his ability to make dramatic and moving statements about the Christian tradition by creating realistic human forms. Giotto achieved this effect by focusing the viewer's attention upon a few monumental figures. Naturalism, the depiction of reality, was a central concern for these painters and sculptors, as it had been for Giotto. But this did not involve simply the faithful copying of nature, the creation of a mirrored image of the physical universe. Instead, these artists selected particular elements of the visible world and organized them rationally and scientifically to create the illusion of reality. For painting, Brunelleschi made the crucial contribution through his invention of perspective, the geometric device for depicting three-dimensional space upon a flat plane surface. The employment of this technique strengthened the impression of realism, enabling the artist to stimulate the viewer's emotions and sensibilities. With mathematical precision, objects could be fixed, and their relations to each other established, in this three-dimensional world. Discovery of the rules of proportion made it possible for Florentine painters to depict the human form realistically in this new spatial order. While mastering these new techniques, they also began to experiment with light and shadow to intensify the sense of reality, and to enlarge the dramatic possibilities of a scene.

This impulse toward a greater realism, a more accurate rendition of the visible world, was the most powerful current in the Florentine artistic revolution. But it was the blending of naturalism with classical forms which gave this movement its distinctive character and vitality. The process by which these two currents merged in this creative relationship defies easy description and analysis. The patriciate's enthusiasm for classical studies is not an adequate explanation. Florentine artists of the early Quattrocento were guild craftsmen, the social equals of stonemasons and retail merchants. Their education was not classical, but vocational and vernacular. Nor is there any concrete evidence to suggest that, in the early and crucial stages of this revolution, they were encouraged by aristocratic patrons to utilize antique forms. This classical interest developed among the artists themselves. Brunelleschi and Donatello were the first men of their generation to examine, thoroughly and systematically, the ruins of ancient Rome. They discovered the principles of classical building and—equally important—the qualities of mind and spirit of classical artists. Through his measurement of columns, pediments, and arches, Brunelleschi worked out the mathematical ratios used by Roman architects, and he also grasped the idea of space as the essential dimension in the visual arts. He spent the rest of his professional career working out the implications of this discovery.

The first creations of the new style were conceived and executed in the second and third decades of the fifteenth century. Donatello's statue of St. Mark (1411–1413), commissioned for Orsanmichele by the guild of linen makers and used clothes' dealers, is generally recognized as the first Renaissance monument. In the decade following the completion of this work, Brunelleschi formulated, and began to implement, his plans for the cathedral dome and for the Foundling Hospital, the city's first classical building. Meanwhile, Donatello was pursuing his revolutionary course in sculpture, working both in marble and bronze. His statue of St. George (1420) was the first piece of free-standing sculpture to be carved since classical times, and his

St. George by Donatello in the Museo Nazionale. (Alinari-Art Reference Bureau)

bronze panel for the baptismal font in the Sienese Baptistery (1427) opened up new and exciting vistas for artists in that medium. The youngest and most precocious member of this revolutionary cadre was the painter Masaccio, born in 1400 and dead by 1428. During his short but prolific career of six years (he entered the painters' guild in 1422), Masaccio revolutionized Florentine painting with such works as the *Trinity* in S. Maria Novella (1427) and his fresco cycle dedicated to the life of St. Peter which he and his partner, Masolino da Panicale, painted in the Brancacci chapel of S. Maria del Carmine (1426–1427).

Masaccio's *Trinity* is a superb example of the new art; it illustrates many of its characteristic features, its ethos, and its purpose. This fresco, recently restored, is attached to the north wall of the nave in S. Maria Novella. In the center of the painting is the crucified Christ, above, the dove symbolizing the Holy Spirit, and in the background, the awe-inspiring figure of God the Father. Standing at the foot of the cross are the Virgin and St. John, while outside the scene are the donor and his wife kneeling in prayer. All of the new techniques invented and developed by Brunelleschi and Donatello are employed in this fresco to create a dramatic, realistic scene of great emotional intensity. Masaccio has utilized perspective brilliantly to create a sense of depth, of three dimensions. To strengthen the impression of space disciplined and organized, he placed his subject in a classical setting: an arched chapel, which might have been designed by Brunelleschi, framed by two classical pilasters and a pediment. Within this geometrically ordered space, the human figures are drawn to scale, and their relation to each other is accurately defined. Masaccio's treatment of space is absolutely novel, without precedent in the history of painting, but in his depiction of the human figure, he followed Giotto. His saints and donors are solid, massive, immobile, like pieces of statuary, and they contribute to the impression of gravity and monumentality, which are trademarks of the great Trecento master. Masaccio had also grasped Giotto's principle that the dramatic impact of a painting is weakened by irrelevant and extraneous detail. But in his portrayal of the nude form, the figure of the dead Christ, the young painter had progressed far beyond his mentor or, indeed, beyond any contemporary artist of his time.

The Trinity with the Virgin by Masaccio in the Church of S. Maria Novella. (Alinari-Art Reference Bureau)

This new style was developed by an artistic community which was experiencing a significant transformation of its structure, its relations with society, and also its self-awareness. These developments—stylistic, social, and psychological—all influenced each other. The fifteenth century witnessed the decline of the traditional view of the artist as craftsman, practicing his metier within a rigid guild structure. The artists who originated the Renaissance style were a special breed who did not function well in the old corporate system. In their intense dedication to their work, they correspond more closely to the modern idea of the artist than to the medieval craftsman. It is instructive to compare the career of Agnolo Gaddi (d. 1396), who, according to Vasari, "was more devoted to trading and commerce than the art of painting," with those of Brunelleschi and Donatello, who never married or devoted much thought to their material concerns. Vasari also relates the anecdote about Paolo Uccello (d. 1475), whose wife reported that "Paolo would remain the night long in his study to work out the lines of his perspective, and then when she called him to come to rest, he replied: 'Oh, what a sweet thing perspective is!' " With their strong personalities and their awareness of their creative talents, these artists chafed under discipline and preferred to work independently. Brunelleschi deliberately sabotaged the work on the cathedral dome until Ghiberti retired from the project and he was given a free hand to execute his plan. Ghiberti wrote in his *Commentaries* that the guild officials responsible for the construction of the Baptistery doors, the Gates of Paradise, "gave me permission to execute it in whatever way I believed would result in the greatest perfection, the most ornamentation and the greatest richness."

Public opinion responded quite slowly to this novel conception of the artist. Until quite late in the century, Florentine architects were still regarded as the passive agents of their patrons, and not the creators of the buildings which they designed. A letter of 1436 sent by the Signoria to the marquis of Ferrara expresses the traditional view of the artist and his vocation. The marquis had commissioned a painted wax image from a firm of Florentine craftsmen, but a quarrel had arisen over the price of the finished work. The priors vouched for the honesty of these men, describing them as "innocent, good and simple." Price was determined solely by the cost of material and labor. The tone of the letter suggested that the marquis should understand that disagreements often occurred in such matters involving ignorant artisans, but that justice required that they be adequately compensated for their labors. But the writings of Archbishop Antonino in mid-century suggest that these traditional attitudes were gradually disappearing. In a brief discussion of painting in his *Summa*, Antonino accepts the painters' claim to be paid "not only by the amount of work but more in proportion to their application and grêater expertness in their trade." Implicit, too, in Antonino's discussion is the assumption that Florentine painters enjoyed considerable freedom in their treatment of subjects, in their selection of motifs.

Contributing to the emancipation of Quattrocento artists from their traditional craft milieu and mentality was the emergence of the idea that painting, sculpture, and architecture should be classified among the liberal arts, and were thus equal in status to poetry, rhetoric, and mathematics. This argument was first advanced in 1435 by Leon Battista Alberti in his treatise on painting, but it was not immediately accepted by Florence's scholarly community. Time was needed for old prejudices to dissolve, and for a tradition of communication and cooperation to develop between artists and humanists. With their extensive knowledge of classical architecture and sculpture, Brunelleschi and Donatello may have stimulated some interest in humanist circles, but the sources are silent on this point. Lorenzo Ghiberti was the first artist to display an interest in classical literature and to be on friendly terms with Bruni, Traversari, and Niccoli. Scattered through his *Commentaries* are fragments of information about classical art which he had culled from Pliny and other ancient authors. Leonardo Bruni had submitted a design to Ghiberti for the second pair of Baptistery doors, the first documented example of humanist collaboration in an artistic enterprise. Although the sculptor did not use these plans, his execution of the Gates of Paradise was profoundly influenced by his contacts with the humanist milieu in Florence. From this source, so Professor Gombrich has argued persuasively, Ghiberti conceived the idea of progress in the arts, and of his mission to surpass all earlier works, including his own first set of Baptistery doors.

There is little concrete information about the public reaction to the new Renaissance style. Within artistic circles, there must have been lively discussion, and perhaps a sharp division between traditionalists and innovators, but no echoes of this controversy—if it arose—can be found in the sources. The old style did not lose favor with the public, but instead enjoyed a revival in the 1420s, when an Umbrian artist, Gentile da Fabriano, introduced the so-called International Gothic style into Florence. This style had its origins in Italian, and particularly Sienese painting of the Trecento; it was further developed and refined north of the Alps, in Avignon and at the Burgundian court. While possessing many of the characteristics of late Trecento Florentine painting, it also exhibited certain differences reflecting the Burgundian influence. Colors were richer; clothing and accoutrements were more elegant; and space was crammed with a plethora of figures, animal and human, which were depicted in very realistic detail. While Masaccio was working on the *Trinity* and the Brancacci frescoes, Gentile da Fabriano was painting his *Adoration of the Magi,* one of the most opulent and flamboyant works in this archaic style. This altarpiece was commissioned by the wealthy statesman and humanist Palla Strozzi, who paid Gentile 300 florins for the work. Apparently, Palla was more old-fashioned in art than in his literary interests. Cosimo de' Medici favored both styles. His palace on the Via Larga was built according to classical principles, but its chapel was decorated by Benozzo Gozzoli with a gaudy and ornate Magi scene strongly reminiscent of the secular, courtly art of the International Gothic.

The coexistence of these antithetical styles, and their persistent popularity throughout the fifteenth century, suggests that each appealed to certain qualities of the Florentine temperament. Those who favored the Renaissance style were attracted by the sense of order, coherence, and regularity, by relationships clearly defined according to mathematical laws. They conceived of space, and of the physical world, as phenomena which could be defined, measured, and controlled by the human mind. Such ideas have their obvious parallels in Florentine experience: in the precision and accuracy of mercantile account books and communal treasury records, in the trend toward systematic and centralized administration, in efforts to control economic and social activity, in the development of a sense of time in history. The qualities of simplicity, restraint, and austerity—all characteristics of the new art—likewise reflect typically Florentine modes of thought and action. With its penchant for opulence, color, and pageantry, the International Gothic style appealed to the aristocratic impulse which became so prominent in the

Adoration of the Magi by Gentile da Fabriano in the Galleria Uffizi. (Brogi-Art Reference Bureau)

Quattrocento. In contrast to the intellectuality and high seri-
ousness of Renaissance art, Gothic art was light and decorative
in tone and feeling. Its treatment of religious subjects was formal
and stylized; it lacked the emotional intensity of a Masaccio
Madonna or an Old Testament prophet carved by Donatello.

When viewed internally, this creative epoch in Florentine
art is a history of discoveries and achievements by individual
artists who work out their particular solutions to esthetic problems. These breakthroughs are copied and absorbed by other
artists; what began as an individual statement becomes a trend,
a movement, a new style. From another viewpoint, this is a
history of artists and their public: the response of the patriciate
to a new style, the degree to which this style defines the values
of the patron class. From a third and still broader perspective,
one may view this artistic development as a dimension of the
collective experience of the community. Like learning and education, Florentine art was functional. It satisfied particular social
needs and was influenced by changes in the nature and priority
of those needs. Artists benefited from periods of prosperity and
suffered in times of crisis; some metiers were active and productive when others languished. The patterns of such vicissitudes
and oscillations in the fifteenth century give us some clues to
the external pressures which influenced the artist and his work.

The first quarter of the fifteenth century was a period of exceptionally intense activity for sculptors and architects who
were working on the large civic enterprises: the cathedral, the
Foundling Hospital, the Baptistery doors, the Orsanmichele statues commissioned by the guilds, the sculptured figures of saints
for the cathedral façade. These commissions were granted by
guild officials; they were collective decisions, the result of lengthy
deliberations and careful scrutiny of candidates. These guildsmen tended to choose "progressive" artists like Donatello and
Brunelleschi to execute their commissions, with the result that
their stylistic innovations were displayed publicly and were visible to the entire community. Painters did not enjoy this public
and corporate patronage; they created altarpieces for parish and
monastic churches and devotional images for private dwellings.
It is possible but difficult to prove that the private and cloistered
nature of this patronage was a factor in the conservatism of

Florentine painters, in their dilatory response to the stylistic innovations of Donatello and Brunelleschi. Masaccio's revolutionary works of 1426–1427 were commissioned by two families, the Brancacci and the Lenzi, as funerary monuments; this was part of a vogue for monumental tombs which became quite strong in the 1420s, after a lapse of several decades, and which seems to have been a manifestation of the aristocratic spirit. But we can only speculate about the reasons for the selection of Masaccio to execute these frescoes. Had his patrons seen examples of his work, and were they aware of his unusual talents? Was he recommended to them by his friend Brunelleschi? Or was he selected because he was young and relatively unknown, and therefore inexpensive?

The 1420s were a period of astonishing creativity in the arts; by contrast, the succeeding decade was undistinguished. Time was required for the second generation to absorb and assimilate the revolutionary achievements of the past; some of the lesser artists never mastered the new concepts and techniques of Donatello and Masaccio. The arts also suffered from the effects of the Milanese wars, the fiscal crisis, and the political disturbances surrounding the Medici restoration in 1434. Public funds for civic monuments were eliminated or drastically curtailed, while private subsidy of the arts declined sharply. The establishment of the Medici regime marked the beginning of a more stable phase in Florentine history, but it also drove into exile a small contingent of wealthy citizens like Palla Strozzi, whose patronage was lost to the community. Not until after 1440, when Florentines enjoyed greater prosperity and security, did the arts experience a revival. This decade inaugurated the age of the great Renaissance palaces built by the Medici, Pitti, and Rucellai; these enterprises employed architects and painters, but not sculptors. Not even the great Donatello found adequate employment in Florence during his last years; he worked abroad, in Padua and Siena, and received some help from his friend Cosimo de' Medici. "In order that Donatello's chisel might not be idle," Vespasiano reported, "[Cosimo] commissioned him to make the pulpits of bronze in S. Lorenzo and the doors of the sacristy." One of the rare public commissions given to sculptors in the 1440's was Bernardino Rossellino's tomb of Leonardo Bruni (d.

1444). It is ironic that this monument to a distinguished human-ist was created at a time when both civic humanism and civic art were in decline.

The artistic scene in mid-Quattrocento Florence is complex, although certain patterns and trends are visible. Most striking is the superiority of the painters: Fra Angelico, Fra Filippo Lippi, Domenico Veneziano, Andrea del Castagno, Uccello. These men were more original and creative than the architects and sculptors, who did not have many opportunities to display their talents, and who produced no worthy successors to Brunelleschi and Donatello. The old tensions and rivalries continue: between reli-gious and secular art, between the austere, geometric Renais-sance style and the colorful, graceful examples of International Gothic. The stylistic divisions are no longer neat and clear-cut, if indeed they ever were, and much of the painting of these middle decades displays ideas and motifs drawn from both traditions. Every Florentine painter of this generation had mastered per-spective and proportion; but some of the greatest artists —Fra Angelico and Fra Filippo Lippi—used these techniques to paint scenes which were linear, delicate, decorative, senti-mental, a sharp contrast to the austere creations of Paolo Uccello and Andrea del Castagno.

Whereas styles were mixed and confused in these years, the qualitative distinction between secular and religious art was very sharp and clear. The best art was religious painting, com-missioned by ecclesiastical communities for their churches and monasteries. For their secular needs—for busts and portraits, wedding chests, and coats of arms—the Florentines tended to employ second-rate artists. One of the busiest workshops was operated by two painters, Apollonio di Giovanni and Marco del Buono, who specialized in the decoration of *cassoni*, the wedding chests which held the trousseaux of Florentine brides. These chests were decorated with scenes from classical history and literature—incidents from Vergil's *Aeneid*, the assassination of Caesar—and occasionally a contemporary event, like the wed-ding scene which decorates the famous Adimari *cassone*, or a tournament held in the Piazza S. Croce. Between 1446 and 1463, over 300 of these *cassoni* were manufactured by this workshop and distributed to patrician households. Stylistically, these paintings were archaic and old-fashioned, a derivation of the International Gothic which did not lose its attraction for the Florentines. For their public buildings and their churches, they insisted upon the highest standards of quality. But in their domestic surroundings, they rejected the monumental style, with its austerity and rigor, in favor of decorative art, which was more conducive to pleasure and relaxation. In art as in other experiences of the mind and the senses, Florentines enjoyed a variety of styles and subjects, each in its proper context, each for its particular purpose.

SEVEN

Epilogue: The Last Years of the Republic

THE LAURENTIAN AGE (1469–1492)

Two themes run through this analysis of Renaissance Florence: the flexible character of the society and its institutions, and the fruitful balance between tradition and innovation. This community was deeply attached to its past, which provided it with guidelines for policy, behavior, and belief. Yet Florentines did not become prisoners of their traditions or their institutions. In this aristocratic society, a degree of economic and social mobility prevented the formation of a rigid caste system. The republic was controlled by a small, select group of patricians, but that domination was not absolute or total. Factional strife, personal enmity, and quarrels over policy frequently divided an unstable and ever-changing ruling class. Although policy was usually formulated within the context of the city's republican and Guelf traditions, it was always subject to change in the light of new experience or particular circumstances. The achievements of Florentine artists and humanists in the early Quattrocento constitute the most striking evidence for the creative possibilities of this felicitous combination of the old and the new.

By the middle decades of the fifteenth century, however, these particular features of the Florentine experience were in eclipse. The most notable characteristic of Florentine (and Italian) history in the later Quattrocento is the spirit of conservatism which pervades every phase of human activity. In politics, in social and economic relations, in religion and culture, institutions have become more rigid, the range of choices and alternatives more limited. Our knowledge of the historical forces behind this conservative trend is rather sketchy, but one factor was the reaction of a fearful and exhausted society to the chaotic political conditions of the early Quattrocento. After mid-century, Italian princes and statesmen abandoned the aggressive policies and postures of their predecessors; they became more cautious and defensive, more committed to the preservation of the status quo. The Italian League established at Lodi in 1454 symbolized this spirit of conservatism and stasis in the diplomatic sphere; it was designed to stabilize the existing political order and, through the concerted action of the signatories, to thwart any attempt to change the system.

The history of Florence during the period of Medici hegemony (1434–1494) reflects this outlook. The regime established after Cosimo's return from exile in 1434, and continued by his son Piero and his grandson Lorenzo, was based upon the close cooperation of the Medici and a small group of patrician families, for their mutual advantage and security. The social composition of this ruling group did not change perceptibly during the sixty years of Medici rule. Cosimo and Lorenzo did introduce certain techniques to secure their control—the selection of priors by hand instead of by lot, the creation of councils with special authority—but these devices had their precedents in earlier regimes. The application of these institutional controls was very gradual and sporadic, and legislative opposition sometimes forced the Medici to abandon temporarily their plans for electoral and constitutional reform. Even though Medici authority in the regime increased progressively, it never became absolute, and the republic was not transformed into an autocratic despotism.

With some exceptions and reservations, the Florentine aristocracy accepted the Medici regime; it was a stabilizing force, which protected and secured its economic and social preeminence. While a segment of the patriciate was excluded from office and a few citizens were exiled as potential threats to the state, the majority enjoyed at least a modicum of the offices and privileges which traditionally had been monopolized by the leading families. Aristocratic opposition to the regime took various forms, the most innocuous being the muted grumblings and resentments voiced privately, and the votes recorded in council meetings against those measures designed to strengthen the authority of the ruling group. The councils maintained a surprisingly independent attitude toward legislative proposals; not infrequently, they rejected laws which the Signoria, carefully selected by the Medicean leadership, had initiated. In 1449 and again in 1455, strong resistance to the regime's electoral controls and its commissions with special powers forced the government to abandon temporarily these instruments for maintaining Medici control of the state. In 1458, the leadership resorted to the convocation of a *parlamento*, an assembly of the entire citizenry, to approve the creation of a *balìa* with special authority to defend the regime. A serious threat to Medici control occurred in 1466, two years after Cosimo's death. Piero de' Medici, less talented than his father, could not suppress the feuding within the leadership cadre, some of whose members—Luca Pitti and Agnolo Acciaiuoli—had visions of supplanting him as the "leading citizen" of Florence. The regime survived this challenge when, at the last moment, Luca Pitti changed sides and joined Piero, who brought troops into the city to overawe the populace.

The most dramatic incident of political opposition was the Pazzi rebellion of 1479, which possesses all of the colorful features of Renaissance conspiracies, including sacrilege and assassination. The Pazzi were an old noble family whose wealth and status had declined in the fourteenth century, and then recovered after 1420 when they established a bank in Rome. In league with Pope Sixtus IV, who hated Lorenzo for thwarting his political ambitions in central Italy, the Pazzi conspired to kill Lorenzo and his brother Giuliano while they were attending mass in the cathedral, and then seize power during the ensuing confusion. Four assassins (including two priests) attacked their victims, killing Giuliano and wounding Lorenzo, who nevertheless managed to escape into the sacristy. Jacopo de' Pazzi rode through the streets shouting "Popolo e libertà!" but the Florentines responded with curses and cries of "Palle!", a reference to the Medici coat-of-arms. Nine of the conspirators were killed (including the archbishop-elect of Pisa, Francesco Salviati), and the Medici's hold upon the city was stronger than it had ever been.

Such forms of protest, ranging from the negative council vote to the *coup d'etat,* were traditional modes of political opposition in Florence. In this conservative environment, both rulers and ruled looked to the past for guidance and justification for their actions. The antidotes to tension and crisis prescribed in 1460 are almost identical to those formulated a century before: civic unity, repression of factionalism, reaffirmation of old civic values. "As long as our ancestors were united," Franco Sacchetti asserted in 1458, "the city was ruled exceedingly well, and the evils started once discord had broken out. No war is more dangerous than civil war, for the suppression of which every effort should be devoted." Another striking example of the static character of Florentine political thinking before Machiavelli is an analysis made of the electoral scrutiny of 1484 by Piero Guicciardini, the father of the historian Francesco. Piero divided the electorate into five categories, of which two—members of old magnate families and artisans from the lower guilds—had only a very minor part in the regime. The bulk of the offices were filled by men from the greater guilds, whom Guicciardini ranked according to family "nobility" and length of service in high office. These criteria of political status had not changed in two centuries. Guicciardini commented bitterly on the "new men" who had pushed their way into power, in terms reminiscent of Giovanni Cavalcanti's tirade against "upstarts and mechanics" a half-century earlier. And his explanation for this influx of parvenus was similar to Donato Velluti's analysis in the 1350s: the powerful citizens "who pull up new men and undo long established citizens."

Only in the sphere of foreign affairs did the Medici regime depart from tradition to pursue a different political course. Symbolizing this innovation was the permanent presence in the Medici palace of Nicodemo da Pontremoli, the ambassador of Francesco Sforza, lord of Milan. Nicodemo was not simply a diplomatic representative of a foreign prince, but an intimate adviser to Cosimo and Piero de' Medici, and the liaison between the Medici and the Sforza. Cosimo had built the Florence-Milan axis in the 1450s despite strong opposition from the citizenry, who were not easily reconciled to their traditional Lombard enemy. Nicodemo was also the symbol of the strong Milanese support for the regime, and on two occasions (in 1458 and 1466), the Medici turned to Francesco Sforza for help during domestic crises. This need to rely upon outside force for survival was a clear sign of weakness, and an ominous portent for the future.

Medicean diplomacy after the peace of Lodi has been praised for its defensive orientation, its dexterity and flexibility, and its contribution to the maintenance of a rough balance of power in the Italian peninsula. This favorable judgment requires some qualification. Florentine foreign policy in the late Quattrocento was not guided, to any significant degree, by those material considerations—food supply, markets, sea outlets—which were so important in the past, nor by ideological concerns, such as friendship with the republic of Venice. Instead, the Medici relied very heavily upon personal ties with individual princes and sought to strengthen those bonds with lavish gifts and elaborate hospitality. This personal diplomacy was most likely to succeed when it was reinforced by mutual interests; Medici loans to Francesco Sforza were repaid when the latter sent troops to Florence to thwart a revolutionary movement. But this system— based upon the dubious loyalty of Italian *signori* and their uncertain tenure of power—was extremely unstable. This concentration upon personal relationships helps to explain why Italian diplomacy of the Laurentian period appears, in retrospect, so superficial, so devoid of meaningful issues. Lorenzo de' Medici played this game with consummate skill, and his personal prestige was an important factor in Florentine diplomatic successes. But he made no serious effort to instruct his partners in the charade about the realities of power politics. Indeed, there is no evidence that he was really aware of the flaws and deficiencies of the system, which became so glaringly apparent after 1494.

While Lorenzo's foreign policy did secure Florentine independence and contributed to the maintenance of a tenuous equilibrium in the peninsula, it also imposed heavy fiscal burdens upon the city and its dominions. The problem of the fisc in the Laurentian period have not been fully explored, but the researches of Louis Marks do permit the formulation of some tentative conclusions. The most significant development was the withdrawal of fiscal policy from the political arena into the hands of specialists, the officials of the *Monte,* who faithfully executed the will of the Medici leadership. This intimate tie between state finance and political power was reinforced by the practice of relying upon private loans, advanced by the officials and their friends, for emergency expenditures; these loans earned a high rate of interest and were guaranteed by the state. Wealthy Florentines with Medici connections thus gained secure profits from the fisc, whereas citizens of modest means suffered most from the partial repudiation of the public debt: reduction of interest rates on old *Monte* shares, delay of repayment, and partial payment of redeemed shares. The history of the Medici fisc is a gloomy tale which displays the regime's least attractive qualities: the despoliation of public funds by the ruling group, the progressive decline of fiscal responsibility, the increasing reliance upon makeshift devices to maintain solvency.

Closely linked to the issues of taxation and public credit is a larger problem: the state of the Florentine economy in the Laurentian period. Some scholars believe that Florence—and Italy—experienced a severe recession in the Quattrocento, while others have argued that the economy was strong and vital, and that decline was sporadic and temporary. Florentine banking, the foundation and sustenance of so many patrician fortunes, was in serious difficulty in the late fifteenth century. Several firms foundered in the 1460s, and the Medici bank declined steadily after Cosimo's death in 1464, as a consequence of adverse business conditions and inept management. The financial difficulties of the Medici may have hurt the city's economy, although the extent of damage is difficult to estimate. Compared to his grandfather Cosimo, Lorenzo had less money available to help friends and associates, to subsidize building and the arts. Yet some businessmen and some enterprises prospered in Laurentian Florence. Richard Goldthwaite's study of the careers of Filippo Strozzi, Gino Capponi, and Giuliano Gondi proves that an entrepreneur with capital and a willingness to take risks could build a large fortune in the late fifteenth century. These merchants were all engaged in international trade and banking, with bases in Naples, Rome, Lyon, and Antwerp. They also invested in cloth industries, both wool and silk, and gained regular if modest profits from these enterprises.

The pattern of aristocratic fortunes in the late Quattrocento thus appears to be as follows: a few spectacular rises and declines, with the majority of patrimonies and incomes remaining quite stable. In the economic sphere, as in politics, caution and conservatism prevailed; men took fewer risks and concentrated upon maintaining rather than increasing their wealth. Though some fortunes were diminished by bad investments, by divisions of property among heirs, and by heavy expenditures on buildings, dowries, and conspicuous consumption, most patrician families lived in substantial comfort if not in luxury. Nearly every aristocratic household owned at least one *contado* farm which provided it with the staples of life and, in good years, a surplus which could be converted into cash. When Niccolò Machiavelli lost his government post and salary in 1512, he was able to subsist, however miserably, upon the income of his small farm near S. Casciano. Perhaps to compensate for diminishing opportunities in trade and industry, more patricians than ever before were utilizing their training in law and the humanities to embark upon professional careers. Lauro Martines has counted thirty-two patrician lawyers who practiced in Florence between 1480 and 1530, compared to fourteen and thirteen in the two previous half-centuries. The widening range of aristocratic occupations is illustrated by the careers of five brothers, the sons of Piero di Jacopo Guicciardini (1454–1513), who had himself combined entrepreneurial activity with politics in the Laurentain period. Piero's second son was Francesco, the famous historian. He practiced law in Florence, served as governor in the Papal States, invested in land and a silk manufacturing firm, and upon retiring from public life in the 1530s, wrote his *History of Italy*. The eldest son, Luigi, had no talent for business and was frequently in economic difficulties; his modest income came from land and the salaries he earned as an official. Bongianni represented yet another aristocratic type: the amateur humanist who lived on his country estate with his books, and took no active part in business or politics. Piero's youngest sons, Jacopo and Girolamo, were both engaged in commerce and manufacturing;

they gained their livelihood from the profits of silk factories and international trading ventures.

While the economic condition of the patriciate remained quite stable in the second half of the Quattrocento, its social outlook did change significantly. The aristocratic impulse became progressively stronger; its imprint is visible in behavior patterns and living styles, as well as in the more abstract realm of ideas and value systems. This was a manifestation of the patriciate's effort to define itself as a special caste, to attribute unique qualities to itself, and to emphasize the gulf which separated its members from the rest of Florentine society. Classical learning had become an essential element in patrician education, and thus a badge of social distinction. The political and psychological curbs upon conspicuous consumption had largely disappeared by Lorenzo's time, as each family sought to surpass its neighbors in the splendor of its wedding ceremonies and funeral corteges, in the size of its dowries, and in the elegance of its living quarters.

These aristocratic, elitist impulses and drives, magnified and reinforced by the Medicean experience, were given concrete form in the palace construction of the late Quattrocento. The palaces were statements of aggrandizement, tangible symbols of a particular family's wealth and status, of its separation from— and elevation above—the rest of the community. Towering over adjacent buildings, violating (in spirit if not in letter) communal legislation which regulated private construction, these palaces were massive monuments to the aristocratic ego, which announced the demise of corporate sanction and social conformity. Illustrating the gulf between conventional etiquette, still bound to traditional behavior patterns, and the private yearnings of the aristocracy is a contemporary account of the construction of Filippo Strozzi's palace in the 1480s. Filippo's son, Lorenzo, reported that his father stated publicly that "a comfortable everyday house was all he needed," hoping that his modest and humble statements would shield him from the jealousy of his neighbors. But Filippo was secretly delighted when his architects drew up plans for a grandiose palace and, despite his grumbling that "it was improper and too expensive," he also favored Lorenzo de' Medici's suggestion for placing rusticated masonry on the palace exterior. Filippo did not build a comfortable

Strozzi Palace. (Alinari-Art Reference Bureau)

home; these huge classical edifices were much less suited for domestic living than, for example, the Davanzati palace built in the late fourteenth century. One authority on Renaissance architecture has commented that "the rooms were mostly grandiose stages for the performance of the rites of commercial and political leadership, and it is hard to imagine where one slept, washed or found privacy."

In one sense, however, these palaces were more private than their medieval predecessors, for they were designed to shield their occupants from contact with the adjacent street. Families no longer assembled in the public loggia, but in the interior courtyard. The gradual disappearance of the loggia from the urban scene in the fifteenth century (the number had dwindled to thirty by the 1470s) was an important social fact, comparable in significance to the destruction of towers belonging to magnate families after 1250. The enclosure in 1517 of the open loggia of the Medici palace signalled that family's special status, its withdrawal from the community life of the neighborhood, for which the loggia had been the natural focus. The replacement of the loggia by the private courtyard was a manifestation of still another social development involving the patrician family. These palaces and courtyards were built by and for single households, or nuclear families. Their construction symbolized the fragmentation of the large, extended family, that of the Strozzi, for example, comprising seventy households in 1380. A wealthy patrician like Filippo Strozzi visualized himself as the founder of a dynasty and lavished his attention upon his direct descendants, not upon the entire Strozzi clan. He felt little sense of kinship for distant relatives and no responsibility for their welfare. He would not dream of participating in a vendetta to avenge an insult to a second cousin; he would pause before loaning money to an impecunious relative. When Donato Velluti wrote his family memoirs in the 1360s, he could identify and describe over 100 members of his blood kin in terms of profession, marriage, children, and personality traits. A century and a half later, Francesco Guicciardini limited his genealogical analysis to his direct lineage, and ignored the collateral branches of the Guicciardini clan. His sense of family, and his class consciousness, had become narrow and exclusive.

Like the aristocratic society that patronized it, Florentine culture in the Laurentian age was elitist. The civic culture of the early Quattrocento had been a product of corporate groups (guilds, commune, churches); it defined and exalted collective values and ideals, both spiritual and secular. Laurentian culture was private, created for a small group of learned and sophisticated *cognoscenti*. The structure of cultural patronage had changed during the Medici period and so, too, did intellectual preoccupations and interests. Those political and moral problems —liberty, republicanism, the active life—which had so passionately interested Leonardo Bruni and his friends had little relevance for Laurentian Florence; indeed, public speculation on these questions would not have been prudent. The quality of historical writing also declined in the late Quattrocento; the histories of Bruni and Poggio Bracciolini had no worthy succes-

Primavera by Botticelli in the Galleria Uffizi. (Alinari-Art Reference Bureau)

sors until the crisis of the 1490s rekindled the Florentine historical imagination. Neoplatonism was the unofficial ideology of Laurentian Florence; its teachings were peculiarly suited to the atmosphere which then prevailed in aristocratic society. The deprecation of man's physical nature and the exaltation of the spirit; the view of the body as the soul's terrestrial prison; the concept of *ascensio,* the soul's struggle upward to achieve unity with God: these ideas appealed to many cultured Florentines who were disenchanted with traditional Christian teaching, and indifferent to the civic orientation of early Quattrocento humanism. As an elitist philosophy, Neoplatonism had a particular attraction for aristocrats. Its tenets could only be grasped by the learned, and only a small minority of its devotees were deemed capable of achieving its ultimate fulfillment, the spiritual union with God. Botticelli's *Primavera* is a product of this environment. This painting is an allegory which combined Neoplatonic and Christian ideas, but its themes and its iconography are so arcane and esoteric that only a sophisticated initiate could understand its message. The *Primavera* vividly illustrates the cultural gap which separated Lorenzo and his intellectual coterie from the rest of Florentine society.

THE REPUBLIC RESTORED, 1494–1512

In the autumn of 1494, King Charles VIII of France led a military force across the Alps into Italy. The king's ultimate objective was the conquest of Naples, but his passage through Tuscany had fateful consequences for Florence. Lorenzo de' Medici had died two years before; his son Piero, a man of limited intelligence and talent, replaced him as head of the regime. Out of loyalty to his Neapolitan ally, King Ferrante, Piero opposed the French enterprise and thus incurred the enmity of Charles VIII. As the king approached Florence with his army, the panic-stricken Piero visited the French camp to make his peace with Charles, and surrendered Pisa and three other fortresses on the Tyrrhenian littoral. Enraged by this craven behavior, the Florentines expelled Piero and his family, thus ending sixty years of Medici domination. While most citizens applauded the restoration of a popular government, they also realized that the situation was not auspicious for the new rigime. The Signoria had to negotiate a peace agreement with King Charles, and avoid a military occupation by the French army. The loss of Pisa was a bitter blow to Florentine pride and a grave threat to the economy, which slumped as a result of the disturbances. Moreover, the surrender of the coastal fortresses weakened Florence's defenses, and intensified the feelings of vulnerability and insecurity which had been aroused by the French invasion.

The psychological impact of these events upon the city was deep and permanent. While life soon returned to normal after the departure of the French army for Rome and Naples, the Florentines did not recover their self-confidence. Never again in their history did they see themselves as the masters of their destiny. Magnifying the intensity of the shock was the deceptive sense of security, which had been bred by years of internal peace and by the peninsula's immunity from foreign invasion. Like most Italians, Florentines had come to believe that the prosperity and peace they enjoyed were the consequences of their virtue and intelligence, of their ability to control their environment. Contrasting the order and security of the Laurentian age with the chaotic situation after 1494, Francesco Guicciardini (writing in the 1530s) argued that Lorenzo was the man primarily responsible for Italy's well-being:

Italy was preserved in this happy state, which had been attained through a variety of causes, by a number of circumstances, but among these by common consent no little credit was due to the industry and virtue of Lorenzo de' Medici. . . . Knowing that it would be very dangerous to himself and to the Florentine Republic if any of the larger states increased their power, he diligently sought to maintain the affairs of Italy in such a balance that they might not favor one side more than other. This would not have been possible without the preservation of peace and without the most careful watch over any disturbance, however small. . . . Such was the state of things, such the foundation of the peace of Italy, so arranged and juxtaposed that not only was there no fear of any present disorder but it was difficult to imagine how, by what plots, incidents or forces, such tranquility might be destroyed. Then, in the month of April 1492 there occurred the death of Lorenzo de' Medici. It was bitter for him, because he was not quite forty-four years of age, and bitter for his republic which, because of his prudence, reputation and intellect in everything honorable and excellent, flourished marvelously with riches and all those ornaments and advantages with which a long peace is usually accompanied. But it was also a most untimely death for the rest of Italy, both because of the work he constantly did for the common safety and because he was the means by which the disagreements and suspicions that frequently arose . . . were moderated and held in check.

Although a sense of pessimism pervaded much of the political discussion in Florence after 1494, there were also signs of a revival of civic spirit and vitality. Sixty years of Medici government had not dampened the Florentine enthusiasm for republicanism; memories of ancient liberties and past glories were a powerful stimulus to the rekindling of traditional sentiments and ideals. The new regime was more broadly representative of the community than any which had governed the city since 1382; its popular character was demonstrated by the establishment of a legislative body, the Great Council, comprising some 3000 members (one-fifth of the male population over twenty-nine) who were eligible for office. To house this assembly, the government ordered the construction of a spacious hall in the Palazzo della Signoria, and for its decoration, commissioned two frescoes by Leonardo da Vinci and Michelangelo, depicting Florentine victories in the battles of Anghiari and Cascina.* These works were civic enterprises, reminiscent of the public commissions for the city's beautification which had been given to Ghiberti and Donatello early in the century. But the political content, the patriotic message, of these frescoes was much more explicit than those embodied in the statues of Biblical figures carved by the sculptors of the early Quattrocento. In 1501, Michelangelo received the republic's last major commission to exalt the civic spirit of the Florentine *popolo:* the giant statue of David.

The man primarily responsible for stimulating this resurgence of republicanism was not a native citizen, but a foreigner and a friar, Girolamo Savonarola. Since coming to Florence in 1491 as prior of the Dominican convent of S. Marco, this native of Ferrara had won renown as a preacher and a prophet. In religious matters, he was a moralist and a traditionalist; he warned his listeners that God would inflict a horrible punishment upon Italy if the people did not repent their sins and live righteously. Thousands who heard his sermons were persuaded that he was a true prophet, the voice of God. The French invasion enhanced his reputation, for he had announced that Charles VIII was the agent of divine punishment; he had also been instrumental in persuading the king to keep his army out of the city. Savonarola played a significant if unofficial role in Florentine politics after the expulsion of the Medici. He was adviser to those citizens who shared his religious and moral outlook, and who constituted a loosely organized faction in the political struggles which marked the post-Medici period. The friar had criticized the Medici for destroying the traditional liberties of the Florentines; he supported a regime which was broadly representative of the community, convinced that a popular (but not a democratic) government would be more stable and more just than one controlled by an oligarchy. His voice may have been crucial in the

---

*Cascina was the site of a Florentine victory over Pisa in 1364. In the battle of Anghiari (1440), a mercenary army in Florentine pay defeated the forces of Niccolò Piccinino, who was serving the lord of Milan, Filippo Maria Visconti.

decision to establish the Great Council; many of his most fervent supporters came from the ranks of artisans and shopkeepers who, through their membership in that body, now participated actively in politics.

Savonarola's main goal, the moral and spiritual regeneration of Florence, was not realistic, and his own fate was sealed because he sought to achieve his objectives within a political context. Inevitably, his program aroused hostility and exacerbated tensions within Florentine society. He was disliked by the Franciscans and by many of the local clergy, who resented his attacks upon the ecclesiastical establishment. His opposition to Medici rule antagonized the supporters of that family, while aristocrats who favored an oligarchic regime deplored his advocacy of popular government. Two elements of his program, in particular, contributed to his downfall: his continued advocacy of the French alliance and his denunciation of Pope Alexander VI. The Borgia pope was angered by the friar's personal attacks upon him, but even more by his support of King Charles VIII. When papal warnings did not deter Savonarola, Alexander excommunicated him; the friar denounced this act as illegal and therefore invalid, and continued to preach. This open violation of a papal order frightened many citizens; the chronicler Luca Landucci reported that "many refused to go to Savonarola's preaching for fear of the excommunication, saying 'just or unjust, it is to be feared.' I myself was one of these who did not go." At that moment (March 1498) when the friar's hold upon the Florentines was weakening, a Signoria dominated by his enemies entered office. In collusion with the pope, the Signoria arrested and tortured Savonarola and forced him to confess that his prophecies were not of divine origin. Luca Landucci recorded his reaction to this news:

He whom we had held to be a prophet, confessed that he was no prophet and had not received from God the things which he preached, and he confessed that many things which had occurred during the course of his preaching were contrary to what he had given us to understand. I was present when this protocol was read, and I marvelled, feeling utterly dumbfounded with surprise. My heart was grieved to see such an edifice fall to the ground on account of having been founded on a lie. Florence had been expecting a new Jerusalem, from which would issue just laws and splendor and an example of righteous life and to see the renovation of the church, the conversion of unbelievers and the consolation of the righteous; and I felt that everything was exactly contrary, and had to resign myself with the thought: "Lord, in thy hands are all things."

On May 28, 1498 in the Piazza della Signoria, Savonarola was hanged and his body burned while thousands of Florentines watched, some with horror and others with grim satisfaction.

Savonarola's ideal had been a Christian society based upon the principles of peace, order, and justice; in seeking to implement his program, he had aroused intense opposition. Yet it would be neither just nor accurate to blame the friar for all of the social and political discord in Florence. The establishment of

The Execution of Savonarola in the Piazza della Signoria by an anonymous sixteenth-century artist. (Alinari-Art Reference Bureau)

a popular regime and the creation of the Great Council had placated the middle strata of Florentine society but had alienated many patricians who believed that public affairs should be reserved for citizens of wealth, status, and experience. The conflict between advocates of oligarchy and popular government was an old theme in Florentine politics; this regime was no more successful in resolving it than its predecessors. The election in 1502 of Piero Soderini as permanent *gonfaloniere* of justice was a concession to the aristocratic pressure for constitutional reform, but it did not satisfy the patricians. Soderini refused to become a tool of the great families but instead sought to maintain a balance between the aristocratic and the popular factions. He managed to hold the regime together for ten years, but he never persuaded the aristocrats to accept the Great Council or the popular republicanism which it symbolized.

As had occurred so often in the past, these internal dissensions were exacerbated by external forces and pressures which imperiled the regime's security and the city's independence. Generations of Florentines had learned to live with the omnipresent dangers from abroad, but rarely if ever had the citizenry felt more insecure and vulnerable than in the years after Charles VIII's invasion. The republic's impotence was advertised by the failure to recover Pisa, despite yearly campaigns launched against the rebel city and its *contado,* and the expenditure of hundreds of thousands of florins. Pisa's revolt encouraged opponents of Florentine rule in other parts of the dominion: in Arezzo, which rebelled in 1502, and also in Pistoia and Volterra. The years between 1499 and 1503 were particularly crucial; they coincided with the efforts of Pope Alexander's son, Cesare Borgia, to build a large and powerful state in central Italy, which, had it survived, would have endangered Florence's independence. But Cesare's power and his state dissolved with Alexander's death in August 1503. Freed from this peril on her eastern frontier, Florence pursued her campaign against Pisa, which finally surrendered in June 1509.

Tradition, economic considerations, and a paramount concern for Pisa's recovery dictated the republic's unswerving loyalty to France; the Valois alliance became the keystone of Florentine foreign policy after 1494. The conquest of Milan in 1499 by

Charles VIII's successor, Louis XII, restored French power to the peninsula, although this did not contribute materially to Pisa's recovery as the king had promised and as the Florentines had hoped. Even though deluded by the French failure to assist her in regaining Pisa, the republic under Soderini's leadership continued to seek its security under the French banner. But each year seemed to bring another peril, and to add yet another complication to the turbulent state of peninsular politics. By Louis XII's invitation, Ferdinand of Aragon made his entree onto the Italian scene in 1501, through his joint conquest with France of the Neapolitan kingdom. Two years later, the Spanish forces drove out their erstwhile allies and created a solid power base in southern Italy, as a counter to the French presence in Milan. In 1506 Pope Julius II began his campaign to gain effective control over the Papal States by occupying Perugia and Bologna. Then he organized an alliance, the league of Cambrai, against Venice, which had occupied some portions of the Papal States in northern Romagna. Partners in this enterprise, which was launched in 1508, included the pope and the monarchs of France, Spain, and Germany; they quickly subdued the Venetians, who sued for peace in 1510. Not satisfied with Venice's abasement, Julius II next moved against the French king, whom he accused of planning to subjugate all of Italy. In the autumn of 1511, he organized a Holy League (comprising Spain, Venice, and England) against France. The outbreak of war between Louis XII and the pope placed Florence in a terrible dilemma, since both princes demanded her help against the other, and both were antagonized by her desperate efforts to remain neutral. Florence's treaty commitments bound her to France, however, and Soderini steadfastly refused to break that obligation. When a French army under Gaston de Foix defeated the forces of the Holy League in June 1512, Florence's safety was apparently secured.

Then, very suddenly, the fortunes of war and politics shifted against Soderini and the republic. Gaston de Foix died of battle wounds; his successor received orders from Louis XII to withdraw the French army from Italy. Florence was abandoned and forsaken; a meeting of Holy League representatives in Mantua decided to crush the republican regime and restore the Medici.

A Spanish army was sent into Tuscany to carry out the League's decision. On August 28, 1512, this force attacked the garrison in Prato, eight miles from Florence, conquered and sacked the city. A demoralized government abandoned the struggle against the Spanish; Piero Soderini fled into exile. A new regime was formed by Medici sympathizers and members of aristocratic families. While this government retained the traditional institutions, offices, and practices of the republic (except the Great Council, which was suppressed), it was essentially a puppet regime controlled and manipulated by the Medici. Lorenzo's second son, Cardinal Giovanni (who became Pope Leo X after Julius II's death in February 1513), governed the city through his relatives and associates. To an even greater extent than in Lorenzo's time, the Medici palace became the headquarters of the Florentine state.

FINALE (1512–1532)

The Florentine Renaissance has been defined in various ways: as a chronological period, as a cultural phenomenon, as a complex of attitudes, ideas, and values. However it is described and interpreted, it was the creation of a free and independent community. Liberty and republicanism were two key elements of the city's historical experience. With the restoration of the Medici in 1512, these foundations (which had long been under attack) finally disintegrated. Slowly and reluctantly, Florentines realized that their golden age had ended, that their traditional liberties were dead, and that they no longer controlled their own destiny. The years between 1512 and 1532 were spent in learning and relearning these painful truths.

Florentines responded to the restoration in different ways. Aristocrats with Medicean sympathies naturally rejoiced in the return of their friends; they looked forward eagerly to their share of the benefits and perquisites of power. Joining them in the courtyards and anterooms of the Medici palace was a group of young and ambitious patricians who accepted the demise of the republic and the advent of despotic government. They too desired to profit from the new system by insinuating themselves into Medici favor. Their elders, however, were reluctant to abandon their dreams of a republican restoration. Some nourished the naive hope that the Medici could be persuaded to give up their privileged status and live as private citizens. Such reactions were typical of aristocrats whose position had not been threatened by the restoration, and who had some expectations of benefiting from Medici largesse. Others, less sanguine about their future under the Medici, pursued different courses. A handful of republican die-hards organized a conspiracy in the spring of 1513 and were beheaded or exiled for their pains. Savonarola's disciples continued to keep the friar's memory alive; they tended to withdraw from public life, convinced that a viable political order in Florence could only be achieved through a moral and spiritual regeneration of the city. Still others retired to their palaces and villas, concentrating upon their private affairs, devoting themselves to literature, music and the arts. A few hardy souls decided to abandon their native city and seek their fortunes elsewhere. The move to Rome of Florence's two greatest artists, Leonardo da Vinci and Michelangelo,* was a sign that Rome had replaced Tuscany as the cultural center of Italy.

The city's fate in these years was inextricably linked to that of Rome; the bond was the Medici pope, Leo X. The policies pursued by that cultured and affable pontiff were seemingly calculated to sustain the illusion that nothing had changed since 1494, that the age of Lorenzo could be recreated in Florence, and that the diplomatic tactics of the fifteenth century were adequate to confront the problems of a new era. In Florence, Leo hoped to reconcile the citizenry to the new regime by retaining the façade of republicanism and by providing a heavy diet of festivals and entertainments. His prodigality and lavish patronage of the arts was a great boon to Rome's economy and to the fortunes of those favorites (including hundreds of Florentines) who received papal commissions, pensions, and gifts. In foreign affairs, Leo was guided by Lorenzo's example. He sought to maintain a balance of power in Italy; he hoped that this

---

*The exodus of artists from Florence had begun before 1512. Michelangelo had traveled between Florence and Rome since 1496; after 1512, he spent most of his time in Rome. Raphael left Florence for Rome in 1508. Leonardo left his native city in 1513 and spent four years in Rome before traveling to France.

would prevent the peninsula's domination by either France or Spain, and would thus preserve the independence of the Papal States and Florence. But the initiative in Italian affairs no longer rested with Rome, or indeed with any peninsular state, but with the great European powers. In 1515, a young and energetic prince, Francis I, became king of France and led an army across the Alps to reconquer the duchy of Milan. The pope had joined his Spanish and Swiss allies in resisting the French invasion, but he quickly negotiated a settlement with Francis after the king's decisive victory at Marignano (September 1515). For the remainder of his pontificate, Leo trod a very circumspect path between the French and the Spaniards, who, from their respective bases in Milan and Naples, waited for a favorable opportunity to expand their power. In the last year of his life, Leo X decided to abandon his cautious policy of neutrality; he made an alliance with the emperor-elect, Charles V, against France. The pope received the news that the French had lost Milan just a few days before his death, in December 1521.

Leo was succeeded by the Flemish cardinal, Adrian of Utrecht, who assumed the title of Hadrian VI. Cardinal Giulio de' Medici, a nephew of the dead pope, retained control of Florence and when Hadrian died in 1523, he was elected to the Holy See. A weaker and less decisive man than his uncle (who was himself no dynamo of energy and forcefulness), the new pontiff, Clement VII, played the key role in Florence's dramatic and turbulent history during his eleven-year pontificate (1523–1534). The security of the Papal States and Florence was in grave jeopardy after the battle of Pavia in 1525, when Francis I was decisively beaten in his campaign to recover Milan. Italy's subjugation by a foreign ruler, so often predicted and feared since 1494, now appeared to be a reality. To restore the power balance in the peninsula, Clement VII made an alliance with France and Venice (the League of Cognac) in May 1526; the objective was the expulsion of Spain from Italy. Armies of the League besieged and finally captured Cremona, but they could not oust the imperial forces from Lombardy. In the spring of 1527, an unpaid and undisciplined throng of imperial troops marched south into Tuscany, threatened Florence, but then bypassed the city and moved toward Rome. On May 6, the troops assaulted the

Roman walls, broke into the city and pillaged it, while Clement VII watched from the security of his fortress, the Castel S. Angelo. When news of Rome's disaster and the pope's plight reached Florence, a group of republicans organized a movement to overthrow the Medici state. With a minimum of violence, the old regime fell and the republic was restored on May 16, 1527.

For nearly two years, Florence's last republic was not challenged by the Medici, nor was it directly menaced by Spanish arms. Clement VII was too weak and demoralized to make any serious efforts to recover the city; he did not return to Rome from his sanctuary in Orvieto until October 1528. Having received no help from his French and Venetian allies, the pope was forced to come to terms with the emperor-elect, Charles V. In the Treaty of Barcelona, signed on June 29, 1529, the two princes formed a defensive alliance. Charles promised to assist Clement VII against Florence, while the pope recognized the emperor's authority in Milan, and so tacitly accepted Spanish hegemony in the peninsula.

Thus was the diplomatic stage set for the final assault upon Florence and her republican regime. For the second time in a generation, Spanish arms were employed to bring Florence to heel and restore the city to the Medici. In April 1529, the leadership of the republic had passed from the moderate Niccolò Capponi (who was apparently willing to negotiate a settlement with Clement VII) to the intransigent Francesco Carducci, an implacable foe of the Medici. With compromise and reconciliation no longer possible, the imperial armies began their siege operations in October 1529. Behind their walls, the citizens repelled the imperial attacks, but they were unable to obtain adequate food supplies for a population swollen by refugees from the *contado*. Hunger and famine weakened the city's will to resist; efforts to break the blocade failed. On August 12, 1530, after a ten-month siege, the regime capitulated and Spanish troops entered the starving city.

Once back in power, the Medici revenged themselves on their enemies. Francesco Carducci and five associates went to the scaffold, in violation of the amnesty provision in the capitulation; other republicans were exiled and their property confiscated. But Clement VII did not have a completely free hand in re-

organizing the city. The emperor was now the arbiter of Florentine affairs; the Medici had to accept the decisions of their new
master. This unpalatable fact was publicized in an imperial
decree of 1531 which recognized Medicean primary in Florence,
but also proclaimed the emperor's sovereign rights over the city
and its territory. On May 1, 1532, the Medici promulgated a
new constitution, which abolished the magistracy of the Signoria (it had survived for 250 years) and named Duke Alessandro de' Medici as head of state. Protected and supported by
Spanish arms, the Medici principate was born.

In that Florentine generation which witnessed the demise of
the republic, two men stand out: Niccolò Machiavelli (1469–
1527) and Francesco Guicciardini (1483–1540). Their lives and
careers were shaped (one might almost say deformed) by these
tragic events. Both men were patricians, although Guicciardini's
family was wealthier and more prominent than Machiavelli's.
In 1498 Machiavelli obtained a position as secretary to the Ten
on War, and for fourteen years, he was an active and influential
figure in the republican regime, an intimate counselor of Piero
Soderini. When the republic fell in 1512, he lost his post and
never again held an office in the Florentine government. Guicciardini's political career began as Machiavelli's ended. He
served the Medici regime in Florence and the Medici papacy in
Rome; for several years he was an administrator in the Papal
States. In the 1520s, he and Machiavelli became close friends,
each attracted by the other's intelligence and passionate interest
in politics. Only Machiavelli's death in 1527 terminated their
relationship; that year also marked a turning point in Guicciardini's career. Too closely identified with the Medici to enjoy
favor with the republican regime of 1527–1530, his willingness to
serve that government had angered Pope Clement VII. After
the return of the Medici in 1530, he again worked for his old
masters. When he lost the trust of Duko Cosimo (who succeeded
the murdered Alessandro as head of state in 1537), he went
into retirement and began to write his *History of Italy*.

Some men respond to disaster (whether private or public)
by denouncing those judged responsible, or by engaging in self-
justification and self-exculpation. Machiavelli and Guicciardini

indulged very sparingly in these fruitless exercises. Instead, they were stimulated by the Italian tragedy to examine the historical events, and to scrutinize the policies which had led to those events. Their reaction to crisis was creative in the highest degree, for it contributed to the formulation of new concepts of politics and of the historical process.

In their views of the human condition, Machiavelli and Guicciardini were much less sanguine than the Quattrocento humanists. They saw men as selfish and egotistical creatures, concerned primarily with their own interest, and rarely if ever capable of generous or selfless action. To control such beings, moral and religious principles were useless; force was the prime requisite. In addition to rejecting the humanist (and the Christian) belief in man's goodness and perfectability, these Florentines expressed doubts about the efficacy of reason in directing human affairs. Too frequently, they argued, men were guided by passion and emotion; moreover, the application of reason to human problems did not guarantee success. Machiavelli and Guicciardini were both committed to rational analysis; but they also believed that fortune and chance played major roles in history and that occasionally, intelligent and knowledgeable men could be crushed by forces outside their control. Since 1494, these men had lived in a world dominated by the irrational and the unpredictable, by the triumph of force and violence over reason and calculation. Their writings reflect this experience in a very direct and immediate way.

Even though their view of human nature and human experience was pessimistic, Machiavelli and Guicciardini were not advocates of resignation and despair. Neither suggested that men should cease to think, or that they should abandon themselves to fate; rather, they should develop and use their minds to the fullest extent. Intelligent and prudent men can avoid some (not all) of fortune's blows, and they should try to understand their environment, even if they cannot always control it. Machiavelli was perhaps more sanguine about human possibilities than his compatriot, possibly because he died first and thus did not witness the full extent of Italy's tragedy. Even in a corrupt society, he believed, men could live decent lives if they were governed by a ruler who possessed some measure of the *virtù*,* which the citizenry lacked. Machiavelli's ideal form of political organization was a republic in which men were so imbued with *virtù* (as were the ancient Romans) that they would willingly sacrifice themselves for the state. Although a regime similar to Rome's republic was not conceivable in the Italy Machiavelli knew, the fates which controlled human destiny might forge another superior model somewhere at some future time. Guicciardini, on the other hand, was very pessimistic about the future of his enfeebled and degraded country. By writing the account of Italy's disaster, he appeared to be saying that men must learn to live in a world without hope. Perhaps he believed that they could achieve some measure of dignity by understanding and accepting their own nature, and their impotence in the toils of an ineluctable fate.

---

*In his *Machiavelli and Guicciardini* (Princeton, 1965, p. 179), Felix Gilbert defines Machiavelli's concept of *virtù:* "The meaning of this term in his writings has many facets; basically it was an italianization of the Latin word *virtus* and denoted the fundamental quality of man which enables him to achieve great works and deeds. In the ancient world man's *virtus* was placed in relation to *Fortuna; virtus* was an innate quality opposed to external circumstances or chance. *Virtù* was not one of the various virtues which Christianity required of good men, nor was *virtù* an epitome of all Christian virtues; rather it designated the strength and vigor from which all human action arose."

Bibliography and Notes

CHAPTER I: THE RENAISSANCE CITY

There is no comprehensive study of Florence's metamorphosis from provincial town to urban metropolis. The fundamental work on medieval Florence's topography is R. Davidsohn, *Forschungen zur Geschichte von Florenz* (Berlin, 1896–1908), IV, 389–530; and his *Geschichte von Florenz* (Berlin, 1896–1927), IV, 247–281; Italian translation, *Storia di Firenze* (Florence, 1956–1965), VII, 475–540. Important studies on the city's relations with its rural hinterland include: J. Plesner, *L'émigration de la campagne à la ville libre de Florence au XIII*e *siècle* (Copenhagen, 1934) and the same author's "Una rivoluzione stradale nel dugento, " *Acta Jutlandica*, I (1938); E. Fiumi, "Sui rapporti fra città e contado," *Archivio storico italiano*, CXIV (1956); and the important but incomplete study of Tuscan agrarian history by E. Conti, *La formazione della struttura agraria moderna nel contado fiorentino* (Rome, 1965——).

A useful guide to contemporary Florence is the Touring Club Italiano's *Firenze e dintorni*, 5th edition (Milan, 1964). A recent, attractive guidebook is Eve Borsook, *The Companion Guide to Florence* (London, 1966). Among the numerous photographic albums of Florence and its environs, two examples may be cited: *Firenze* in the *Attraverso l'Italia series* (Milan: Touring Club Italiano, 1962). and A. von Borsig, *Tuscany* (London, 1955). There is a good collection of old drawings and maps of Florence in R. Ciullini, "Di una raccolta di antiche carte e vedute della citta di Firenze," *L'universo*, V (1924). Artists' impressions of the medieval quarters of the city before the demolitions of the nineteenth century are in C. Ricci, *Cento vedute di Firenze antica* (Florence, 1906), and H. Railton, *Pen Drawings of Florence* (Cleveland, n.d.). The most comprehensive survey of the city's ancient buildings is W. Limburger, *Die Gebäude von Florenz* (Leipzig, 1910). W. Braunfels has written a general survey of urban building in medieval

Tuscan towns: *Mittelalterliche Stadtbaukunst in der Toskana* (Berlin, 1953). The demolition of the Mercato Vecchio and its environs in the 1880s inspired the writing and publication of several descriptive studies: *Studi storici sul centro di Firenze* (Florence, 1889); *Il centro di Firenze. Studi storici e ricordi artistici* (Florence, 1900); G. Carocci, *Il Mercato Vecchio di Firenze* (Florence, 1884) and the same author's *Firenze scomparsa* (Florence, 1898).

Students of Florentine architecture have concentrated much of their attention upon churches. The results of these researches have been assembled by W. and E. Paatz, *Die Kirchen von Florenz*, 6 vols. (Frankfurt am Main, 1940–1954). The cathedral, and particularly Brunelleschi's cupola, has been the subject of intensive study. A brief analysis, with superb illustrations, is in W. Braunfels, *Der Dom von Florenz* (Olten, 1964); a survey of the literature and the scholarly controversies in H. Saalman, "Santa Maria del Fiore, 1294–1418," *Art Bulletin*, XLVI (1964), 471–500. The construction of the Loggia dei Lanzi has been described by K. Frey, *Die Loggia dei Lanzi* (Berlin, 1885), the Palazzo della Signoria by A. Lensi, *Palazzo Vecchio* (Milan-Rome, 1929). The other major public buildings have not yet found a modern historian.

The data on urban rents was culled from the *catasto* records for the years 1427, 1430, and 1433, and particularly the volumes of the first *catasto* of 1427; *Archivio di Stato di Firenze* [ASF], *Catasto*, 64–81. The specific citations of rental figures are: *Catasto*, 64, fol. 302r; 80, fol. 73v; 81, fols. 518r–518v; 491, fol. 289v.

The documentation for a history of Florentine urban planning is sketchy, particularly for the medieval centuries. Braunfels, *Mittelalterliche Baukunst*, has references to some of the early legislation on urban planning; his sources may be supplemented by documents printed in Davidsohn, *Forschungen*, IV, 441–514; and G. Gaye, *Carteggio inedito d'artisti dei secoli XIV, XV, XVI* (Florence, 1839), I, appendix. The quotation from Salutati's *Invective* is in P. Ruggiers, *Florence in the Age of Dante* (Norman, Okla., 1964), ix. The decrees of the tower officials are in ASF, *Giudice degli Appelli*, 71, no pagination, 15 June 1397; 72, no pag., 9 Aug. 1401; 74, no pag., 4 July and 30 Aug. 1415; 74, no pag., 11 Oct. 1421; 79, part 2, fol. 180r. Some of the decrees of these officials, in the *Archivio del Parte Guelfa* of the *Archivio di Stato*, were damaged in the 1966 flood; see *Archivio storico italiano*, CXXIV (1966), 439–441. The decree authorizing the widening of the streets around the cathedral is printed in C. Guasti, *S. Maria del Fiore* (Florence, 1887), 284. The project to enlarge the square of S. Lorenzo is described in ASF, *Deliberazioni dei Signori e Collegi, ordinaria autorità*, 44, fols. 18v–19r, 18 March 1434. The enlargement and embellishment of the Piazza della Signoria has been documented in *Frey, Loggia dei Lanzi*. A good study on the cathedral *opera* is A. Grote, *Das Dombauamt in Florenz*, 1285–1370 (Munich, 1959); references to the *opere* of other ecclesiastical foundations are in Frey, *Loggia*, 154–156; *ASF, Provvisioni*, 72, fols. 72v-73v, and R. Morcay, S. *Antonin fondateur du couvent de Saint-Marc archevêque de Florence (1389–1459)*, (Paris and Tours, 1914), 47.

Our knowledge of private building in medieval and Renaissance Florence is quite limited. There is some information on early domestic architecture in J. W. Brown, *The Builders of Florence* (London and New York, 1907); A. Haupt, *Palast-architektur von Ober-italien und Toskana*, II (Berlin, 1888); B. Patzak, *Palast und Villa in Toskana*, 2 vols. (Leipzig, 1912–1913); and A. Schiaparelli, *La casa fiorentina ed i suoi arredi* (Florence, 1908). Data on particular buildings are found in Limburger, *Gebäude von Florenz*, and in G. and C. Thiem, *Toskanische Fassaden-Dekoration in Sgraffito und Fresko 14. bis 17. Jahrhundert* (Munich, 1964). The latter work also contains some excellent illustrations and a comprehensive bibliography. The building plans for a small Florentine house of the mid-fourteenth century are described in P. Sanpaolesi, "Un progetto di costruzione per una casa del secolo XIV," in *Atti del IV Convegno Nazionale di storia dell' architettura* (Milan, 1939), 259–266. A concise survey of the work of the great Quattrocento Florentine architects is P. Murray, *The Architecture of the Italian Renaissance* (New York, 1963). Luca Landucci's reference to the construction of the Strozzi palace is in his *Florentine Diary* (London, 1927), 48.

Antonio Pucci's description of the Old Market is in *Delizie degli eruditi toscani*, ed. I. di San Luigi (Florence, 1770–1789), VI, 267–274. The role of the Tartar slaves in Florentine society has been described by I. Origo, "The Domestic Enemy: the Eastern Slaves in Tuscany in the Fourteenth and Fifteenth Centuries," *Speculum*, XXX (1955), 321–366, with illustrations. Leon Battista Alberti's description of the Piazza della Signoria is in E. Borsook, *Companion Guide to Florence*, 42.

The celebration of the feast of St. John the Baptist is described by Davidsohn, *Storia di Firenze*, VII, 562–564. The selections from the anonymous chronicler of the 1380s are in *Diario d'anonimo fiorentino dall'anno 1358 al 1389*, in *Cronache dei secoli XIII e XIV*, ed. A. Gherardi (Florence, 1876), 400, 463–467, 525–526. The revolution of 1378 is described in my *Florentine Politics and Society, 1343–1378* (Princeton, 1963) and my article, "The Ciompi Revolution," in *Florentine Studies*, ed. N. Rubinstein (London, 1968), 314–356. The three accounts of the Black Death in Florence are: Matteo Villani, *Cronica*

(Florence, 1846), I, chaps. 1–2; *Cronaca fiorentina di Marchionne di Coppo Stefani,* ed. N. Rodolico, *Rerum Italicarum Scriptores,* new ed., XXX, part 1 (Città di Castello, 1903–1955), rubric 634; G. Boccaccio, *The Decameron,* trans. J. Rigg (London, 1906), I, 5–12. D. Herlihy has compiled a list of the years of famine and plague in the city of Pistoia, 30 miles from Florence; *Medieval and Renaissance Pistoia* (New Haven, 1967), 105.

CHAPTER II: THE ECONOMY

The most comprehensive bibliography on Florentine economic history is in A. Sapori, *Studi di storia economica (secoli XIII-XIV-XV),* 3rd edition (Florence, 1956). Briefer compilations are printed in Sapori, *Le marchand italien au moyen âge* (Paris, 1952), 1–14; G. Brucker, *Florentine Politics and Society,* 403–406; and R. de Roover, *The Rise and Decline of the Medici Bank 1397–1494* (Cambridge, Mass., 1963), 391–408. Sapori and De Roover have made significant contributions to our knowledge of Florentine economic development, as has E. Fiumi in his study, "Fioritura e decadenza dell' economia fiorentina," *Archivio storico italiano,* CXV–CXVII (1957–1959).

Alfred Doren's studies of the guild system and the woolen cloth industry are somewhat dated: *Das Florentiner Zunftwesen vom XIV. bis zum XVI. Jahrhundert* (Stuttgart, 1908), and *Die florentiner Wollentuchindustrie vom vierzehnten bis zum sechzehnten Jahrhundert* (Stuttgart, 1901). My "revisionist" analysis of the Ciompi Revolution appears in *Florentine Studies,* ed. Rubinstein, 314–356. The account book of Niccolò Strozzi and his partner is in *ASF, Carte Strozziane,* series III, 278; that of Lippo di Dino and Francesco di Vanni in *ibid.,* series II, 5.

Donato Velluti's account of his son's apprenticeship is in his *Cronica domestica di Messer Donato Velluti* (Florence, 1914), 311. Francesco Pegolotti's mercantile manual has been edited by A. Evans, *La pratica della mercatura* (Cambridge, Mass., 1936). Selections from Francesco Datini's correspondence are printed in F. Melis, *Aspetti della vita economica medievale* (Siena, 1962), I, 35, 36, 214–215. Buonaccorso Pitti's chronicle has been translated by Julia Martines: *Two Memoirs of Renaissance Florence. The Diaries of Buonaccorso Pitti and Gregorio Dati,* ed. G. Brucker (New York, 1967). The documents pertaining to Francesco Davizzi and Domenico Lanfredini are in *Carte Strozziane,* series III, 112, fol. 90r; and *Biblioteca Nazionale di Firenze* [BNF], II, V, 7, fol. 5r. The Venetian scandal involving letters of credit is described in *ASF Mercanzia,* 1187, fols. 67v–70r. Andrea Lamberteschi's tax declaration is in *Catasto*, 68, fols. 34r–34v. The plight of Bartolo Petriboni and Francesco Bernadetti is recounted in *Mercanzia*, 1177, fols. 58r–75r; that of Bernardo Davanzati in *ASF*, *Acquisti e Doni*, 296, no pag.

The protocols of the Arte della Lana are an important source for the difficulties experienced by the cloth industry in the 1370s; some of the evidence is cited in Doren, *Wollentuchindustrie*, 303–317, and in my article in *Florentine Studies*, 323–325. The Datini letters describing the city's economic troubles during the Milanese war are in the *Archivio di Stato*, *Prato*, *Archivio Datini*, vols. 1064, 987, and 868, no pag. The comment on the Florentine economy by Rinaldo Rondinelli is in *ASF*, *Consulte e Pratiche*, 40, fols. 209v. Giovanni Rucellai's reference to economic conditions is printed in *Giovanni Rucellai ed il suo Zibaldone*, ed. A. Perosa (London, 1960), I, 46, 60–62. The legislation granting tax exemptions and a debt moratorium is in *Provvisioni*, 114, fols. 63v–64r; 117, fol. 45v; 118, fols. 116v–117v; 122, fols. 2r–3r. The proposal to allow Jews to settle in Florence was made in August 1431; *Consulte e Pratiche*, 49, fols. 184v–185r. U. Cassuto has described the establishment of a Jewish colony in 1437; *Gli ebrei a Firenze nell'età del Rinascimento* (Florence, 1918), 17–23.

The prosperity of the Florentine silk industry in the fifteenth century is documented by G. Corti and J. G. Da Silva, "Note sur la production de la soie à Florence, au XVe siècle," *Annales*, XX (1965), 309–311. Statistics from the cloth enterprises of the Fortini were gleaned from *Catasto*, 80, fol. 567r. The vicissitudes of woolen cloth production in the late fifteenth century are described by Doren, *Wollentuchindustrie*, 416–425. Florence's development as a maritime power is discussed by M. Mallett, *The Florentine Galleys in the Fifteenth Century* (Oxford, 1967).

CHAPTER III: THE PATRICIATE

Many of the sources for economic history listed by Sapori, *Le marchand italien au moyen âge*, 1–14, are also useful for social history. A recent and important work on the Florentine patriciate is L. Martines, *The Social World of the Florentine Humanists 1390–1460* (Princeton, 1963), which supersedes the older analysis of A. von Martin, *Sociology of the Renaissance* (New York, 1963). There is some material on the patriciate in Brucker, *Florentine Politics and Society*, 27–56. A study of particular importance is P. Jones, "Florentine Families and Florentine Diaries in the Fourteenth Century," *Studies in Italian Medieval History presented to Miss E.M. Jamison* (Rome, 1956), 183–205. Richard Goldthwaite's *Private Wealth in Renaissance Florence* (Princeton, 1968) is a valuable contribution to the subject.

References to the Alberti, Spini, and Morelli families are in L. Passerini, *Gli Alberti di Firenze* (Florence, 1869), II, 7–9; *Carte Strozziane*, ser. II, 13, fol. 15r; G. Morelli, *Ricordi*, ed. V. Branca (Florence, 1955), 81–83. Francesco Davanzati's letter concerning the Peruzzi marriage is in *ASF*, Conventi Soppressi, no. 78, vol. 315, fol. 287r. The Del Bene family is the subject of a recent monograph: H. Hoshino, "Francesco di Iacopo Del Bene cittadino fiorentino del Trecento," *Istituto giapponese di cultura*, Rome; *Annuario*, IV (1966–1967), 29–119. The letters on marriage written by Giovanni del Bene are in *ASF*, *Archivio Del Bene*, 51, no pag. There is information on the Castellani in Martines, *Social World*, 199–210; and on the Vespucci, in G. Arciniegas, *Amerigo and the New World* (New York, 1955). The petition of Andrea Salterelli is in *Provvisioni*, 84, fols. 229v-231r. Giovanni Morelli's advice concerning marriage is printed in his *Ricordi*, 208–209. The letters received by Forese Sacchetti are in the *Conventi Soppressi*, no. 78, vol. 323.

The statements concerning merchants by Gregorio Dati and Bernardo da Castiglionchio are reported in Martines, *Social World*, 32; the opinion on banking, in Melis, *Aspetti*, 213. Giovanni Morelli's views on business activity are in his *Ricordi*, 225–243; his biography of his father is in *ibid.*, 143–159. The denunciation of the Bardi is in *ASF*, *Atti del Esecutore degli Ordinamenti di Giustizia*, 1223, fol. 4r. Donato Velluti's description of his shiftless relative, Piero Pitti, is in his *Cronica domestica*, 138–139. The reference to Giovanni Capponi is in Martines, *Social World*, 25. Paolo Sassetti's reference to his disgraced cousin Letta is in *Carte Strozziane*, ser. II, 4, fol. 67r. Morelli describes the illicit amours of his cousin in his *Ricordi*, 162–163.

Bicci de' Medici's testament is in *ASF*, *Atti Notarili*, L 290, vol. 3, fols. 17r-19r. Vespasiano da Bisticci's reference to Cosimo de' Medici is in *The Vespasiano Memoirs* (London, 1926; Harper Torchbook reprint, New York, 1963), 218–219. Donato Velluti's account of Bernardo's religious crisis is in *Cronica domestica*, 40–41. Gregorio Dati's struggle for moral improvement is described in *Two Memoirs of Renaissance Florence*, 124–125.

A selection of Lapo Mazzei's letters to Francesco Datini was edited by C. Guasti: *Lettere di un notaro a un mercante* (Florence, 1880). Lapo's analysis of his friendship with the merchant is printed in vol. I, 191; his letter expressing his fears concerning Datini's preoccupation with the world was translated by I. Origo, *The Merchant of Prato* (New York, 1957), 236–237. The letter describing Lapo's encounter with Bartolo Pucci is in the Guasti edition, II, 56–58. Baldetta Manetti's complaint about her son is in *ASF, Arte del Cambio*, 65, fol. 43v. Niccolò Bastari's letter is in *Conventi Soppressi*, no. 78, vol. 313, fols. 94r–94v; Remigio Lanfredini's denunciation of his father is in *BNF*, II, V, 7, fols. 137r-138r. Antonio Rustichi's memoirs are in *Carte Strozziane*, ser. II, 11. The reference to Luca da Panzano's vendetta is in *Archivio storico italiano*, ser. 5, IV (1889), 149–152; Angelo Ricoveri's hiring of an assassin is described in *Atti del Esecutore*, 1269, fols. 79r–80v. Simone della Tosa's references to the crimes committed by his relatives are in *Cronichette antiche di vari scrittori*, ed. D. Manni (Florence, 1733), 163–166. Luigi Guicciardini's account of his kinsman's crimes is in *Carte Strozziane*, ser. I, 16, fols. 4r–5r.

There is a discussion of Guido del Palagio's career in the preface of Giovanni da Prato's *Il Paradiso degli Alberti*, ed. Wesselofsky (Bologna, 1867), I, 93–96. Lapo Mazzei's letters concerning Guido are in the Guasti edition, I, 125; II, 63. Vespasiano da Bisticci's biographies of Cosimo de' Medici and Palla Strozzi are in *The Vespasiano Memoirs*, 213–245. "Il Zibaldone Quaresimale" of Giovanni Rucellai is the source of our knowledge about this patrician; it was edited by A. Perosa, *Giovanni Rucellai ed il suo Zibaldone*.

CHAPTER IV: POLITICS

A concise summary of the origins and development of the Italian commune is in the recent study by J. K. Hyde, *Padua in the Age of Dante* (Manchester and New York, 1966), 9–26. Florence's political history to 1330 is analyzed in the monumental work of R. Davidsohn, *Geschichte von Florenz*, 4 vols. (Berlin, 1896-1927; Italian translation, Florence, 1956–1965), and by M. Becker, *Florence in Transition*, I (Baltimore, 1967). F. Schevill, *History of Florence* (New York, 1936; Harper Torchbook edition, New York, 1963) is dated but still useful. G. Brucker, *Florentine Politics and Society*, chap. 2, contains an analysis of republican institutions in the mid-fourteenth century. A recent, informed account of Florentine politics prior to 1434 is C. Bayley, *War and Society in Renaissance Florence* (Toronto, 1961). Two recent and important books on Florentine government are: N. Rubinstein, *The Government of Florence under the Medici 1434–1494* (Oxford, 1966) and L. Martines, *Lawyers and Statecraft in Renaissance Florence* (Princeton, 1968). Both works examine the institutional and technical aspects of Florentine government, which are neglected in this essay.

I have used Thomas Bergin's translation of Dante's comments on Filippo Cavicciuli (*Inferno*, VIII, 54–57; Crofts Classics); and John Ciardi's translation of Dante's conversation with Ciacco (*Inferno*, VI,

55–72, Mentor Classic). The references to the statements by Alessandro Alessandri, Matteo Tinghi, and Rinaldo Gianfigliazzi are in *Consulte e Pratiche*, 27, fol. 57r; 26, fol. 224r; 42, fol. 17v. Palla Strozzi's speech of 1430 in opposition to tax reform is in *Carte Strozziane*, series III, 125, fols. 126r–127v. The Del Bene correspondence describing the dispute with Filippo Adimari is in *Carte Del Bene*, 51 and *Acquisti e Doni*, 301, no pag. Giovanni Cavalcanti's comments on taxation are in his *Istorie fiorentine*, ed. G. di Pino (Milan, 1944), I, chap. 11. The appeals for tax relief by Barone di Cose and his fellow petitioners are in *Provvisioni*, 82, fols. 22r–23v; 87, fols. 62v–64r; 91, fol. 27r; 92, fols. 183v–184r; 95, fols. 224v–225r; 101, fol. 203r. The letters of Lanfredino Lanfredini and Donato Acciaiuoli are in *BNF*, II, V, 7, fol. 9r and Carte Del Bene, 49, no. 289. The conversation between the widow Margherita and Antonio di Piero is recorded in *Atti del Podestà*, 4080, fols. 23r–23v. R. de Roover has written a brief summary of the *catasto* in his *Rise and Decline of the Medici Bank*, 21–31.

L. Martines discusses the Florentine judicial system in his *Lawyers and Statecraft*, 130–145, and appends a bibliography, 215–217. Marchionne Stefani described a rector's misdeeds in his *Cronaca fiorentina*, rub. 938. The cases of judicial malfeasance in 1387 and 1400 are in *ASF*, *Atti del Capitano*, 2107, no pag.; *Atti del Esecutore*, 1680, fols. 91r–92r; *Provvisioni*, 76, fols. 41r–42v. The letters written by Francesco de Coppoli to Forese Sacchetti are in *Conventi Soppressi*, 78, vol. 325, nos. 338, 365. The examples of *bollettini* are in *Atti del Capitano*, 2605, fols. 5v–6r; and in *ASF*, *Deliberazioni dei Signori e Collegi, ordinaria autorità*, 32, fols. 10r–10v. The complaint of the two accused kidnappers is in *Provvisioni*, 115, fol. 7r.

The statements of the Ciompi conspirators, Luca di Guido and Antonio di Recco (somewhat suspect because extracted by torture) are in *Atti del Capitano*, 1197 bis, fols. 130r–132r; 1198, fols. 31r–35r. The Ciompi plot of July 1383 is described in *Atti del Esecutore*, 960, fols. 45r–47v. The revolutionary plans of the Alberti in 1411–1412 are outlined in *Atti del Esecutore*, 1759, fols. 103r–108r; 1763, fols. 3r–4r; 1785, fols. 14v–16r.

Buonaccorso Pitti's account of his unpleasant experiences with the Ricasoli, *Two Memoirs of Renaissance Florence*, 88–97, is corroborated by the criminal court records; *Atti del Podestà*, 4272, no pag., 17 Dec. 1412; and *Atti del Esecutore*, 1808, fols. 68r–69r. Cavalcanti's judgments on internal politics prior to 1434 are in *Istorie fiorentine*, book I, prologue, chaps. 1, 7, 10–11; book II, chaps. 1–4, 7, 21–23; book III, chaps. 1–10. C. Gutkind has written a laudatory biography of Cosimo: *Cosimo de' Medici Pater Patriae 1389–1464* (Oxford, 1938). Evidence of Cosimo's close ties with *condottieri* has been collected by C. Bayley,

War and Society in Renaissance Florence, 120–124, 227. Cosimo's letter to Pius II is printed in Janet Ross, *Lives of the Early Medici as Told in their Correspondence* (London, 1910), 66–69.

The fiscal problems resulting from escalating war costs in the Trecento are described by M. Becker, "Economic Change and the Emerging Florentine Territorial State," *Studies in the Renaissance,* XIII (1966), 7–39. The letter ordering the S. Gimignano census is in *Carte Strozziane,* series III, 103, fol. 30r. U. Procacci summarizes the literary evidence pertaining to Florence's fiscal crisis in the 1420s in "Sulla cronologia delle opere di Masaccio e di Masolino," *Rivista d'arte,* XXVIII (1953), 3–35.

Baron's *The Crisis of the Early Italian Renaissance* has recently been published in a second edition (Princeton, 1965). A similar approach is developed by N. Valeri, *L'Italia nell'età dei principati* (Milan, 1949), by E. Garin, "I cancellieri umanisti della Repubblica fiorentina da Coluccio Salutati a Bartolomeo Scala," *Rivista storica italiana,* LXXI (1959), 185–208; and D. Hay, *The Italian Renaissance in its Historical Background* (Cambridge, 1961), chap. 5. Among the historians who stress the material factors in foreign policy are C. Bayley, *War and Society in Renaissance Florence;* D. Bueno de Mesquita, *Giangaleazzo Visconti* (Cambridge, 1941), and P. Partner, "Florence and the Papacy in the Earlier Fifteenth Century," *Florentine Studies,* ed. Rubinstein, 381–402. Political and institutional similarities between republics and despotisms are emphasized in P. Jones, "Communes and Despots: the City State in Late Medieval Italy," *Transactions of the Royal Historical Society,* 5th series, XV (1965), 71–96; Bueno de Mesquita, "The Place of Despotism in Italian Politics," in *Europe in the Late Middle Ages,* eds. J. Hale et al., (London and Evanston, Ill., 1965), 301–331; and L. Martines, *Lawyers and Statecraft,* chap. 11. A survey of the background of these scholarly positions is in Baron, *Crisis,* 1st ed., 379–390.

The letters of Ser Giacomo Manni are in *Archivio di Stato, Siena, Concistoro,* vols. 1816–1819. The records of the *Consulte e Pratiche,* 24, fols. 59v–83v, for these months corroborate Manni's testimony.

The most informed analyses of Florentine foreign policy in the late Trecento and early Quattrocento (in addition to the works already cited) are: N. Rubinstein, "Florence and the Despots," *Transactions of the Royal Historical Society,* 5th series, II (1952), 21-45; P. Partner, "Florence and the Papacy," *Europe in the Late Middle Ages,* 76–121, and his "Florence and the Papacy in the Earlier Fifteenth Century"; and P. Herde, "Politik und Rhetorik in Florenz am Vorabend der Renaissance," *Archiv für Kulturgeschichte,* XLVII (1965), 141–220. A good account of the internal quarrels over foreign policy in the early Quattrocento is in Bayley, *War and Society*, chap. 2. Hans Baron quoted the 1424 statement by Rinaldo degli Albizzi, *Crisis*, 2nd ed., 376.

CHAPTER V: THE CHURCH AND THE FAITH

The religious history of Renaissance Florence before Savonarola is largely unexplored; there are no adequate surveys and few good monographs. The best general study of the European church in the fourteenth and early fifteenth centuries is E. Delaruelle, E. Labande, and P. Ourliac, *L'église au temps du Grand Schisme et de la crise conciliare (1378–1449)*, 2 vols. (Paris, 1962–1964). R. Brentano has brilliantly described and analyzed the thirteenth century Italian church in his *Two Churches. England and Italy in the Thirteenth Century* (Princeton, 1968). Some details of fourteenth century ecclesiastical life in Florence can be found in R. Davidsohn's section on religion in his *Geschichte von Florenz*, IV (Italian trans., vol. IV, part III, Florence, 1965). Millard Meiss has written a good analysis of the Florentine religious mentality in the Trecento: *Painting in Florence and Siena after the Black Death* (Princeton, 1951; Harper Torchbook edition, New York, 1964).

The testament of Francesco Niccoli is in *Conventi Soppressi*, 122 (S. Spirito), vol. 75, fols. 34r–36r. Domenico Lanfredini's letter is in *BNF*, II, V, 7, fols. 5r–5v. The condemnations of Adoardo Peruzzi and Antonio di Tome are in *Atti del Podestà*, 3672, fols. 41r–44r; and *Giudice degli Appelli*, 99, fols. 161r–163r.

Certosa's real estate holdings are listed in *Conventi Soppressi*, 51 (Certosa), vol. 213. The statistics on ecclesiastical landholding in the fifteenth century were collated from E. Conti, *La formazione della struttura agraria moderna nel contado fiorentino*, III, part 3 (Rome, 1965). Pandolfo Ricasoli's assault against the rector of the Chianti church is described in *Atti del Esecutore*, 964, fol. 31r.

Lanfredino Lanfredini's letter concerning Bernardo Angioleri is in *BNF*, II, 7, fol. 175r. The circumstances of Bene del Bene's appointment to the church of S. Maria sopra Porta are described in my article, "An Unpublished Source on the Avignonese Papacy; the Letters of Francesco Bruni," *Traditio*, XIX (1963), 355–358, 362–365. Buonaccorso Pitti's description of the Altopascio incident is in *Two Memoirs of Renaissance Florence*, 85–86. Gregorio Dati's debt to his brother Leonardo is noted in *ibid.*, 140. The details of the Corsini's involvement in episcopal finances are in *Il libro di ricordanze dei Corsini (1362–1457)*, ed. A. Petrucci (Rome, 1965), xviii–xx, 26–43.

Aspects of church-state relations in Trecento Florence are described in two articles by M. Becker, "Florentine Politics and the Diffusion of Heresy in the Trecento," *Speculum*, XXXIV (1959), 60–75, and "Some Economic Implications of the Conflict between Church and State in Trecento Florence," *Medieval Studies*, XXI (1959), 1–16; and R. Trexler, *Economic, Political and Religious Effects of the Papal Interdict on Florence, 1376–1378* (Frankfurt am Main, 1964). The antipapal comments by Maffeo di Ser Francesco are recorded in *Consulte e Pratiche*, 26, fol. 64v, 17 July 1387.

The letter complaining about the Franciscan provincial is in *ASF, Dieci di Balià, Legazione e Commissarie*, 2, fol. 46v. An example of a protest against papal appointment of foreigners to Florentine benefices is in *ASF, Missive*, 22, fols. 112r–112v. The provision sequestering revenues of benefices held by absentees is in *Provvisioni*, 95, fol. 63r. Complaints against the transfer of Bishop Visdomini are found in several sources: *Consulte e Pratiche*, 35, fols. 67r–68r; *Missive*, 25, fol. 27r; *ASF, Signori e Collegi, Legazione e Commissarie*, 1, fol. 113r. Pope Eugenius' anger over an unauthorized imposition of a forced loan on the clergy is described in *BNF, Magliabechiana*, XXV, 518, fol. 46r. Peter Partner has collected some useful data on clerical taxation in his "Florence and the Papacy in the earlier Fifteenth Century," *Florentine Studies*, 401–402. Lauro Martines also discusses this problem in his *Lawyers and Statecraft*, 251–270. His study of "Rotal and Cameral Lawsuits," *ibid.*, 270–286, is the basis for my paragraph on the increase of judicial appeals from Florentine to Roman courts.

Sentences of the episcopal court against Jacopo Agli are in *Giudice degli Appelli*, 78, fols. 78r, 92r, 129r. The Signoria's penalty against Archbishop Ricci's brother is in *ibid.*, 80, fol. 282r. Criticism of the episcopal process against the Duke of Anjou is in *Consulte e Pratiche*, 21, fols. 96r–96v. The reprimand of the indiscreet friars who criticized Urban VI is in *ibid.*, 26, fol. 18r. The sentences of exile against the Pistoiese clerics is in *Missive*, 29, fol. 98v. The condemnation of Messer Francesco Bartolini is in *Atti del Esecutore*, 2107, no pag., 17 May 1399; the cancellation of the sentence in *Provvisioni*, 91, fols. 60r–62v. The request for permission to condemn the Aretine canon is in *Missive*, 24, fols. 99v–100v. Paolo Sassetti described the controversy over naming an incumbent to the parish church of S. Piero Buonconsiglio in *Carte Strozziane*, series II, 4, fols. 99v–100v.

The account book of Giuliano Benini, rector of S. Jacopo di Campo Corbellino, is in *Conventi Soppressi*, 132, vol. 484. A partial list of Florentines buried in S. Maria Novella is printed in *Delizie degli eruditi toscani*, IX, 123–217. The variety of activities, roles, and contributions of Florentine Dominicans is illustrated in the *"Necrologio" di Santa Maria Novella,* ed. S. Orlandi (Florence, 1955). The contributions of the monastic *studia* to Florentine education are analyzed by C. Davis, "Education in Dante's Florence," *Speculum,* LX (1965), 420–435. The visitation record of the Vallombrosan general Francesco Altoviti is in *Conventi Soppressi,* 260, vol. 217. Conditions in the convent of S. Caterina de Cafaggiolo are described in Nicholas V's letter, printed in R. Morcay, *Saint Antonin fondateur du couvent de Saint-Marc archêveque de Florence (1389–1459),* (Paris and Tours, 1914), 482; those in the convent of Monticelli in two letters of Eugenius IV, *Archivio Segreto Vaticano* [ASV], Rome, *Reg. Vat.,* 373, fols. 126v–128r. The escapades of three young Florentines in S. Silvestro are described in *Atti del Capitano,* 2766, fols. 25r–26r. The law providing for the supervision of convents by communal authorities is in *Provvisioni,* 111, fol. 45r; Pope Eugenius' protest against this provision is in ASV, *Reg. Vat.,* 374, fols. 76v–77r. The Signoria's complaints over Eugenius' consolidation policy were voiced in a letter to the Cardinal of S. Marco, *Missive,* 34, fol. 126v. Ser Lodovico della Casa's report on his daughter is copied in *Catasto,* 497, fol. 462r. The personnel of the convents of S. Verdiana, S. Felicita and S. Appolinaria are listed in *Conventi Soppressi,* 260, vol. 217, and in the Carnesecchi papers, *Acquisti e Doni,* 293, no pag.

Dom Lorenzo Martini's ledger of S. Trinita's petty expenditures is in *Conventi Soppressi,* 89, vol. 45. Ambrogio Traversari's description of his visitation travels is printed in A. Dini Traversari, *Ambrogio Traversari e i suoi tempi* (Florence, 1912), 11–139. S. Antonino's career is most fully described in the biography by R. Morcay, *Saint Antonin,* which contains a valuable appendix of documents.

Francesco Datini's account of his pilgrimage was translated by Iris Origo, *The Merchant of Prato,* 361–362. Francesco di Tommaso Giovanni described the Florentine reaction to the 1453 earthquake, *Carte Strozziane,* series II, 16. The religious crisis during the interdict of 1376–1378 has been analyzed by R. Trexler, *Effects of the Papal Interdict on Florence,* 104–161. References to the *flagellanti* in 1377 are found in *ibid.,* 123–127; the law of 1388 prohibiting their public assembly and parading is in *Provvisioni,* 77, fol. 215r. Contemporary descriptions of the Bianchi are numerous, an indication of the impact which this phenomenon made on the Florentine mentality. Two examples: R. Piattoli, "Un documento datiniano intorno alle processioni dei Bianchi," *Archivio storico pratese,* X (1931), 33; Buonaccorso Pitti's account in *Two Memoirs of Renaissance Florence,* 62. The regime's efforts to handle the prison issue are described in *Provvisioni,* 88, fols. 147v–148v.

Information on the Fraticelli heresy in Florence may be found in D.

Douie, *The Nature and Effect of the Heresy of the Fraticelli* (Manchester, 1932) and M. Becker, "Florentine Politics and the Diffusion of Heresy," *Speculum, XXXIV*, 60–75. Expressions of communal hostility to the Fraticelli are recorded in *Missive*, 18, fols. 125v–126r; *Provvisioni*, 71, fols. 175v–176r; *Consulte e Pratiche*, 22, fols. 71v, 108r; 25, fol. 56v; 26, fols. 187r–187v. The trial of the artisans who led an assault against Inquisition officials is in *Atti del Podestà*, 3178, fols. 136r–136v. The condemnation of Fra Michele da Calci, and the anonymous account of his ordeal, has been edited by F. Flora, *Storia di Fra Michele Minorita* (Florence, 1946). The three heresy cases of the early fifteenth century are found in ASV, *Reg. Vat.*, 342, fols. 36v–38v (Jacopo Palladini), *Giudice degli Appelli*, 74, part 2, fol. 139r (the priest Antonio Stefani), and Morcay, *Saint Antonin*, 430–431 (Giovanni Cani).

A brief survey of Florentine confraternities is provided by G. Monti, *Le confraternite medievali dell'alta e media Italia* (Venice, 1927), I, 253–265. The law of 1419 suppressing them is in *Provvisioni*, 109, fols. 160v–162v. The statutes of the society of S. Maria della Scala are in *BNF, Magliabechiana, XXXII*, 43. My impressions concerning the social orientation of Florentine religious bequests in the fifteenth century were influenced by David Herlihy's book, *Medieval and Renaissance Pistoia* (1967).

Piero Girolami's reference to his family's obligations to ecclesiastical foundations is in *Catasto*, 68, fol. 276v. Iliarione de' Bardi's memoirs, in *Conventi Soppressi*, 79, vol. 119, describe his charitable expenditures. The history of Bonifazio Lupi's hospital is in G. Richa, *Notizie istoriche delle chiese fiorentine* (Florence, 1754–1761), V, 310–315. Statistics on the rapid increase in the landholdings of charitable foundations are extracted from E. Conti, *La formazione della struttura agraria moderna nel contado fiorentino*, III, part 3. Niccolò da Uzzano's bequest to the Studio is printed in *Statuti della Università e Studio Fiorentino*, ed. A. Gherardi (Florence, 1881), 230–339.

The Florentine visit of Fra Manfredo of Vercelli is described in D. Buoninsegni, *Storia della città di Firenze*, 14; his influence on Ginevra Mannelli is reported in the Signoria's letter to the Sienese government; *Missive*, 31, fol. 78v. Buoninsegni, 90–91, 114, describes the pilgrimage to Rome during the Jubilee year of 1450 and the impact of the Crusade preacher, Maestro Giovanni of Naples. The reference to the Bible-reading custom of Tedaldo Tedaldi is in *Atti del Capitano*, 2740, fol. 101r. Sacchetti's criticisms of vows are stated in his *Trecento novelle*, no. 109. Buoninsegni, 110, comments on the Lana guild's acquisition of relics for the cathedral; the story of S. Reparata's arm is told by Matteo Villani, *Cronica*, III, chaps. 15–16.

CHAPTER VI: CULTURE

The preeminent role of Florence in the culture of Renaissance Italy has focused attention upon her poets, humanists, and artists. Every general work on Renaissance culture devotes many pages to the Florentine achievement. Subjects which have been most thoroughly investigated are Dante and the literary culture of his time, the humanists, and the artists. Two lesser known aspects of Florentine culture, the legal and the mercantile, are the subjects of recent books: L. Martines, *Lawyers and Statecraft in Renaissance Florence* (Princeton, 1968) and C. Bec, *Les marchands écrivains à Florence 1375–1434* (Paris and The Hague, 1967).

My views about the relationship between Florentine culture and society owe much to D. Hay, *The Italian Renaissance in its Historical Background.*

Meetings of Florentine intellectuals are described by A. Della Torre, *Storia dell'Accademia platonica di Firenze* (Florence, 1902). The social status of humanists is described by L. Martines, *Social World of the Florentine Humanists.* The libraries of Piero Alberti and Ser Matteo Gherardi are inventoried in *Atti del Podestà*, 3784, fols. 29r–31v; and *Conventi Soppressi*, no. 83, vol. 102, part 9. Bec, *Les marchands écrivains*, 117, 307, comments on the reading of Lapo Mazzei and Giovanni Rucellai. The popular reaction to the sorcerer's conviction in 1383 is described in Brucker, "Sorcery in Early Renaissance Florence," *Studies in the Renaissance*, X (1963), 22–23.

In his article, "Florence, a City that Art Built," published in *History and the Social Web* (Minneapolis, 1955), 135–174, A. Krey emphasizes the role of the Florentine artisans and their skills in the development of a sense of quality and an appreciation of beauty. Rosso Orlandi's letter to Piero Davanzati concerning the purchase of cloth is in *Conventi Soppressi*, no. 78, vol. 315, no pag. Jacopo de' Pazzi's letter to Filippo Strozzi is in *Acquisti e Doni*, vol. 293, no pag. G. Rucellai describes his park in *Giovanni Rucellai ed il suo Zibaldone*, I, 20–21. The Signoria's letters to the Camaldoli are in *Missive*, 25, fol. 24r; 26, fol 58r. Kristeller's comment on the quality of concreteness in humanist writing is in *Renaissance Thought* (New York, 1961), 20.

Giovanni Villani's statistics on Florentine school population are in his *Cronica*, XI, chap. 94. The sad tale of Antonio di Manno is described in *Mercanzia,* 1179, fol. 233r. Filippo Balducci's letter eulogizing Florence is cited in L. Martines, *Lawyers and Statecraft,* 105–106. I thank my colleague, Randolph Starn, for transcribing the document. Ugolino of Montecatini's letter to Jacopo del Bene is in *Carte Del Bene,* 49, fol. 20lr.

The eulogy to Arnolfo di Cambio is printed in Gaye, *Carteggio inedito d'artisti dei secoli XIV, XV, XVI* (Florence, 1839–1840), I, 445–446. Leonardo Bruni's tax exemption is noted in Martines, *Social World,* 168, 171; Poggio Bracciolini's petition is in *ASF, Balìe,* 25, fols. 45v–46r. Brunelleschi's patent is printed in Gaye, I, 547–549. Giovanni Villani's comments on Dante are recorded in his *Cronica,* IX, chap. 136. The plans to erect tombs for five distinguished Florentines are described in *Provvisioni,* 85, fols. 282r–283r.

The discussion of the Florentine Studio is a summary of my article, "Florence and its University, 1348–1434," in *Action and Conviction in Early Modern Europe,* eds. J. Seigel and T. Rabb (Princeton, 1969). The account of Medicean patronage is based upon E. Gombrich's article, "The Early Medici as Patrons of Art," in *Italian Renaissance Studies,* ed. E. F. Jacob (London, 1960).

The early history of Italian humanism is traced by P. Kristeller, "Humanism and Scholasticism in the Italian Renaissance," in his *Renaissance Thought.* Petrarch's career is summarized in E. H. Wilkins' *Life of Petrarch* (Chicago, 1961); and Salutati's in B. Ullman, *The Humanism of Coluccio Salutati* (Padua, 1963). A recent important book by J. Seigel, *Rhetoric and Philosophy in Renaissance Humanism* (Princeton, 1968) was published after this chapter was written. Andrea de' Pazzi's derogatory reference to classical studies is in his son Piero's biography in Vespasiano da Bisticci, *The Vespasiano Memoirs* (London, 1926; Harper Torchbook edition, New York, 1963), 310. The Signoria's letter concerning the use of Latin in diplomatic correspondence is in *Missive,* 24, fol. 43r. Gino Capponi's remark about Piero Baroncelli's oratory is in *Consulte e Pratiche,* 39, fol. 117r.

Hans Baron's *chef d'oeuvre* is *The Crisis of the Early Italian Renaissance* (Princeton, 1955, revised 2nd ed., 1966). J. Seigel's article, " 'Civic Humanism' or Ciceronian Rhetoric?," *Past and Present,* no. 34 (July, 1966), contains references to the scholarly judgments of Baron's interpretation. Baron's reply, "Leonardo Bruni: 'Professional Rhetorician' or 'Civic Humanist'?" is in no. 36 (April, 1967) of the same journal. For my understanding of the significance of historical perspective in Florentine thought, I am indebted to Baron's work, to M. Gilmore's article, "The Renaissance Conception of the Lessons of History," in *Humanists and Jurists* (Cambridge, Mass., 1963), chap. 1;

to L. Green's article, "Historical Interpretation in fourteenth century Florentine Chronicles," *Journal of the History of Ideas*, XXVIII (1967), 161–178; and above all to the first chapter of W. Bouwsma's book, *Venice and the Defense of Republican Liberty* (Berkeley, 1968).

Volumes 35–42 of the *Consulte e Pratiche* contain the deliberations for the years 1401–1414. The records for the critical summer of 1402 are in vol. 35, fols. 127v–151r. The crisis in Florence's relations with Ladislaus begins in the spring of 1409 (*ibid.*, 39, fols. 135v–166v; 40, fols. 3r–25r). The most intense criticism of Florentine war policy was voiced between September 1412 and June 1413 (*ibid.*, 41, fols. 135r–190r; 42, fols. 1r–36v). Messer Piero Beccanugi's speech on the value of historical perspective is in *ibid.*, 42, fol. 21r. Other historical references during these months are in *ibid.*, 41, fol. 175r; 42, fols. 3r, 10r, 12v–14r, 16v, 24v, 26r, 36r. The earliest discussion of Florence as a possible council site occur in September 1407 (*ibid.*, 38, fols. 69r–82v). The debate continued in the early months of 1408 (*ibid.*, 39, fols. 5v–7r) and reached a climax in the summer and autumn of that year (*ibid.*, fols. 75v–88r). Forthcoming is an expanded, fully documented version of my arguments on changes in Florentine attitudes and perspectives, as revealed in these deliberations. In his *Lawyers and Statecraft*, 289–296, L. Martines discusses another aspect of changing views and policies in the early Quattrocento: the role of lawyers in Florence's withdrawal of obedience from Pope Gregory XII and the acceptance of the conciliar idea (1408–1409).

The selection from Manetti's biography of Brunelleschi is printed in E. Holt, *Documentary History of Art*, I (New York, 1957), 168. Giovanni Morelli's comments on education are in his *Ricordi*, 270–273; those of Alberti in *Opere volgari*, ed. C. Grayson, I (Bari, 1960), 68–72.

The literature on Florentine art in the fourteenth and fifteenth centuries is vast. I have found the following works of particular value: A. Blunt, *Artistic Theory in Italy* (Oxford, 1940), P. and L. Murray, *The Art of the Renaissance* (New York and Washington, 1963), P. Francastel, *Peinture et société* (Lyon, 1951), M. Meiss, *Painting in Florence and Siena after the Black Death*, H. Janson, *The Sculpture of Donatello* (Princeton, 1957), R. Krautheimer, *Lorenzo Ghiberti* (Princeton, 1956), M. Wackernagel, *Der Lebensraum des Künstlers in der florentinischen Renaissance* (Leipzig, 1938). For "materialist" interpretations of the artistic revolution, one may consult F. Antal, *Florentine Painting and its Social Background* (London, 1948), and A. Hauser, *The Social History of Art*, II (New York, 1952). Two perceptive discussions of art style are M. Shapiro, "Style," in A. Kroeber, ed., *Anthropology Today* (Chicago, 1953), and J. Ackerman,

"A Theory of Style," *Journal of Aesthetics and Art Criticism*, XX (1962), 227–237.

The *Commentaries* of Lorenzo Ghiberti are edited by J. von Schlosser (Berlin, 1912); E. Holt has translated selections in her *Documentary History of Art*, I, 151–167. Antonio Manetti's *Vita di Filippo di ser Brunellesco* was edited by E. Toesca (Florence, 1927); a translated excerpt is in Holt, I, 167–179. A standard source for information on Florentine artists is G. Vasari's *Lives of the Painters, Sculptors and Architects* (several English editions).

The status of Florentine architects in the Quattrocento is discussed by E. Gombrich, "The Early Medici as Patrons of Art." The Signoria's letter to the marquis of Ferrara is in *Missive*, 34, fols. 123r–123v. Antonino's views on art have been analyzed by C. Gilbert, "The Archbishop on the Painters of Florence, 1450," *Art Bulletin*, XLI (1959), 75–85. Alberti's treatise, *On Painting*, has been translated by J. Spencer (New Haven, 1956). Ghiberti's classical interests are described by Krautheimer, *Ghiberti*, 306–314, and by E. Gombrich, "The Renaissance Conception of Artistic Progress," published in his *Norm and Form* (London, 1966), 5–8. The religious orientation of the Renaissance style, contrasted with the secular concern of International Gothic, is emphasized by Gilbert, *Art Bulletin*, XLI, 83. F. Hartt's article, "Freedom in Quattrocento Florence," *Essays in Memory of Karl Lehmann*, ed. L. Sandler (New York, 1964), 119, discusses the civic commissions of sculptors and architects, and the private and ecclesiastical commissions of painters. I have borrowed C. Gilbert's scheme of artistic cycles in Florence from his Antonino article, *Art Bulletin,* XLI, 85–88. The sudden popularity of monumental tombs in the 1420s is noted by J. Coolidge, "Further Observations on Masaccio's Trinity," *Art Bulletin*, XLVIII (1966), 382–384. The artistic scene in mid-fifteenth century Florence is succinctly analyzed in P. and L. Murray, *Art of the Renaissance*, 89–120. The information on the *cassone* workshop is derived from E. Gombrich's article, "Appollonio di Giovanni," *Norm and Form*, 11–28.

EPILOGUE: THE LAST YEARS OF THE REPUBLIC

A good introduction to the Laurentian age is the collection of essays in *Florence au temps de Laurent le Magnifique* [*Collection Ages d'Or et Réalites*, vol. 2] (Paris, 1965). F. Catalano has developed his thesis of the character of the late Quattrocento in "La crisi italiana alla fine del secolo XV," *Belfagor*, XI (1956). A more positive view of the

Italian scene in these years is P. Pieri, *Il Rinascimento e la crisi militare italiana*, 2nd ed. (Turin, 1952).

The best biographical study on Lorenzo, covering only his early years, is A. Rochon, *La jeunesse de Laurent de Médicis* (1449–1478), (Paris, 1963). The traditional interpretation of Lorenzo is summarized in C. Ady, *Lorenzo de' Medici and Renaissance Italy* (London, 1955). The definitive constitutional history of the Medici period has been written by N. Rubinstein, *The Florentine Government under the Medici, 1434–1494* (Oxford, 1966). L. Martines's recent work, *Lawyers and Statecraft in Renaissance Florence*, has much valuable material on politics during the Medici period; the bibliography is exemplary. Two studies on the Florentine economy in the Quattrocento are particularly valuable: R. de Roover, *The Rise and Decline of the Medici Bank*, and R. Goldthwaite, *Private Wealth in Renaissance Florence*.

Franco Sacchetti's statement of 1458 and Piero Guicciardini's views on the social bases of Florentine politics are cited in N. Rubinstein, *Florentine Government under the Medici*, 94, 213–217. L. Marks' study on the fisc, "The Financial Oligarchy in Florence under Lorenzo," is in *Italian Renaissance Studies*, ed. Jacob, 123–147. L. Martines's calculations on the number of patrician lawyers are summarized in his *Lawyers and Statecraft*, 75. The careers of Piero Guicciardini's sons are described by R. Goldthwaite, *Private Wealth in Renaissance Florence*, 131–155. In *The Architecture of Michelangelo* (New York, 1961), I, 76–79, J. Ackerman discusses Filippo Strozzi's palace and comments on the social and political significance of Quattrocento palaces in Florence. Mrs. Isabelle Hyman of New York University sent me information on the Medici loggia; I am grateful to her for that and other information on building projects and problems in Quattrocento Florence. The cultural milieu of Laurentian Florence has been described by E. Garin, *Italian Humanism* (New York, 1965), 78–113; L. Martines, *The Social World of the Florentine Humanists*, 286–302; and A. Chastel, *Art et humanisme à Florence au temps de Laurent le Magnifique* (Paris, 1959).

There is a good select bibliography on Florentine history after 1494 in Felix Gilbert, *Machiavelli and Guicciardini* (Princeton, 1965), 305–315. Francesco Guicciardini's analysis of Lorenzo's role in maintaining the *pax italiana* is translated by C. Grayson in Guicciardini's *History of Italy and History of Florence*, ed. J. Hale (New York, 1964), 86–87, 89. F. Chabod's essays in *Machiavelli and the Renaissance* (London, 1958) are fundamental for this period. The political problems confronting the republican regime are discussed in chaps. 1 and 2 of Gilbert's work. R. Ridolfi's *Life of Girolamo Savonarola* (London, 1959) is a sound biography of the friar. Luca Landucci's description of Savonarola's end is in his *Diary*, 139. Ridolfi's *Life of Niccolo Machiavelli* (London, 1963) and *Life of Francesco Guicciardini* (London, 1967) provide full accounts of the careers of these men. The significance of their thought is analyzed by Gilbert, *Machiavelli and Guicciardini*, chaps. 4, 7.

The selections on pages 36 and 270–271 are from Luca Landucci, *A Florentine Diary from 1450 to 1516*, translated by Alice de Rosen Jervis, printed by permission of E. P. Dutton and Company, Inc., and J. M. Dent & Sons, Ltd. The quotations on pages 112 and 203 are from Iris Origo, *The Merchant of Prato*, printed by permission of Alfred A. Knopf, Inc. The quotation on page 268 is from Francesco Guicciardini, *History of Florence and History of Italy*, translated by Cecil Grayson, edited by John Hale. It is printed by permission of Washington Square Press.

Notes on Florentine Scholarship

The first edition of *Renaissance Florence* was published in 1969. It was both a work of synthesis, and an exploration of significant themes in Florentine experience during the fourteenth and fifteenth centuries. The book relied heavily upon the scholarship of pre-World War II Florentine historians (Davidsohn, Salvemini, Ottokar, Doren, Rodolico), and upon their successors (Hans Baron, Paul Oskar Kristeller, Felix Gilbert, Nicolai Rubinstein), whose academic careers had been interrupted by Nazi persecution in Germany and by the war. It also exploited the work of a new generation of post-war historians, predominantly Anglo-American, who published their first articles and monographs in the late 1950s and 1960s: Marvin Becker, Richard Goldthwaite, David Herlihy, Philip Jones, Lauro Martines, Anthony Molho, Randolph Starn, Richard Trexler, Donald Weinstein. A collection of articles by a representative group of these scholars, *Florentine Studies*, was published in 1968, under the editorship of Nicolai Rubinstein. In their subject matter and methodology, these articles reflect quite accurately the scholarly interests of that post-war generation. Most are based upon intensive archival research, exploring in depth specific, sharply defined topics. Most, too, are concerned with political and socio-economic themes, largely but not exclusively pertaining to the city's ruling elite. Perhaps the most distinctive characteristic of this scholarship is the lack of an ideological dimension. Possibly reacting against the Italian predilection for viewing the past in terms of current political concerns, Anglo-American historians of Florence have tended to avoid such issues as class conflict, that were so important for Salvemini and Ottokar.

By the 1960s, Florence had become the most intensively studied city in pre-industrial Europe. During the 1970s, the tempo of research and publication escalated at a geometric rate. Some twenty historical monographs were published in English during that decade, ten more in Italian (including the translated work of a Russian scholar), and four in French. Among the more significant and meritorious contributions of this international scholarly consortium are books that employ traditional methodology and explore familiar problems: Dale Kent's study of the rise of the Medici (1978), Hidetoshi Hoshino's monograph on the woolen cloth industry and the Lana guild (1980), and John Najemy's work on the political role of the guilds (1982). Supplementing this mainstream scholarship have been innovative works by scholars who have explored new areas and topics, developed new methodologies, and challenged standard interpretations of Florence's past.

The methods and concepts of the social sciences have inspired new directions and themes of recent historical writing on Renaissance Florence. Quantification has been a strong impulse in contemporary historical research on both sides of the Atlantic, and Florentine history has not escaped its pervasive influence. The city's unusually rich archival records have attracted several scholars who have mastered quantitative techniques. David Herlihy and Christiane Klapisch-Zuber published their demographic and economic profile of urban and rural Tuscany (1976), based on computerized data culled from the 1427 *catasto*. Samuel Cohn, Jr., in his *The Laboring Classes in Renaissance Florence* (1980) and Ronald Weissman, in his *Ritual Brotherhood in Renaissance Florence* (1982) have used quantitative methods to organize their data and to develop their interpretations. The forthcoming study of Florentine marriage patterns and dowries by Julius Kirshner and Anthony Molho, which is based upon dowry and *catasto* records, relies heavily upon the computer. So, too, does David Herlihy's current project: a compilation of biographical data on Florence's officeholding class between 1380 and 1530. Social and cultural anthropology has been another important resource for Florentine historians. References to anthropological studies on kinship structures are cited frequently in F. W. Kent's book on Florentine families (1977). Social network analysis figures prominently in the recent monographs by Cohn on Florence's laboring classes, and by Weissman on confraternities. In the preface to his important book, *Public Life in Renaissance Florence*, Richard Trexler defines the focus of his study as "the interrelated nature of different types of formal behavior."

The significance of this recent scholarship is still being evaluated, but some tentative conclusions may be drawn. Our knowledge of demographic and economic trends has increased substantially, thanks to the studies of Herlihy and Klapisch-Zuber, Charles de la Roncière, Giuliano Pinto and Hidetoshi Hoshino. In his *The Building of Renaissance Florence* (1980), Richard Goldthwaite has formulated a general interpretation of the city's economic development. Though controversial, this synthesis should focus the attention of economic historians on the important issues still unresolved. The political and institutional history of Florence now rests upon a solid documentary foundation, but the relationship between politics and socio-economic developments remains unclear, and very much in dispute. We have learned much in recent years about specific forms of sociability—families, guilds, confraternities, neighborhoods—but the dynamics of this social order is not well understood. The history of Florentine religion has attracted widespread interest in recent years, although much still remains to be explored. Studies in Florentine cultural history have been, for the most part, highly technical and specialized. No general works have appeared that are comparable to the bold and comprehensive syntheses published in the 1940s and early 1950s by Paul Oskar Kristeller, Hans Baron and Eugenio Garin.

So diverse in subject matter, in methodology and conceptualization, the current scholarship on Renaissance Florence does not lend itself to neat definition and categorization. Nor can one predict the future direction of research, since no dominant historiographical tradition has emerged. To integrate and synthesize this scholarship would be a formidable task, and the time may not be ripe. But with that ultimate goal in mind, some useful preparatory work could be done: for example, the identification of major problems; the ordering of research priorities; the exploration of significant relationships between social and cultural phenomena, such as Michael Baxandall's stimulating study of the connections between painting and experience in the Quattrocento (1972). Heretofore, comparative history has not attracted Florentine historians, but under the aegis of the Harvard University Center for

Italian Renaissance Studies, comparative studies of Florence and Venice, and of Florence and Milan, have been inaugurated. These are encouraging signs for the future of Florentine historiography.

Gene Brucker

Berkeley
July, 1982

Bibliographical Supplement

The Historiography of Renaissance Florence since 1969

CHAPTER I: THE RENAISSANCE CITY

A recent important contribution to the history of Florentine urbanism is R. Goldthwaite, *The Building of Renaissance Florence. An Economic and Social History* (Baltimore, 1980). Other monographs and articles on Florentine building are: F. Sznura, *L'espansione urbana di Firenze nel dugento* (Florence, 1975); G. Fanelli, *Firenze: architettura e città* (Florence, 1973); L. Ginori Lisci, *I palazzi di Firenze*, 2 vols. (Florence, 1972); R. Goldthwaite, "The Building of the Strozzi Palace," *Studies in Medieval and Renaissance History*, X (1973), 97–194; and "The Florentine Palace as Domestic Architecture," *American Historical Review*, LXXVII (1972), 977–1012; N. Rubinstein, "The Piazza della Signoria in Florence," in *Festschrift Herbert Siebenhüner*, ed. E. Hubala and G. Schweikhart (Wurzburg, 1978), 19–30; I. Hyman, *The Palazzo Medici and a Ledger for the Church of San Lorenzo* (Ann Arbor, 1977); F. W. Kent, "The Rucellai Family and its Loggia," *Journal of the Warburg and Courtauld Institutes*, XXXV (1972), 397–401; B. Preyer, "The Rucellai Loggia," *Mitteilungen des Kunsthistorischen Instituts in Florenz*, XXI (1977), 183–98; and "The Rucellai Palace," in *A Florentine Patrician and His Palace* (London: Warburg Institute, 1981), 153–225; F. W. Kent, " 'Più superba de quella de Lorenzo': Courtly and Family Interest in the Building of Filippo Strozzi's Palace," *Renaissance Quarterly*, XXX (1977), 311–23; C. Elam, "Lorenzo the Magnificent and the Florentine Building Boom," *Art History*, I (1978), 43–66.

CHAPTER II: THE ECONOMY

Our knowledge of the Florentine economy in the Renaissance has been much expanded in recent years, with the publication of a cluster of important books. David Herlihy and Christiane Klapisch-Zuber have published the results of their computer-based research on the Florentine *catasto* of 1427: *Les Toscans et leurs familles* (Paris, 1978). Another significant contribution: C. de la Roncière, *Florence, centre économique régional au XIVᵉ siècle*, 4 vols. (Aix-en-Provence, 1976). R. Goldthwaite, *The Building of Renaissance Florence*, develops a synthetic view of Florence's economic development in the fourteenth and fifteenth centuries. H. Hoshino has written an important study of the Florentine woolen cloth industry which supersedes the older work by Doren: *L'arte della lana in Firenze nel basso medioevo* (Florence, 1980). M. Bernocchi has published a massive work on Florentine coinage: *Le monete della Repubblica fiorentina*, 4 vols. (Florence, 1974–78). In his edition of *Il libro del Biadaiolo. Carestia e annona a Firenze dalla metà del '200 al 1348* (Florence, 1978), G. Pinto discusses grain prices and food shortages prior to the Black Death. The business career of a Trecento entrepreneur is described by C. de la Roncière, *Un changeur Florentin du Trecento: Lippo di Fede del Sega (1285 env.–1363 env.)* (Paris, 1973). G. Holmes has written on the Medici as papal bankers; *Florentine Studies*, ed. N. Rubinstein (London, 1968), 357–80; R. Goldthwaite discusses the Medici bank in the context of the Florentine banking structure; *I Medici e la banca nel Quattrocento fiorentino* (Milan, 1980). A recent monograph on a provincial economy is Judith C. Brown, *In the Shadow of Florence. Provincial Society in Renaissance Pescia* (New York, 1982).

CHAPTER III: THE PATRICIATE

The Society of Renaissance Florence, ed. G. Brucker (New York, 1971) contains translations of documents pertaining to Florentine social organization and experience in the fourteenth and fifteenth centuries.

The Florentine patrician family has been studied intensively in recent years. F. W. Kent has written an analysis of three patrician lineages, in which he develops a general interpretation of Florentine family structure: *Household and Lineage in Renaissance Florence. The Family Life of the Capponi, Ginori and Rucellai* (Princeton, 1977). P. Malanima has published a monograph on an important Quattrocento family: *I Ricardi di Firenze* (Florence, 1977). Herlihy and Klapisch-Zuber, *Les Toscans et leurs familles*, contains much information on the Florentine family, as does, too, Thomas Kuehn, *Emancipation in Late Medieval Florence* (New Brunswick, 1982). On marriage and dowries: C. Klapisch-Zuber, "Zacharie, ou le père évincé. Les rites nuptiaux toscans entre Giotto et le concile de Trente," *Annales*, XXXIV (1979), 1216–43; J. Kirshner, "Pursuing Honor While Avoiding Sin: the *Monte della Doti* of Florence," *Studi senesi*, LXXXIX (1977), 175–258; A. Molho and J. Kirshner, "The Dowry Fund and the Marriage Market in Early Quattrocento Florence," *Journal of Modern History*, L (1978), 403–38.

Recent revisionist studies on Florentine personalities who were discussed in Chapter III: Francesco Datini and Lapo Mazzei: R. Trexler, *Public Life in Renaissance Florence* (New York, 1980), 131–58; Giovanni Morelli: *ibid.*, 159–86; Cosimo de' Medici: A. Molho, "Cosimo de' Medici: *Pater Patriae* or *Padrino?*" *Stanford Italian Review*, I (1979), 5–33; Giovanni Rucellai: F. W. Kent's biography in *A Florentine Patrician and His Palace*, 9–95.

On the problem of "individualism": M. Becker, "Individualism in the Early Italian Renaissance: Burden and Blessing," *Studies in the Renaissance*, XIX (1972), 273–97.

CHAPTER IV: POLITICS

Political developments in Italian city-states have been summarized in D. Waley, *The Italian City-Republics* (London, 1969); S. Bertelli, *Il potere oligarchico nello stato-città medievale* (Florence, 1978); and L. Martines, *Power and Imagination. City-States in Renaissance Italy* (New York, 1979). General studies on Florentine political experience in the fourteenth and fifteenth centuries: G. Brucker, *The Civic World of Early Renaissance Florence* (Princeton, 1977); G. Guidi, *Il governo della città repubblica di Firenze del primo Quattrocento*, 3 vols. (Florence, 1980); J. Najemy, *Corporatism and Consensus in Florentine Electoral Politics, 1280–1400* (Chapel Hill, 1982); and his "Guild Republicanism in Trecento Florence," *American Historical Review*, LXXXIV (1979), 53–71; D. Kent, "The Florentine 'Reggimento' in the Fifteenth Century," *Renaissance Quarterly*, XXVIII (1975), 575–638.

Three important articles on the late Trecento: A. Molho, "Politics and the Ruling Class in Early Renaissance Florence," *Nuova Rivista Storica*, LII (1968), 401–20; R. Witt, "Florentine Politics and the Ruling Class, 1382–1407," *Journal of Medieval and Renaissance Studies*, VI (1976), 243–67; P. Herde, "Politische Verhaltensweisen der Florentiner Oligarchie 1382–1402," in *Geschichte und Verfassungsgefüge. Frankfurter Festgabe für Walter Schlesinger* (Weisbaden, 1973), 156–249. The Ciompi Revolution figures prominently, though not exclusively, in S. Cohn, Jr., *The Laboring Classes in Renaissance Florence* (New York, 1980). In *Florentine Studies*, ed. N. Rubinstein, is a cluster of articles on themes discussed in this chapter: M. Becker on the Florentine territorial state; C. M. de la Roncière on indirect taxes; P. Partner on Florentine relations with the papacy; M. Mallett on Pisa's incorporation into the Florentine dominion; N. Rubinstein on the constitutional development during the Medici period. The political and fiscal crisis of the 1420s and early 1430s is the subject of two important monographs: D. Kent, *The Rise of the Medici. Faction in Florence 1426–1434* (Oxford, 1978); A. Molho, *Florentine Public Finances in the Early Renaissance* (Cambridge, Mass., 1971). A significant and neglected topic, civic ritual, is explored by R. Trexler in *Public Life in Renaissance Florence* and in *The Libro Ceremoniale of the Florentine Republic* (Geneva, 1978). The social and political structure of a *gonfalone* is the subject of a monograph by D. and F. W. Kent, *Neighbors and Neighborhood in Renaissance Florence: the District of the Red Lion in the Fifteenth Century* (Locust Valley, N. Y., 1982).

CHAPTER V: THE CHURCH AND THE FAITH

R. Trexler has published extensively on the religious history of late medieval and Renaissance Florence; his *Public Life in Renaissance Florence* summarizes many of his conclusions. His important articles in this field include: "Florentine Religious Experience: the Sacred Image," *Studies in the Renaissance*, XIX (1972), 7–41; "Florence, by the Grace of the Lord Pope. . . .," *Studies in Medieval and Renaissance History*, IX (1972), 115–215; "Ritual Behavior in Renaissance Florence: the Setting," *Medievalia et Humanistica*, n. s., IV (1973), 125–44; "Le célibat à la fin du moyen âge: les religieuses de Florence," *Annales*, XXVII (1972), 1329–50; "Ritual in Florence: Adolescence and Salvation in the Renaissance," in *The Pursuit of Holiness in Late Medieval and Renaissance Religion*, ed. C. Trinkaus and H. Oberman (Leiden, 1974), 200–64; "The Episcopal Constitutions of Antoninus of Florence," *Quellen und Forschungen aus Italienischen Archiven und Bibliotheken*, LIX (1979), 244–72. Trexler has also published *The Spiritual Power. Republican Florence under Interdict* (Leiden, 1974); and has edited *Synodal Law in Florence and Fiesole, 1306–1518* (Vatican City, 1971).

Recent work on confraternities: R. Hatfield, "The Compagnia de' Magi," *Journal of the Warburg and Courtauld Institutes*, XXIII (1970), 107–61; R. Weissman, *Ritual Brotherhood in Renaissance Florence* (New York, 1981). On lay piety: R. Trexler, "Charity and the Defense of Urban Elites in the Italian Communes," in F. Jaher, ed., *The Rich, the Well Born and the Powerful* (Urbana, Ill., 1973), 64–109; C. M. de la Roncière, "Pauvres et pauvreté à Florence au XIVᵉ siècle," in M. Mollat, ed., *Études sur l'histoire de la pauvreté (Moyen Âge-XVIᵉ siècle)* (Paris, 1974), II, 661–745; M. Becker, "Aspects of Lay Piety in Early Renaissance Florence," *The Pursuit of Holiness in Late Medieval and Renaissance Religion*, 177–99. On heresy: J. Stephens, "Heresy in Medieval and Renaissance Florence," *Past and Present*, no. 54 (1972), 25–60.

CHAPTER VI: CULTURE

The late medieval context of Italian Renaissance culture is analyzed by J. Larner, *Culture and Society in Italy 1290–1420* (London, 1971). W. Anderson has written a richly textured biography of Dante: *Dante the Maker* (London, 1980). D. Thompson and A. Nagel have edited and translated humanist sources on Dante, Petrarch and Boccaccio: *The Three Crowns of Florence* (New York, 1972). Thompson has also translated a collection of Petrarch's letters: *Petrarch. A Humanist Among Princes* (New York, 1971). C. Trinkaus has published a collection of Petrarch essays: *The Poet as Philosopher. Petrarch and the Formation of Renaissance Consciousness* (New Haven, 1979).

An assessment of Hans Baron's impact on Renaissance studies is incorporated in *Renaissance Studies in Honor of Hans Baron*, ed. A. Molho and J. Tedeschi (Dekalb, Ill., 1970). That *Festschrift* also contains several articles on Florentine Renaissance subjects. R. Pecchioli examines the concept of civic humanism in " 'Umanesimo civile' e interpretazione 'civile' dell'umanesimo," *Studi storici*, XIII (1972), 3–33. Salutati's life and writings are explored by D. De Rosa, *Coluccio Salutati: il cancelliere e il pensatore politico* (Florence, 1980); and by R. Witt, *Hercules at the Crossroads. The Life, Works, and Thought of Coluccio Salutati* (Durham, N. C., 1981). E. Spagnesi has written a comprehensive account of Florentine culture at the end of the Trecento: *Utiliter edoceri. Atti inediti degli ufficiali dello Studio Fiorentino (1391–96)* (Milan, 1979).

G. Holmes has written a synthesis of early Quattrocento culture: *The Florentine Enlightenment 1400–50* (London, 1969). Examples of the political and social writings of Florentine humanists have been translated in *Humanism and Liberty. Writings on Freedom from Fifteenth-Century Florentines*, ed. R. Watkins (Columbia, S. C., 1978); and *The Earthly Republic. Italian Humanists on Government and Society*, ed. B. Kohl and R. Witt (Philadelphia, 1978). Cultural themes are prominent in the collection of articles published in *Florence and Venice: Comparisons and Relations*, vol. I: *Quattrocento*; vol. II: *Cinquecento* (Florence, 1980); and in *Essays Presented to Myron P. Gilmore*, ed. S. Bertelli and G. Ramakus, 2 vols. (Florence, 1978). M. Phillips discusses the vernacular tradition of Florentine historical writing in "Machiavelli, Guicciardini and the Tradition of Vernacular Historiography in Florence," *American Historical Review*, LXXXIV (1979), 86–105.

M. Baxandall has published two valuable studies on the social and cultural context of Florentine painting: *Giotto and the Orators* (Oxford, 1971); and *Painting and Experience in Fifteenth Century Italy* (Oxford, 1972). S. Edgerton, *The Renaissance Discovery of Linear Perspective* (New York, 1975) explores an important aspect of the artistic revolution. Bruce Cole has published a synthetic study of Florentine art 1375–1430: *Masaccio and the Art of Early Renaissance Florence* (Bloomington, 1980). R. Goldthwaite's *The Building of Renaissance Florence* contains much information on Florentine architects and architectural practice, and a provocative thesis on the relationship between the city's economy and social order, and her artistic achievement.

EPILOGUE: THE LAST YEARS OF THE REPUBLIC

Four volumes of the correspondence of Lorenzo de' Medici have now been published, under the general editorship of N. Rubinstein: *Lettere* (Florence, 1977–). A. Brown has written a biography of a leading official of the Medici regime: *Bartolomeo Scala 1430–1497 Chancellor of Florence. The Humanist as Bureaucrat* (Princeton, 1979). J. Hale has summarized the current scholarship on the Medici in his *Florence and the Medici. The Pattern of Control* (London, 1977). D. Weinstein's *Savonarola and Florence* (Princeton, 1970) is the best historical analysis of the Dominican's Florentine career. R. Trexler, *Public Life in Renaissance Florence*, 428–90, contains an original and provocative interpretation of the Laurentian period and the Savonarola episode. R. Cooper has written a perceptive analysis of Pier Soderini's career: "Pier Soderini: Aspiring Prince to Civic Leader," *Studies in Medieval and Renaissance History*, n. s. I (1978), 67–126. Two monographs on influential Florentine figures of the early Cinquecento are R. Devonshire Jones, *Francesco Vettori* (London, 1972); and M. Bullard, *Filippo Strozzi and the Medici* (Cambridge, 1980).

J. Pocock's *The Machiavellian Moment* (Princeton, 1975) sets Florentine political thought of the early Cinquecento into a broad European context. M. Phillips has written on Guicciardini's evolution as an historian: *Francesco Guicciardini: The Historian's Craft* (Toronto, 1977). Randolph Starn's analysis of Tuscan exile experience ranges from the thirteenth to the mid-sixteenth century: *Contrary Commonwealth: The Theme of Exile in Medieval and Renaissance Italy* (Berkeley and Los Angeles, 1982).

INDEX